croo
croo

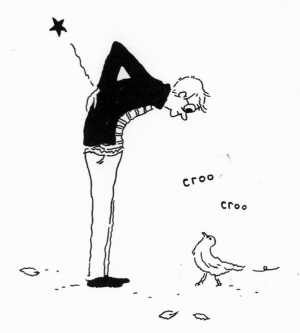

PETTY

pascal girard

THEFT

Translation by
Helge Dascher

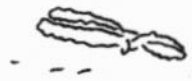

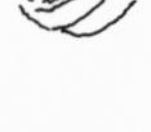

Drawn & Quarterly

First published in French as La Collectionneuse by Éditions La Pastèque.

www.drawnandquarterly.com
www.pascalgirard.com

First paperback edition: May 2014
Printed in China

10 9 8 7 6 5 4 3 2 1

Drawn & Quarterly and Pascal Girard acknowledge the financial contribution of the Government of Canada through the Canada Book Fund, the Canada Council for the Arts, and the National Translation program for our publishing activities and for support of this edition.

Library and Archives Canada Cataloguing in Publication
Girard, Pascal
[Collectionneuse. English]
        Petty Theft/ Pascal Girard; translator, Helge Dascher.
Translation of: La Collectionneuse.
ISBN 978-1-77046-152-9 (pbk.)
        1. Graphic novels. 2. Montréal (Québec)-- Fiction. 3. Montréal (Québec)-- Comic books, strips, etc. I. Dascher, Helge, 1965-, translator II. Title. III. Title: Collectionneuse. English
PN6733.G57C6413 2014   741.5'971   C2013-906212-2

Published in the USA by Drawn & Quarterly,
a client publisher of
Farrar, Straus and Giroux
Orders: 888.330.8477

Published in Canada by Drawn & Quarterly,
a client publisher of
Raincoast Books
Orders: 800.663.5714

Published in the United Kingdom by Drawn & Quarterly
a client publisher of
Publishers Group UK
info@pguk.co.uk

Thanks to Rebecca, Michel, Méli, Victor, and everyone at Drawn & Quarterly.

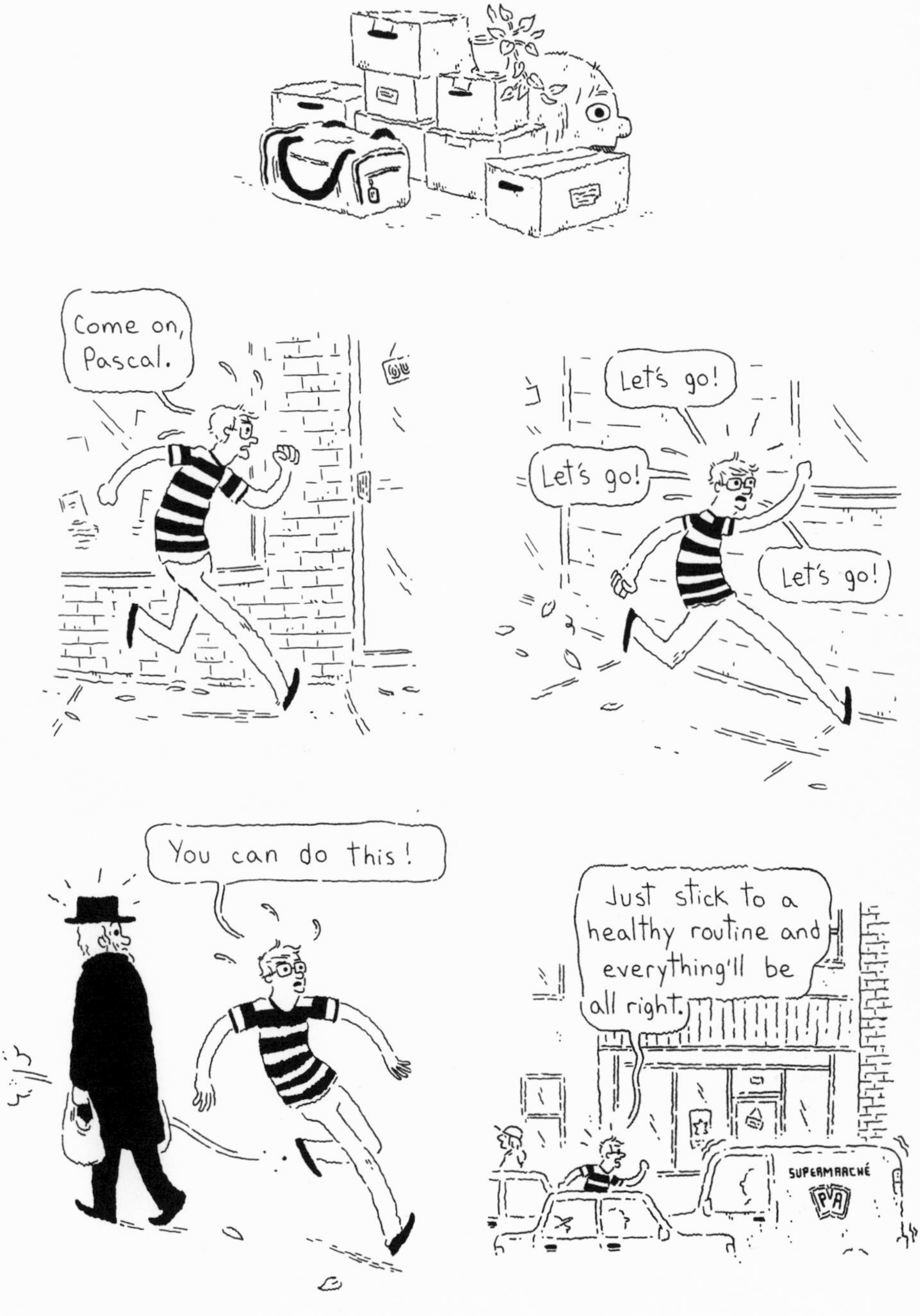
Come on, Pascal.
Let's go!
Let's go!
Let's go!
You can do this!
Just stick to a healthy routine and everything'll be all right.
SUPERMARCHÉ

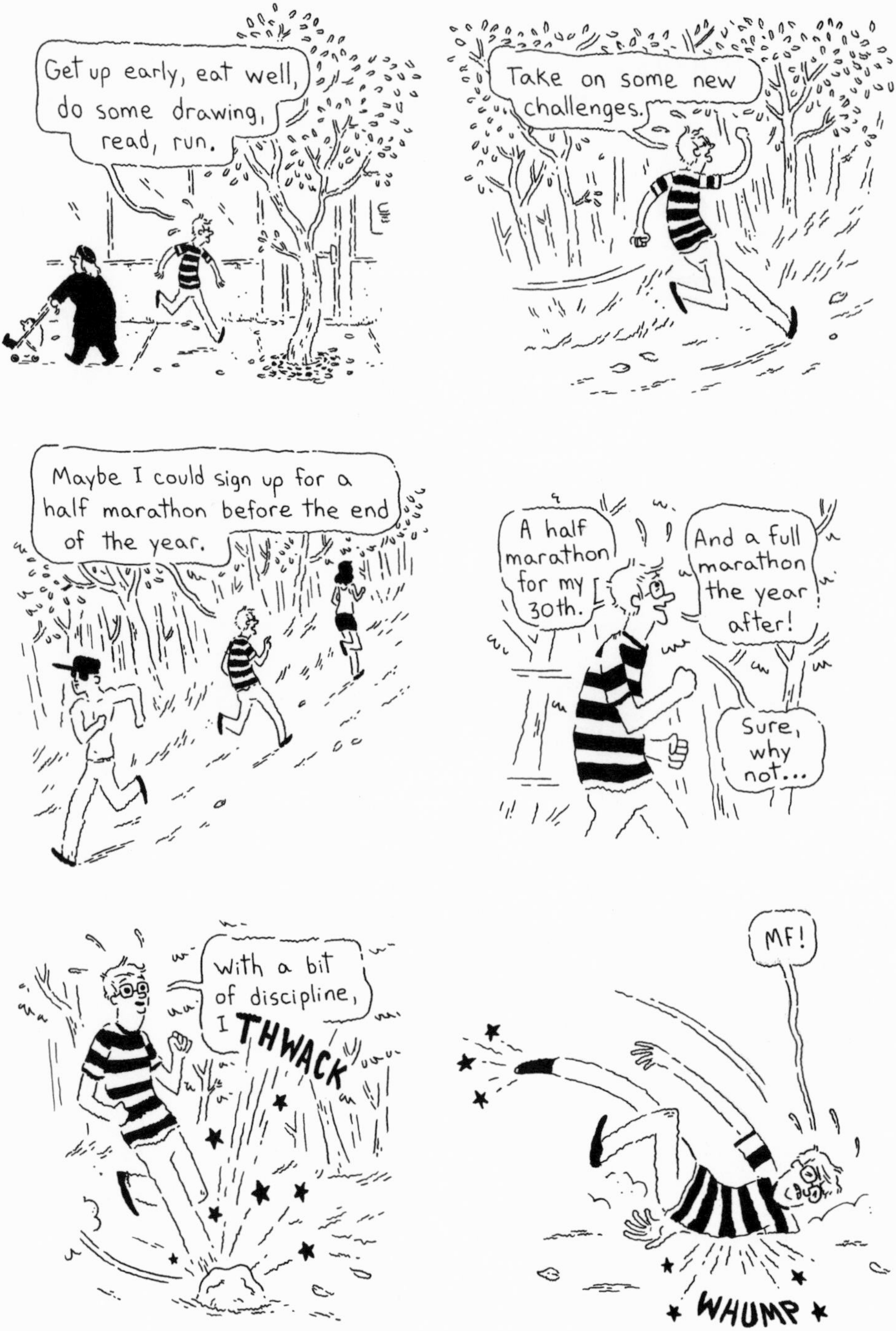
Get up early, eat well, do some drawing, read, run.
Take on some new challenges.
Maybe I could sign up for a half marathon before the end of the year.
A half marathon for my 30th.
And a full marathon the year after!
Sure, why not...
With a bit of discipline, I
THWACK
MF!
WHUMP

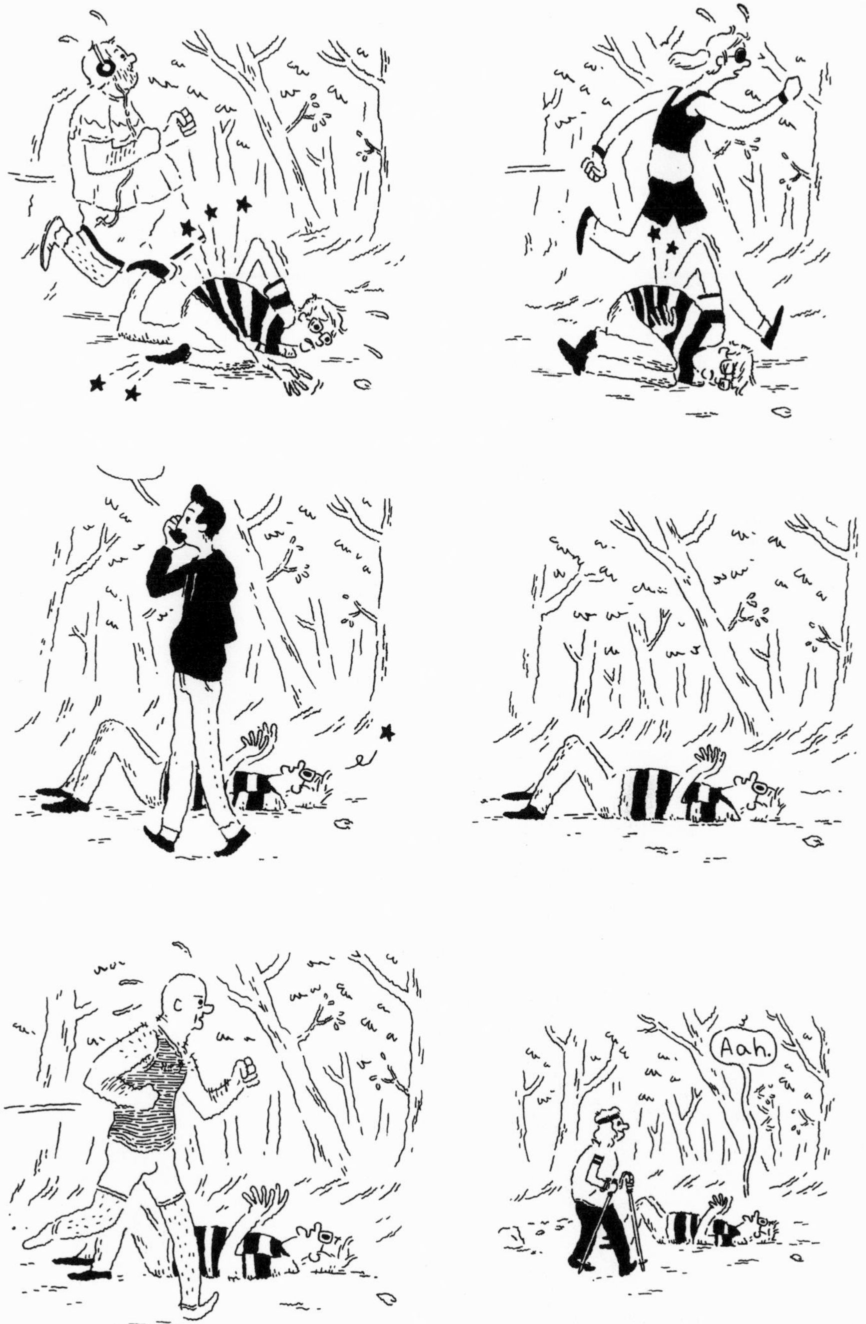
Aah.

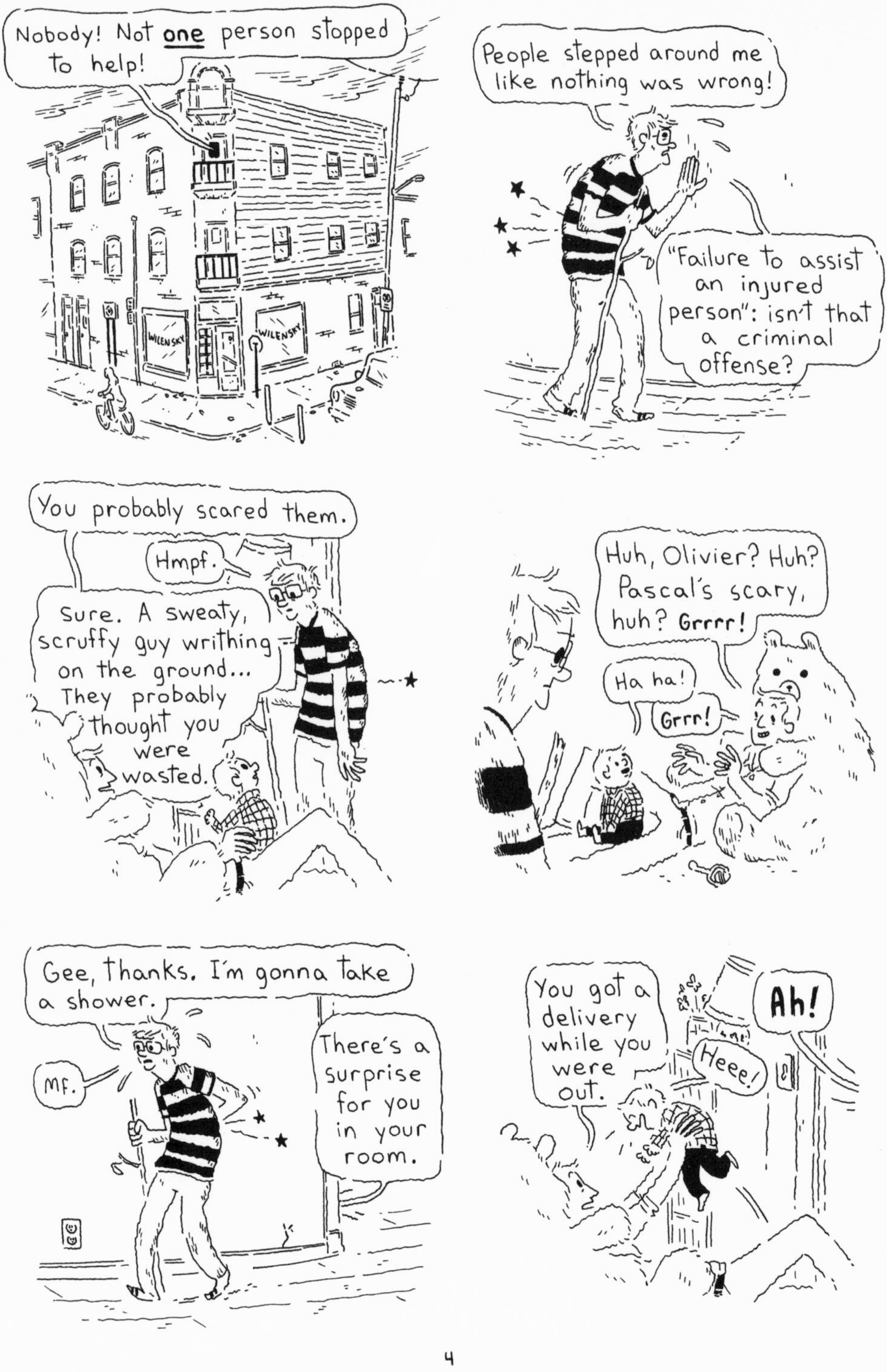

Nobody! Not one person stopped to help!
WILENSKY
WILENSKY
People stepped around me like nothing was wrong!
"Failure to assist an injured person": isn't that a criminal offense?
You probably scared them.
Hmpf.
Sure. A sweaty, scruffy guy writhing on the ground... They probably thought you were wasted.
Huh, Olivier? Huh? Pascal's scary, huh? Grrrr!
Ha ha!
Grrr!
Gee, Thanks. I'm gonna take a shower.
Mf.
There's a surprise for you in your room.
You got a delivery while you were out.
Ah!
Heee!

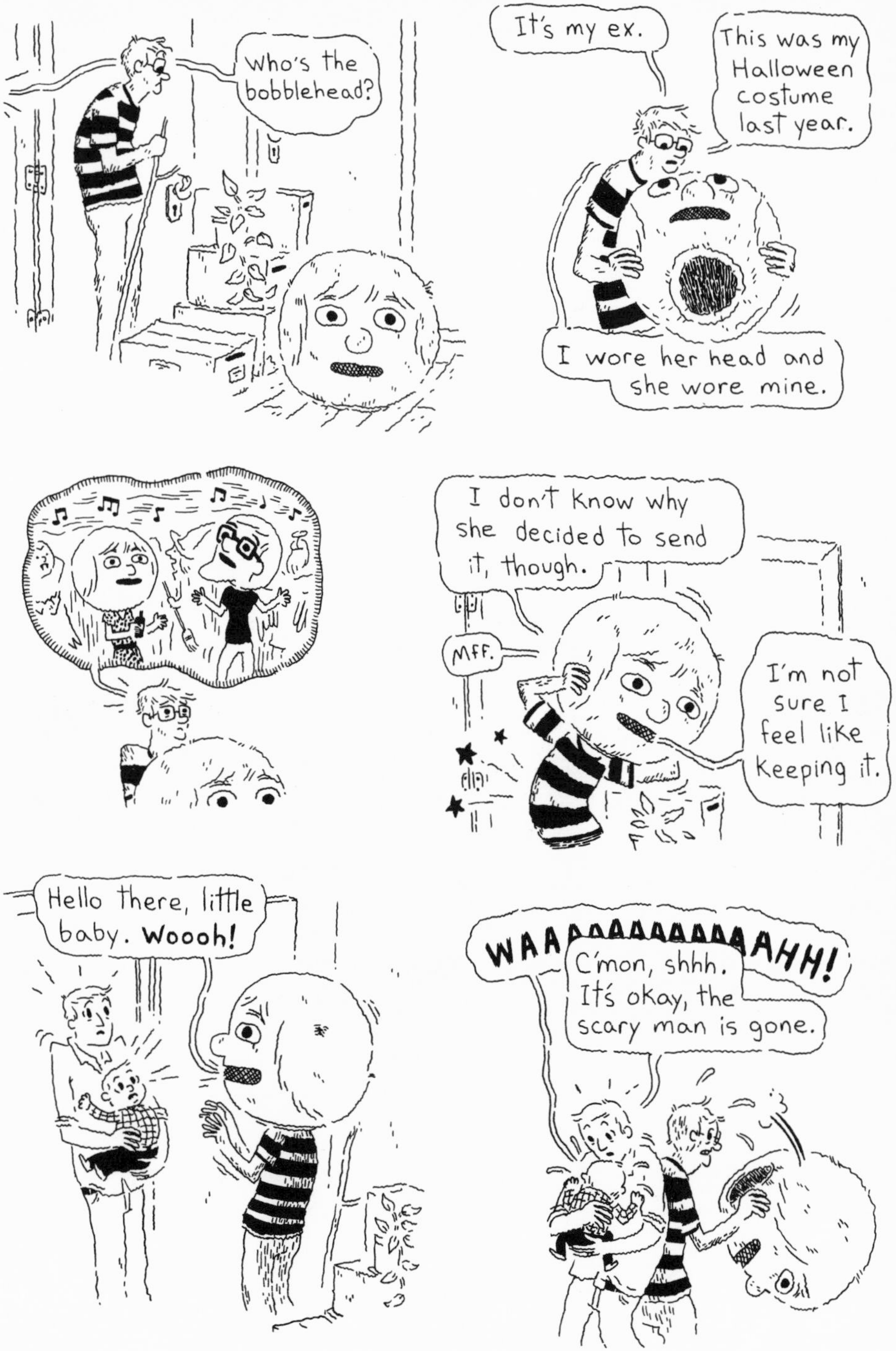
Who's the bobblehead?
It's my ex.
This was my Halloween costume last year.
I wore her head and she wore mine.
I don't know why she decided to send it, though.
Mff.
I'm not sure I feel like keeping it.
Hello there, little baby. **Woooh!**
WAAAAAAAAAAAAHH!
C'mon, shhh. It's okay, the scary man is gone.

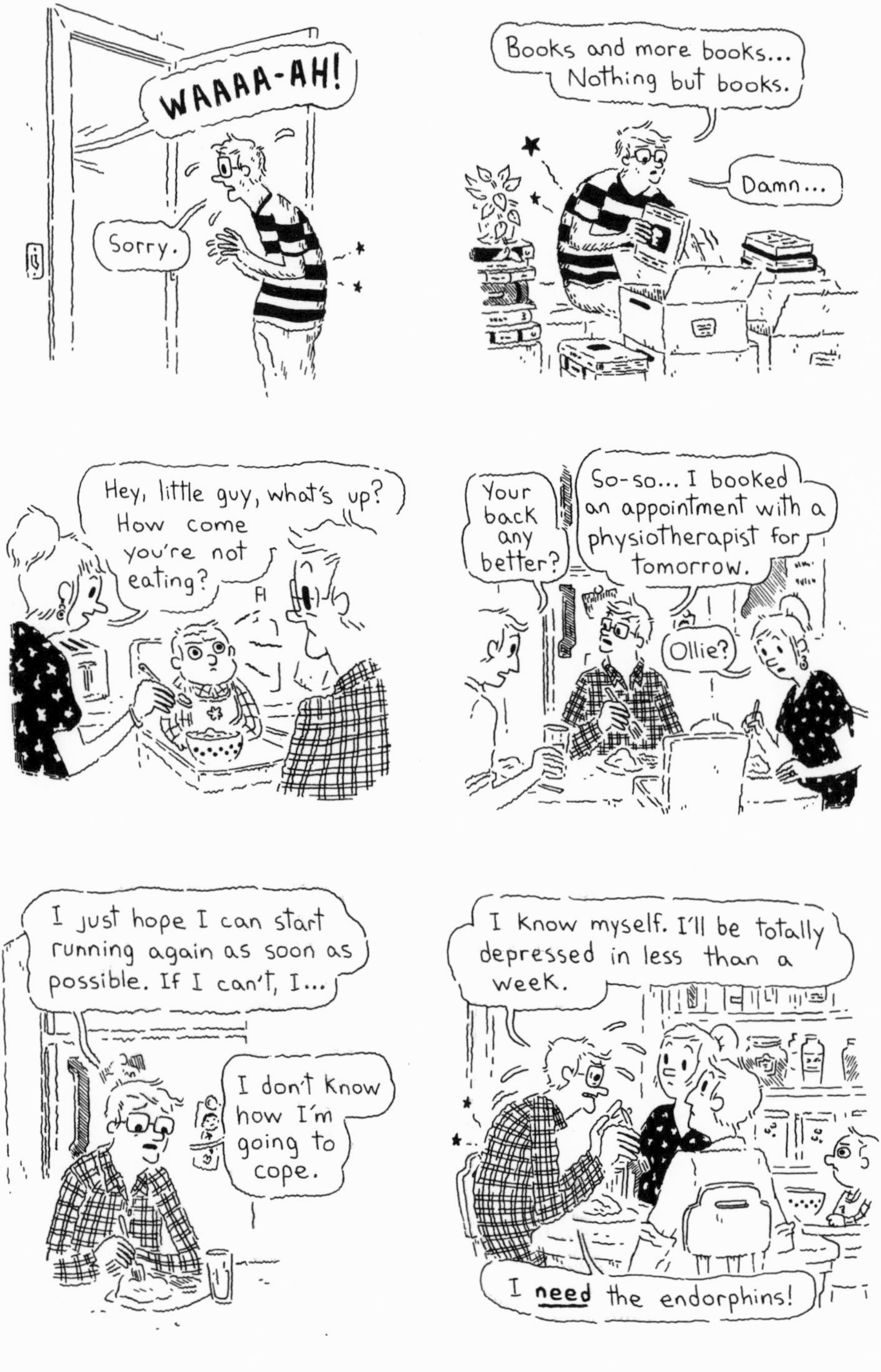
WAAAA-AH!
Sorry.
Books and more books... Nothing but books.
Damn...
Hey, little guy, what's up? How come you're not eating?
Your back any better?
So-so... I booked an appointment with a physiotherapist for tomorrow.
Ollie?
I just hope I can start running again as soon as possible. If I can't, I...
I don't know how I'm going to cope.
I know myself. I'll be totally depressed in less than a week.
I **need** the endorphins!

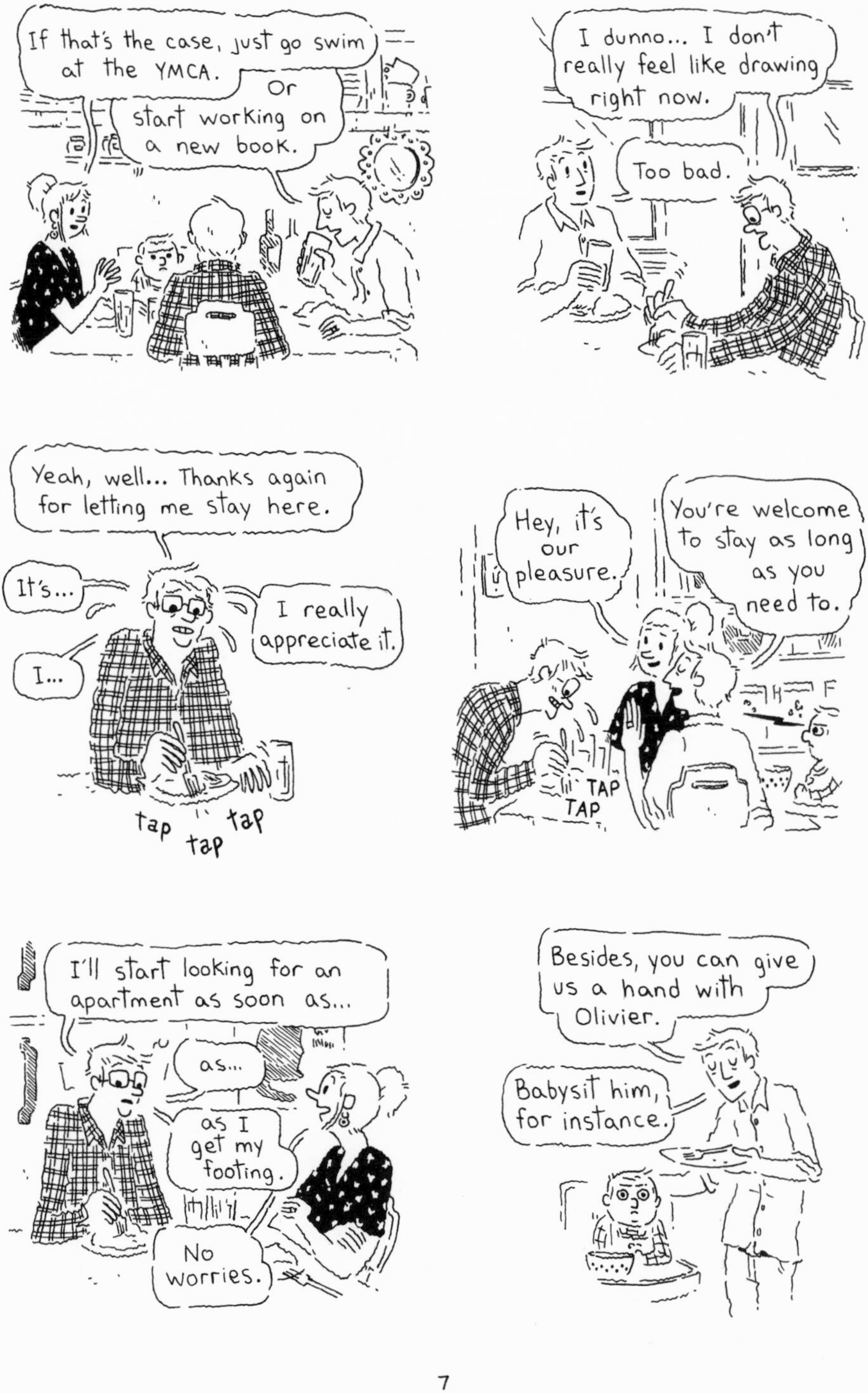
If that's the case, just go swim at the YMCA.
Or start working on a new book.
I dunno... I don't really feel like drawing right now.
Too bad.
Yeah, well... Thanks again for letting me stay here.
It's...
I...
I really appreciate it.
tap tap tap
Hey, it's our pleasure.
You're welcome to stay as long as you need to.
TAP TAP
I'll start looking for an apartment as soon as...
as...
as I get my footing.
No worries.
Besides, you can give us a hand with Olivier.
Babysit him, for instance.

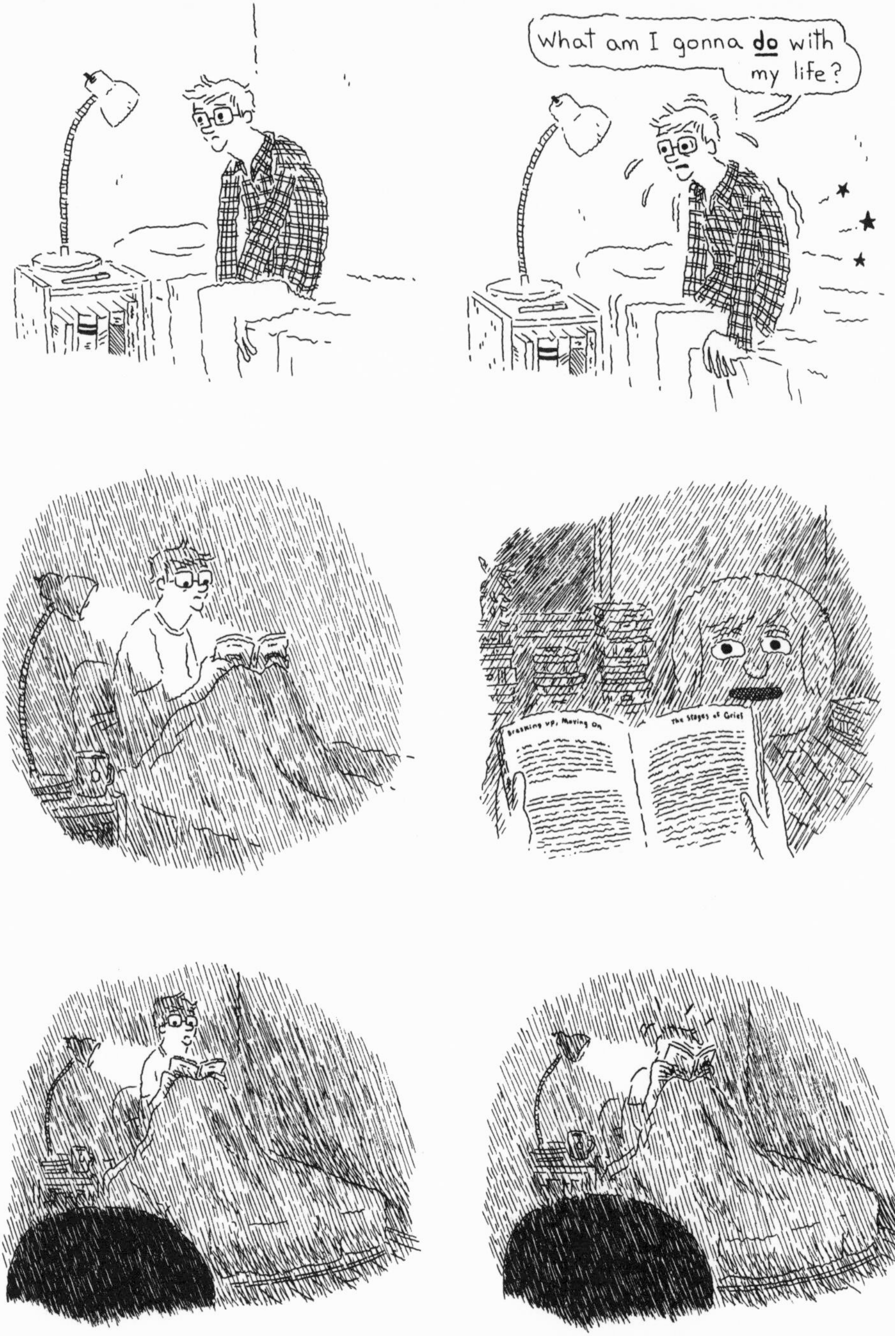

What am I gonna **do** with my life?
Breaking up, Moving On
The Stages of Grief

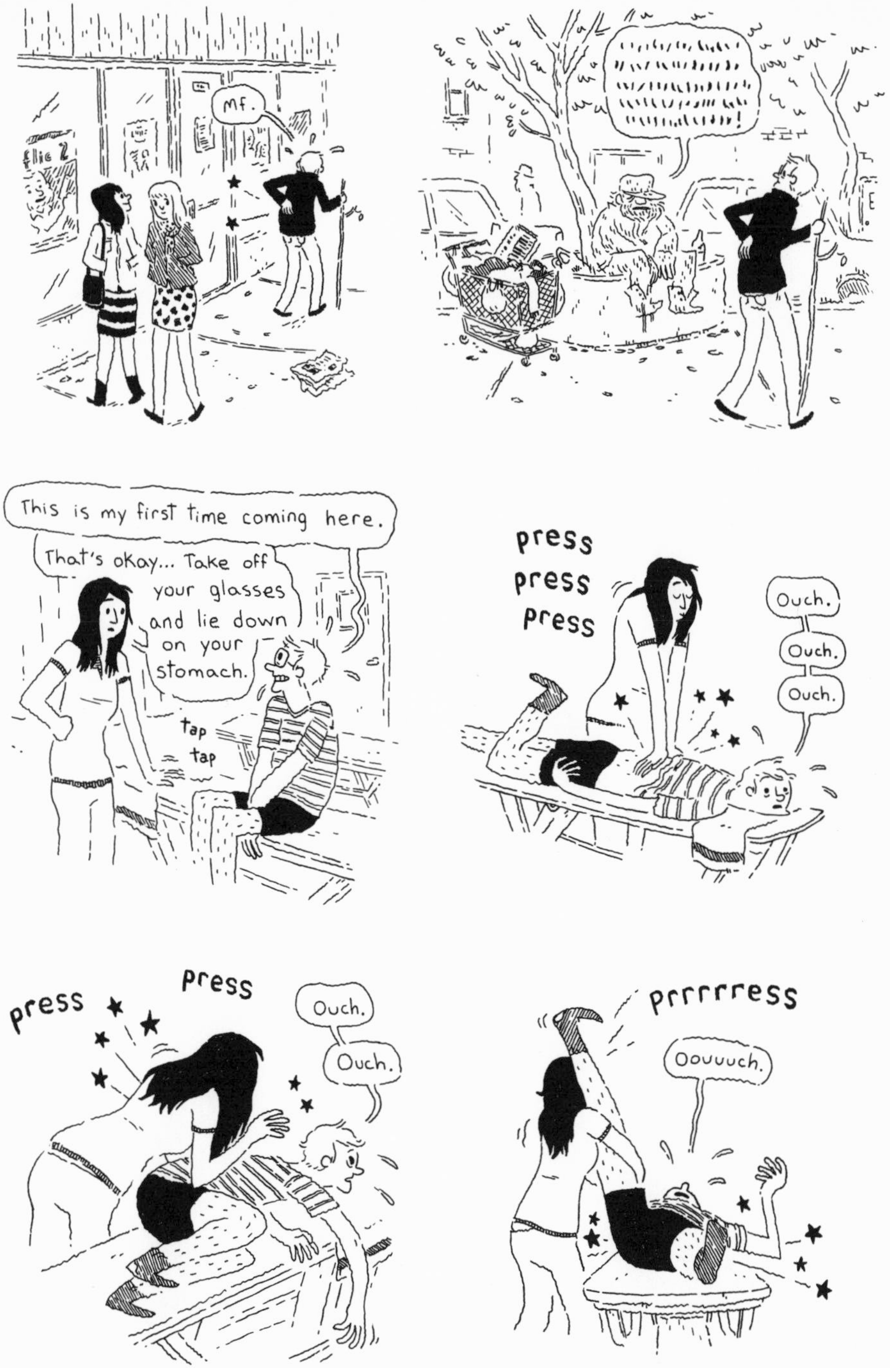

Mf.
This is my first time coming here.
That's okay... Take off your glasses and lie down on your stomach.
tap
tap
press
press
press
Ouch.
Ouch.
Ouch.
press
press
Ouch.
Ouch.
Prrrrress
Oouuuch.

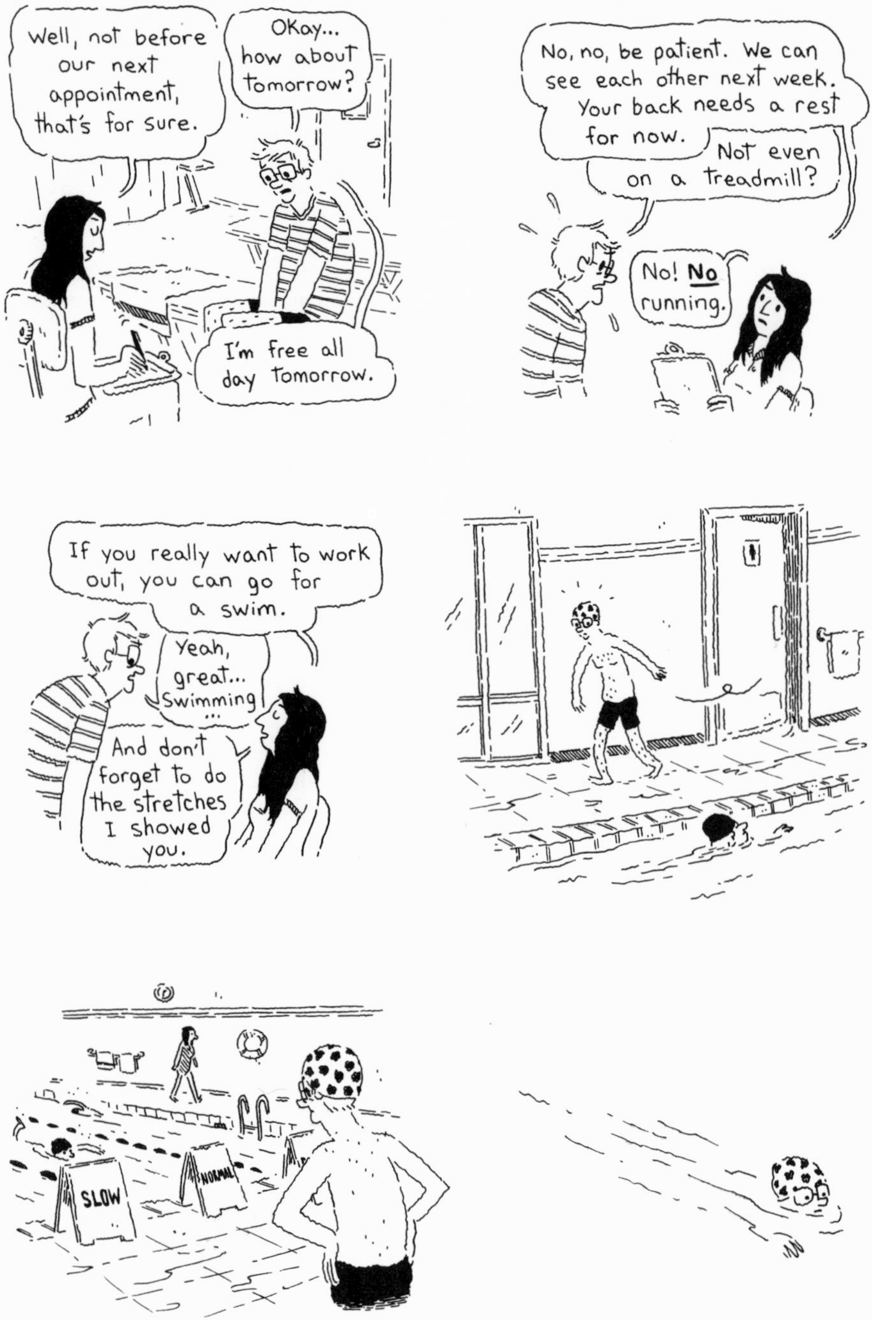

Well, not before our next appointment, that's for sure.
OKay... how about tomorrow?
I'm free all day tomorrow.
No, no, be patient. We can see each other next week. Your back needs a rest for now.
Not even on a treadmill?
No! **No** running.
If you really want to work out, you can go for a swim.
Yeah, great... Swimming...
And don't forget to do the stretches I showed you.
SLOW
NORMAL

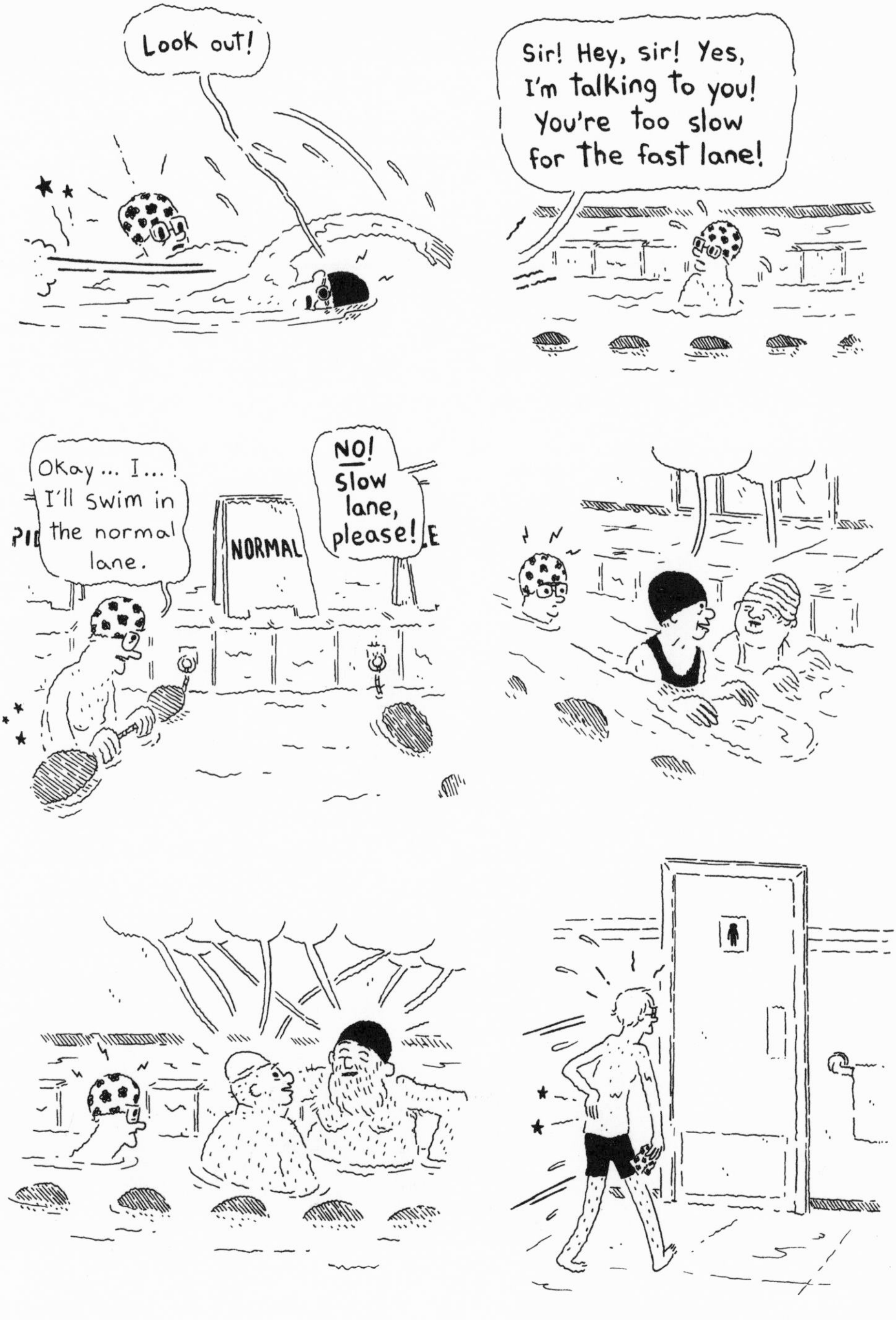
Look out!
Sir! Hey, sir! Yes, I'm talking to you! You're too slow for the fast lane!
Okay ... I ... I'll swim in the normal lane.
NORMAL
NO! Slow lane, please!

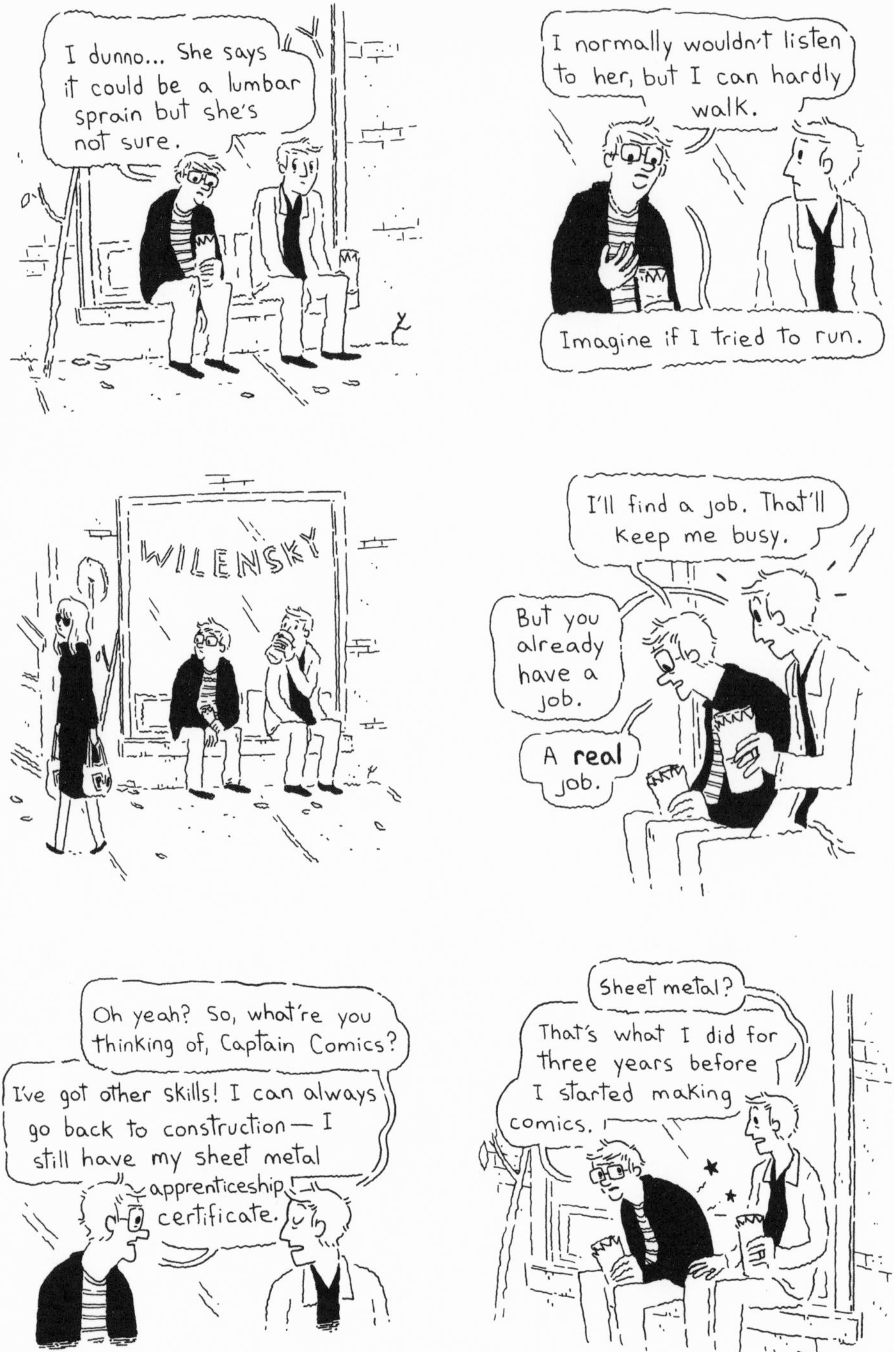

I dunno... She says it could be a lumbar sprain but she's not sure.
I normally wouldn't listen to her, but I can hardly walk.
Imagine if I tried to run.
WILENSKY
I'll find a job. That'll keep me busy.
But you already have a job.
A **real** job.
Oh yeah? So, what're you thinking of, Captain Comics?
I've got other skills! I can always go back to construction— I still have my sheet metal apprenticeship certificate.
Sheet metal?
That's what I did for three years before I started making comics.

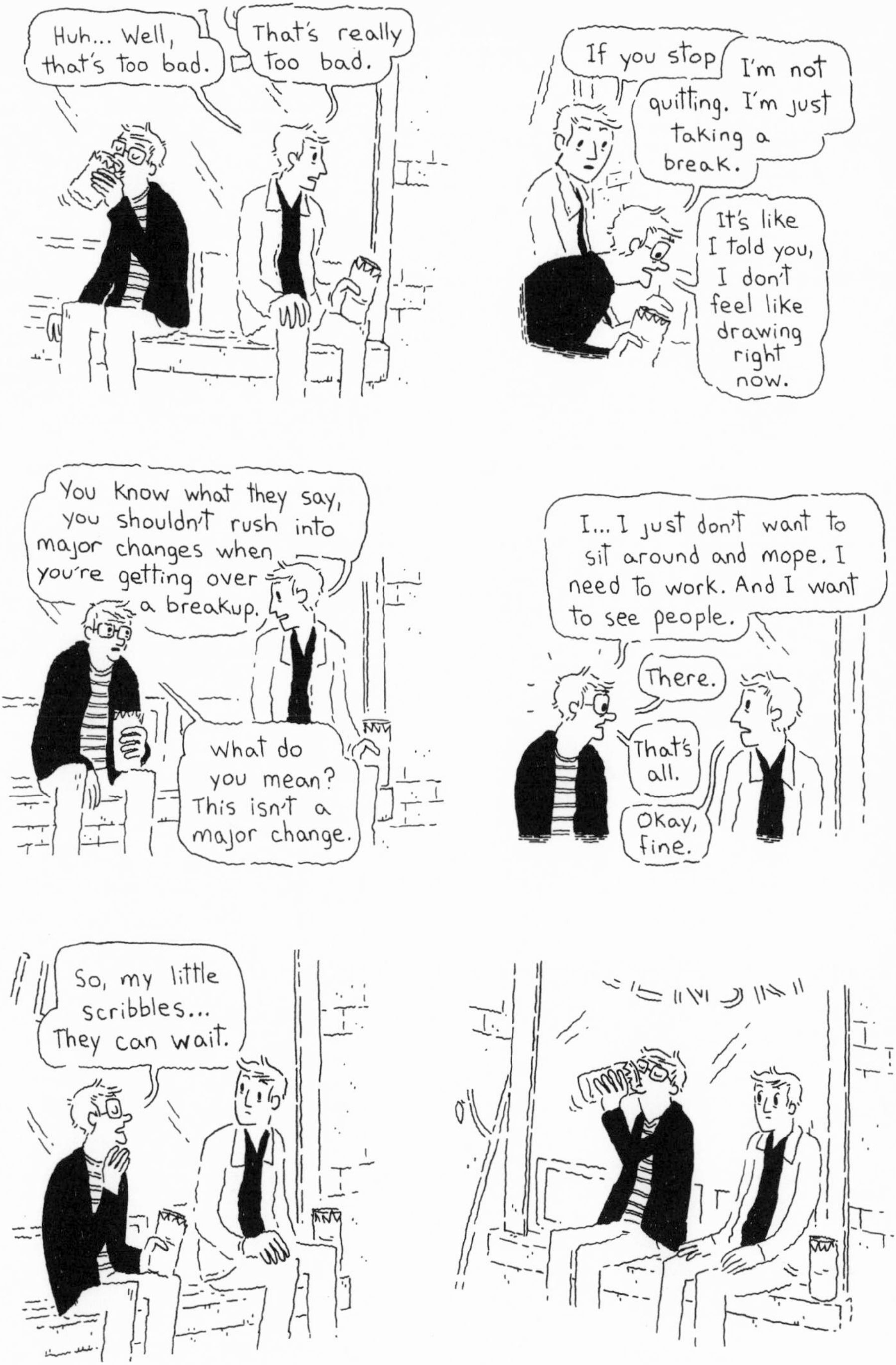
Huh... Well, that's too bad.
That's really too bad.
If you stop
I'm not quitting. I'm just taking a break.
It's like I told you, I don't feel like drawing right now.
You know what they say, you shouldn't rush into major changes when you're getting over a breakup.
What do you mean? This isn't a major change.
I... I just don't want to sit around and mope. I need to work. And I want to see people.
There.
That's all.
Okay, fine.
So, my little scribbles... They can wait.

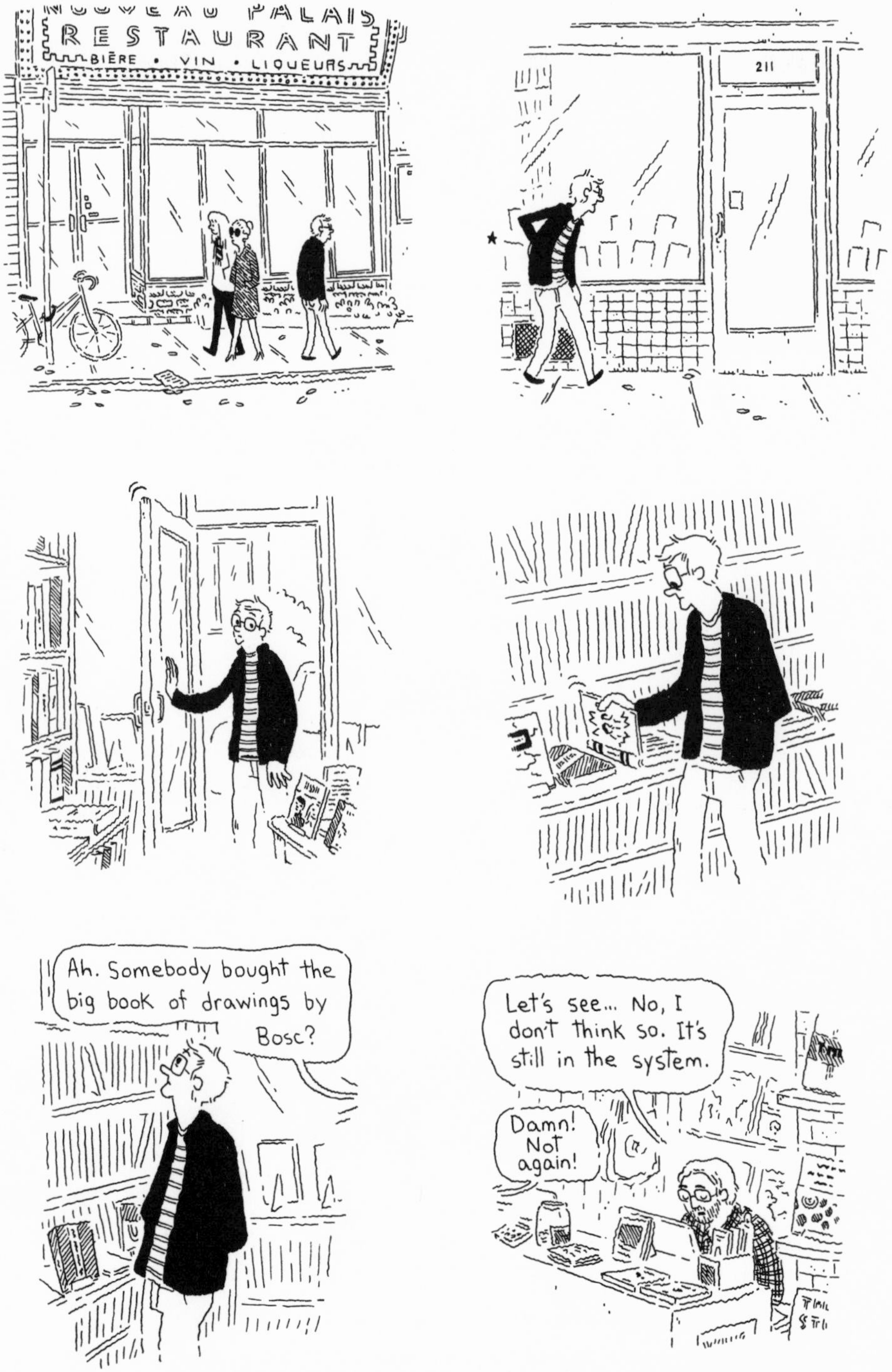
RESTAURANT
BIÈRE • VIN • LIQUEURS
211
Ah. Somebody bought the big book of drawings by Bosc?
Let's see... No, I don't think so. It's still in the system.
Damn! Not again!

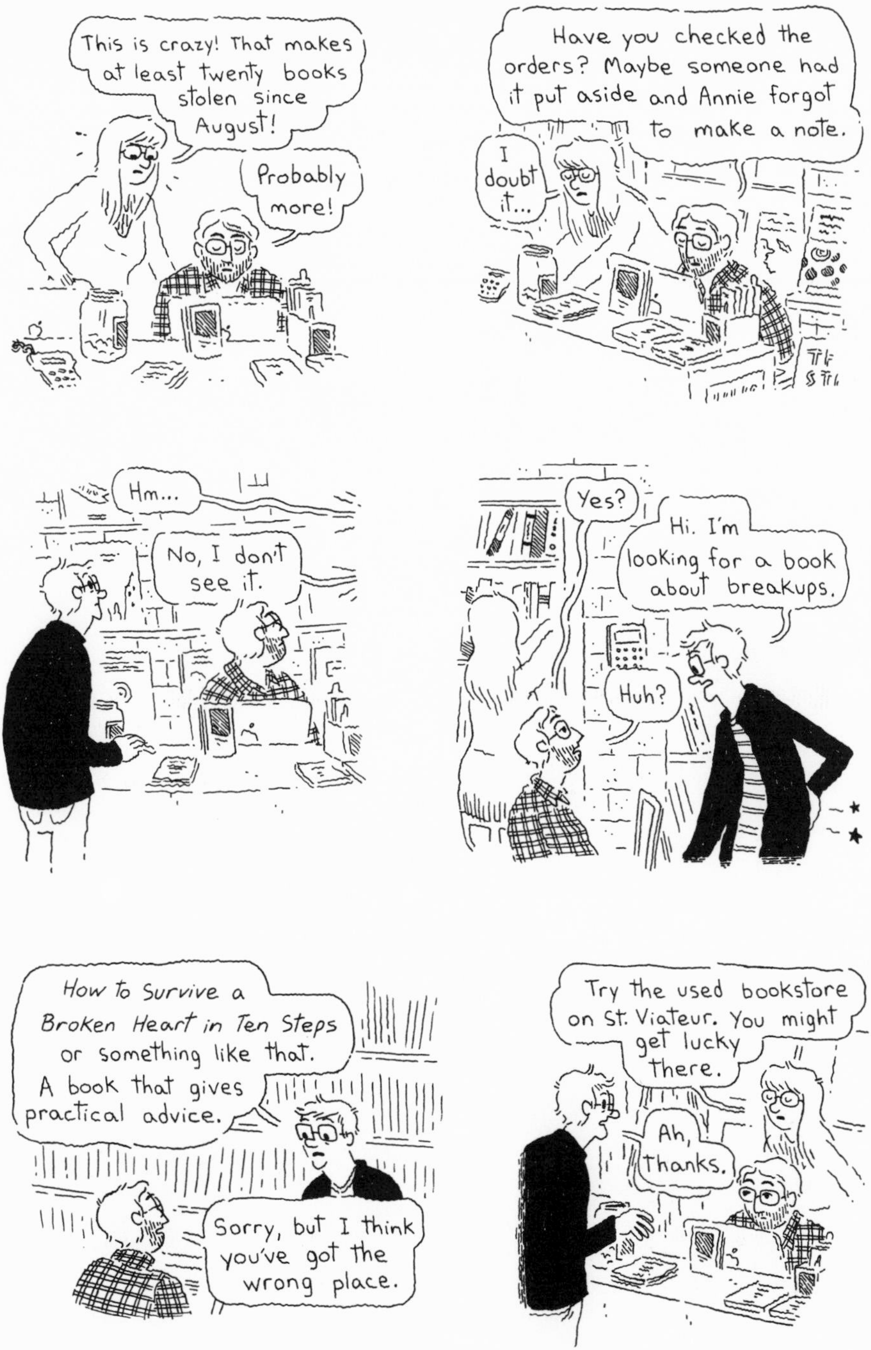
This is crazy! That makes at least twenty books stolen since August!
Probably more!
Have you checked the orders? Maybe someone had it put aside and Annie forgot to make a note.
I doubt it...
Hm...
No, I don't see it.
Yes?
Hi. I'm looking for a book about breakups.
Huh?
How to Survive a Broken Heart in Ten Steps or something like that. A book that gives practical advice.
Sorry, but I think you've got the wrong place.
Try the used bookstore on St. Viateur. You might get lucky there.
Ah, thanks.

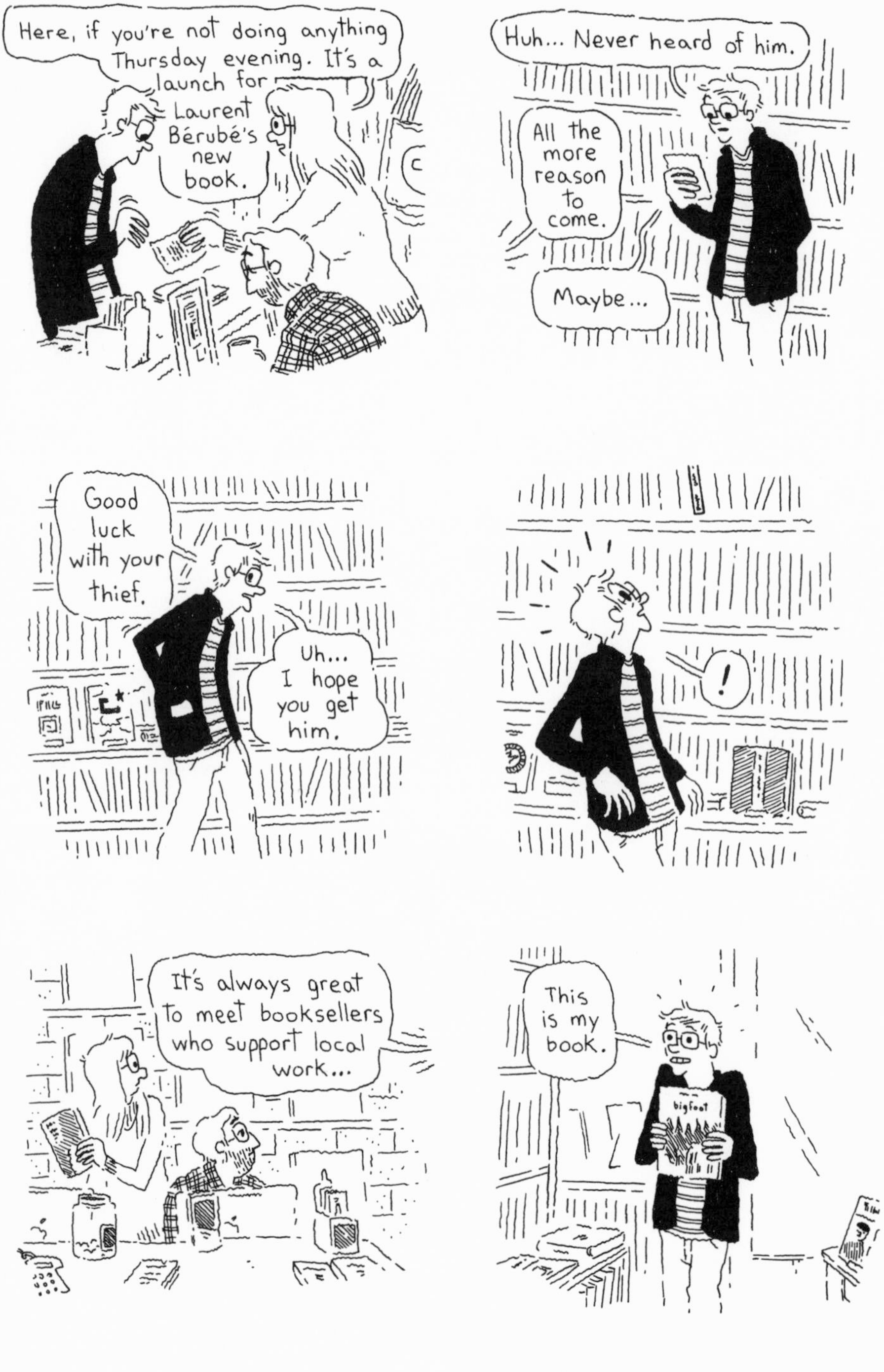
Here, if you're not doing anything Thursday evening. It's a launch for Laurent Bérubé's new book.
Huh... Never heard of him.
All the more reason to come.
Maybe...
Good luck with your thief.
Uh... I hope you get him.
!
It's always great to meet booksellers who support local work...
This is my book.
bigfoot

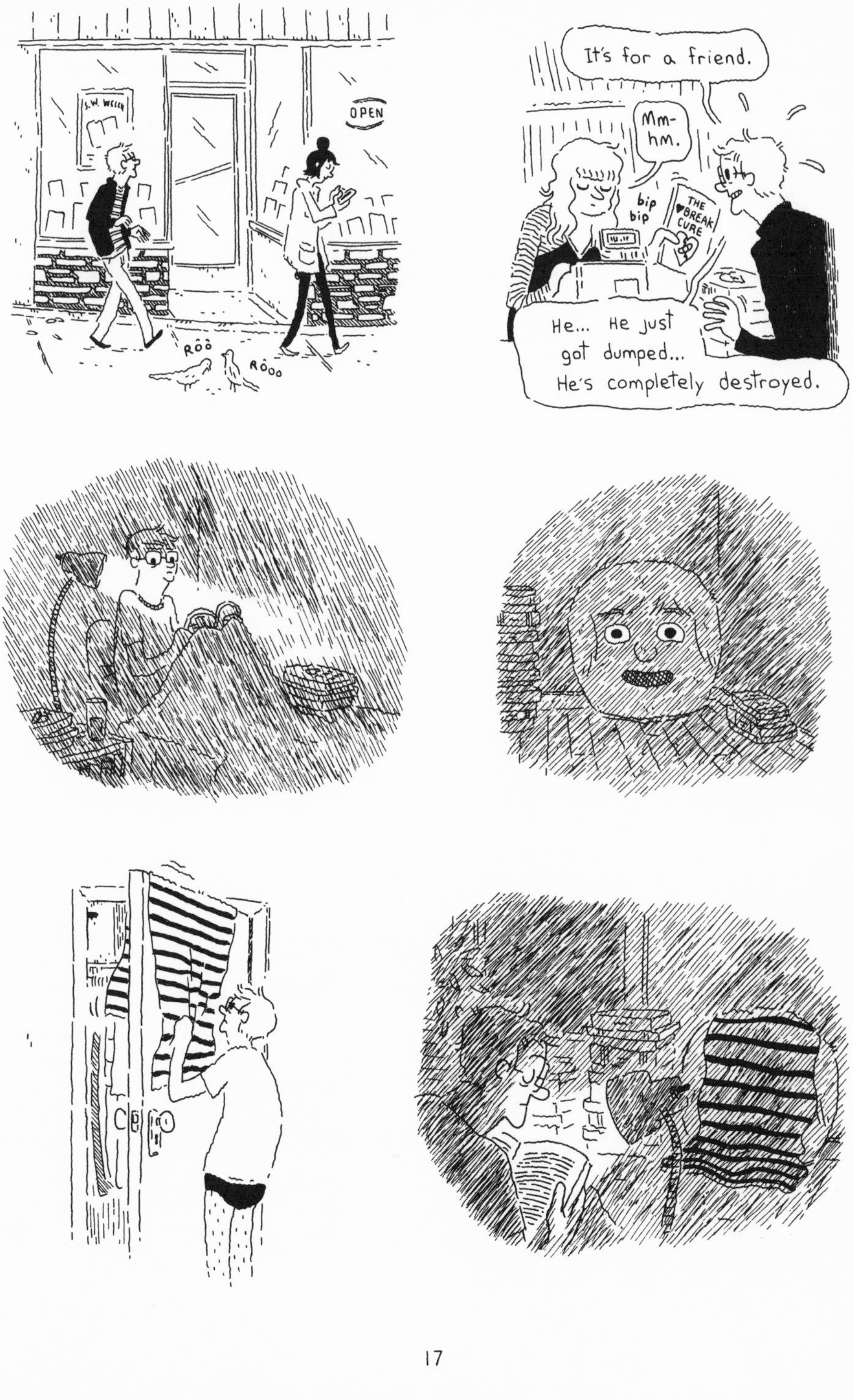
OPEN
RÔÔ
RÔÔO
It's for a friend.
Mm-hm.
bip bip
THE BREAK CURE
He... He just got dumped... He's completely destroyed.

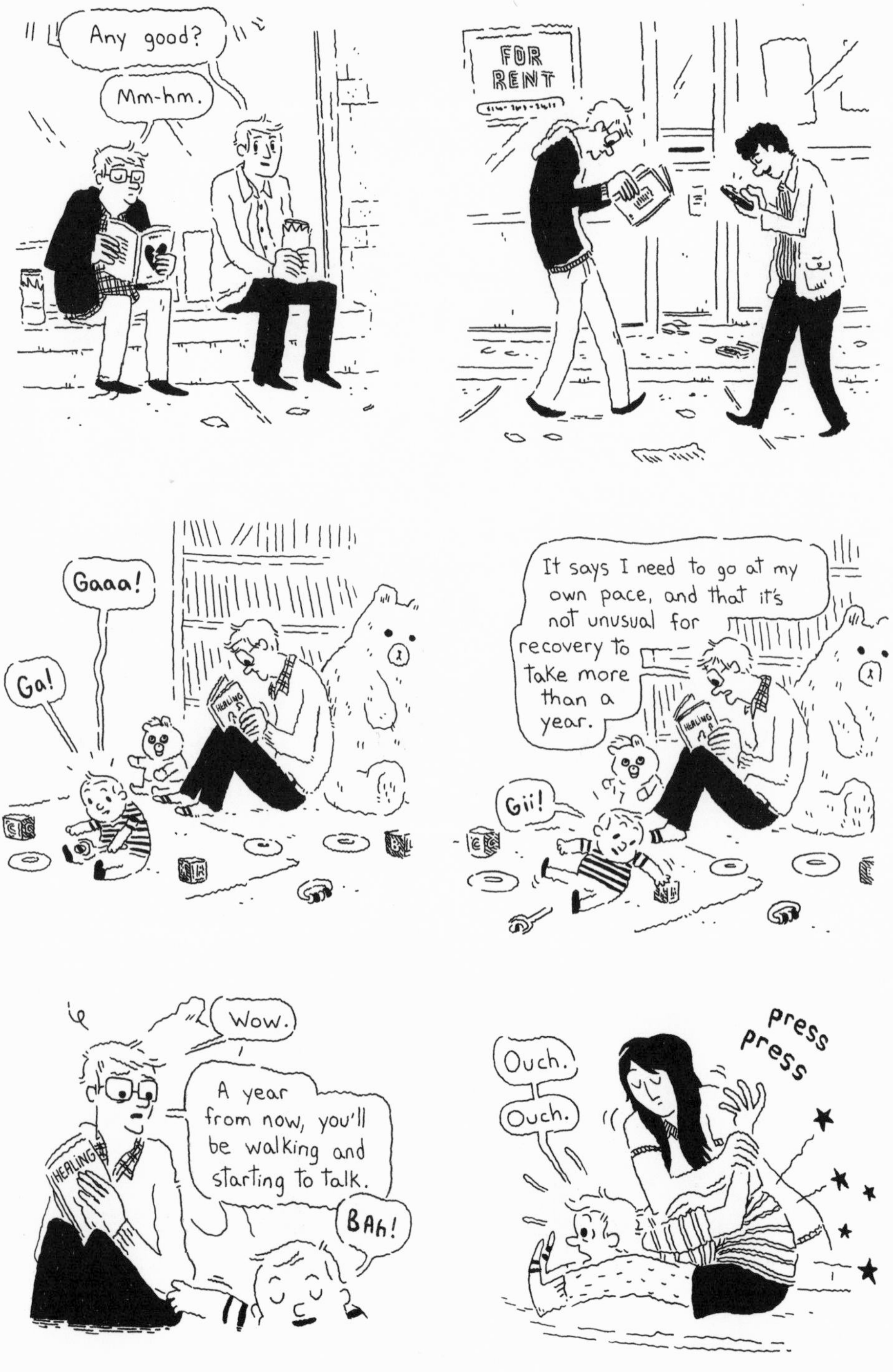
Any good?
Mm-hm.
FOR RENT
Gaaa!
Ga!
HEALING
It says I need to go at my own pace, and that it's not unusual for recovery to take more than a year.
Gii!
HEALING
Wow.
A year from now, you'll be walking and starting to talk.
BAh!
HEALING
Ouch.
Ouch.
press
press

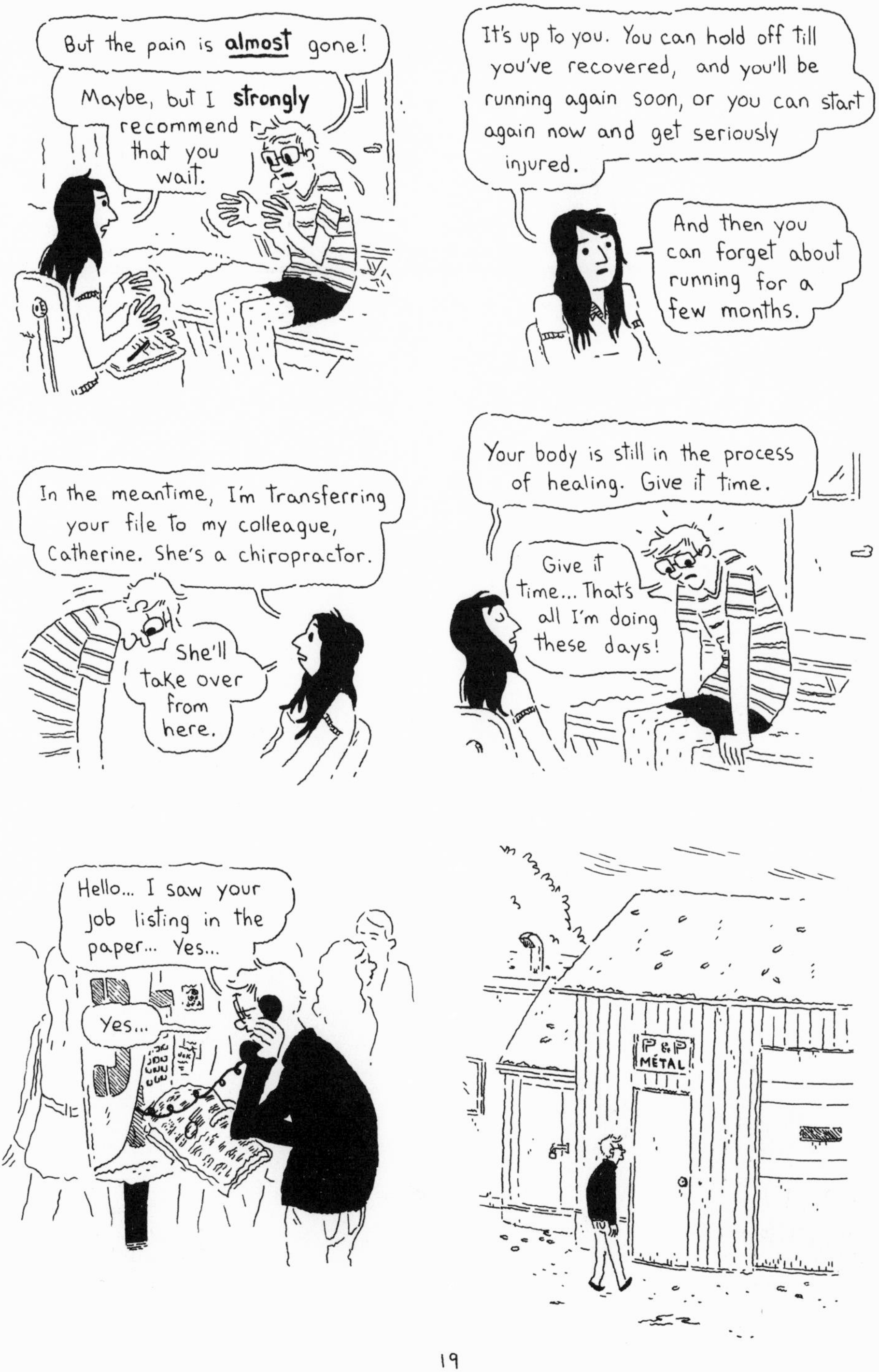
But the pain is **almost** gone!
Maybe, but I **strongly** recommend that you wait.
It's up to you. You can hold off till you've recovered, and you'll be running again soon, or you can start again now and get seriously injured.
And then you can forget about running for a few months.
In the meantime, I'm transferring your file to my colleague, Catherine. She's a chiropractor.
She'll take over from here.
Your body is still in the process of healing. Give it time.
Give it time... That's all I'm doing these days!
Hello... I saw your job listing in the paper... Yes...
Yes...
P & P MÉTAL

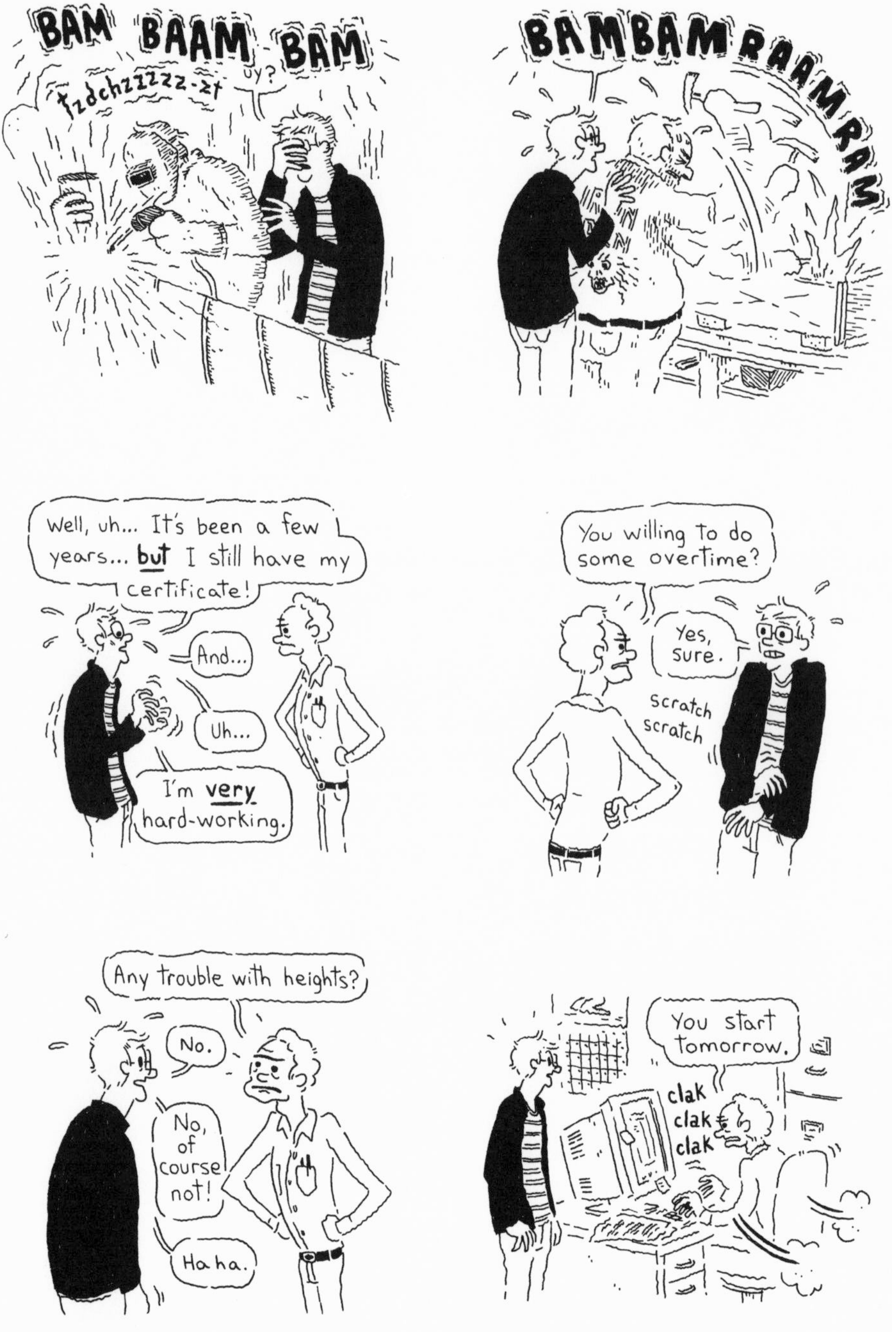
BAM BAAM BAM
tzdchzzzzz-zt
uy?
BAMBAMRAAMRAM
Well, uh... It's been a few years... **but** I still have my certificate!
And...
Uh...
I'm **very** hard-working.
You willing to do some overtime?
Yes, sure.
scratch scratch
Any trouble with heights?
No.
No, of course not!
Ha ha.
You start tomorrow.
clak clak clak

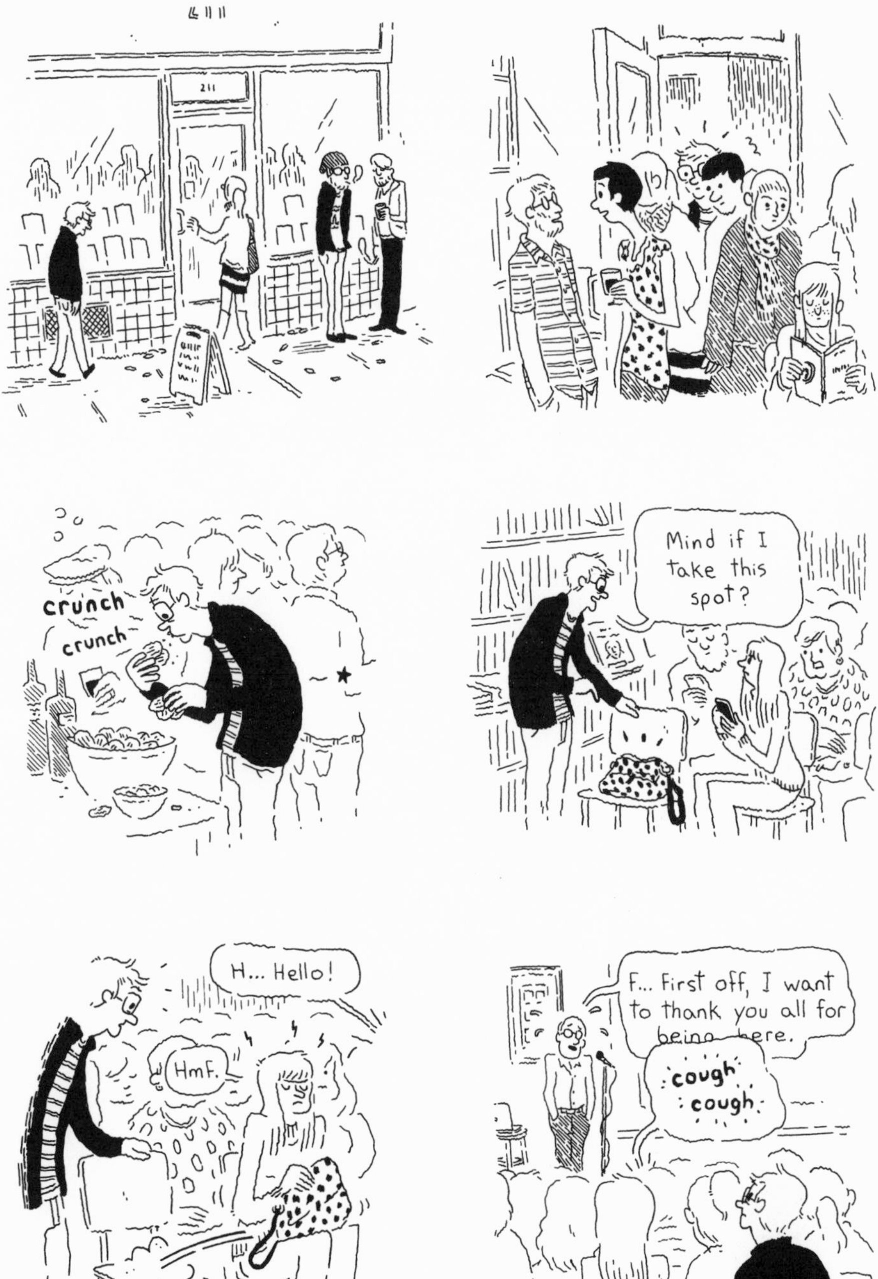
crunch
crunch
Mind if I take this spot?
H... Hello!
HmF.
F... First off, I want to thank you all for being here.
cough
cough

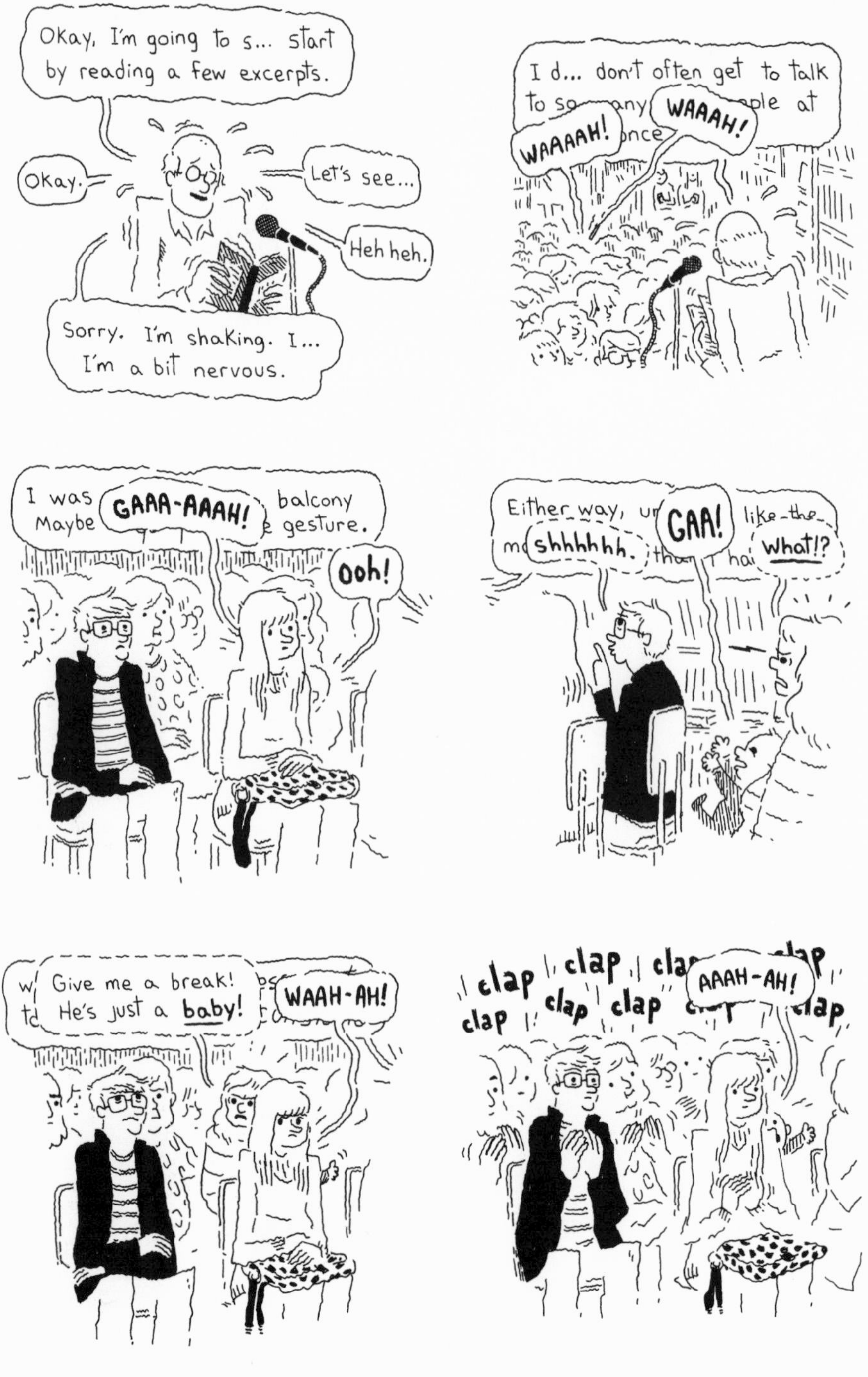
Okay, I'm going to s... start by reading a few excerpts.
Okay.
Let's see...
Heh heh.
Sorry. I'm shaking. I... I'm a bit nervous.
I d... don't often get to talk
WAAAAH!
WAAAH!
GAAA-AAAH!
Ooh!
GAA!
shhhhhh.
What!?
Give me a break! He's just a baby!
WAAH-AH!
clap
clap
clap
clap
clap
clap
AAAH-AH!

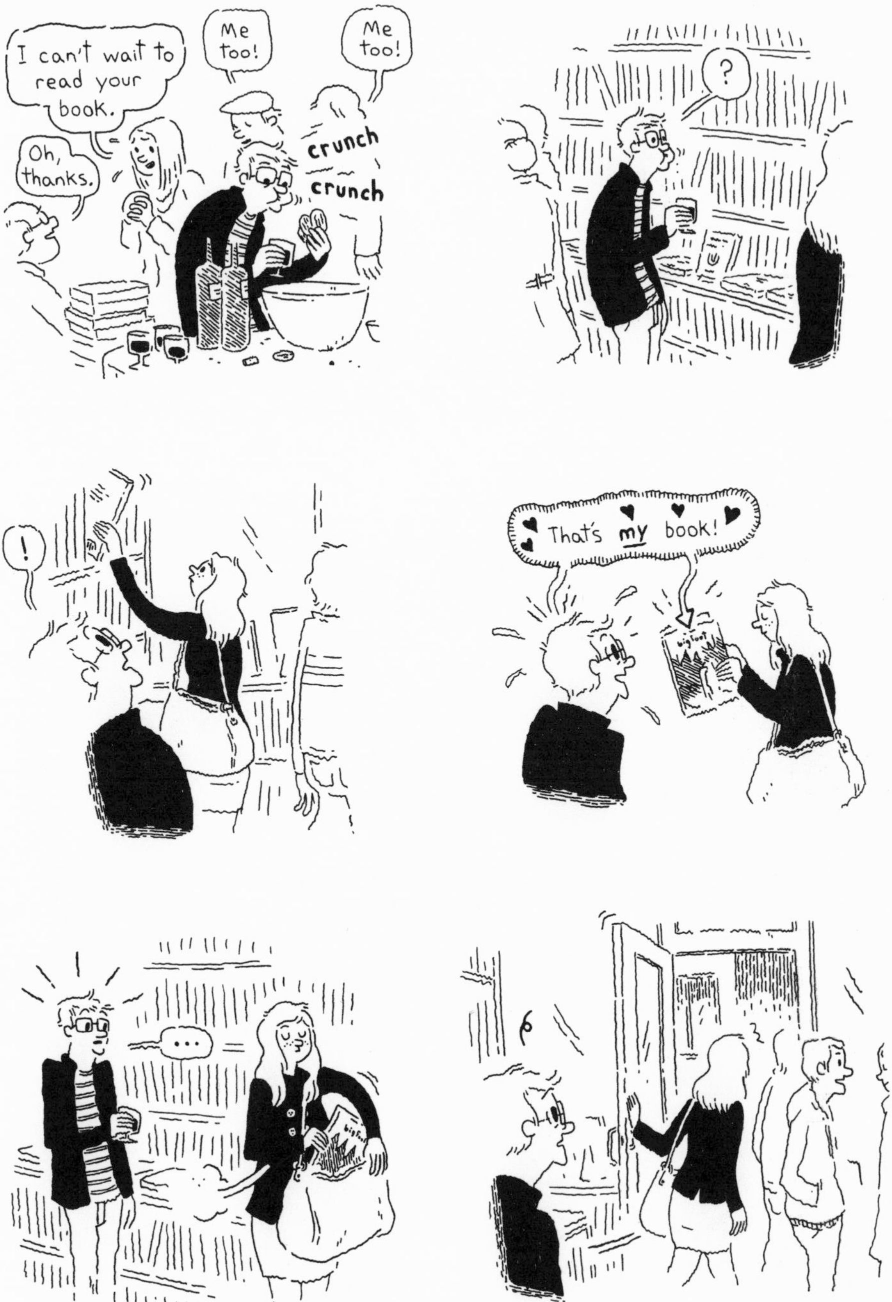
I can't wait to read your book.
Me too!
Me too!
Oh, thanks.
crunch
crunch
?
!
That's my book!
bigfoot
...
bigfoot

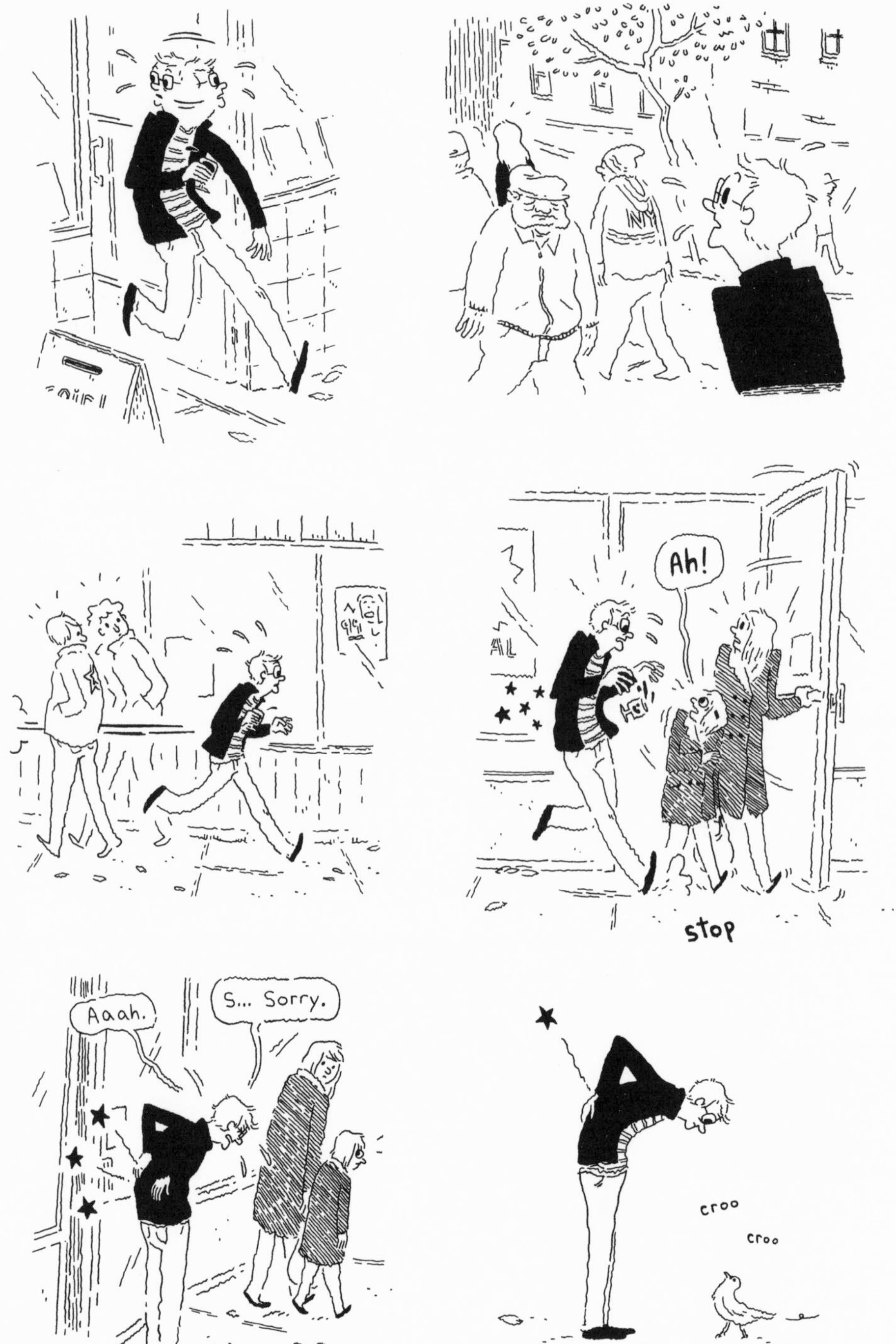
NY
Ah!
stop
Aaah.
S... Sorry.
croo
croo

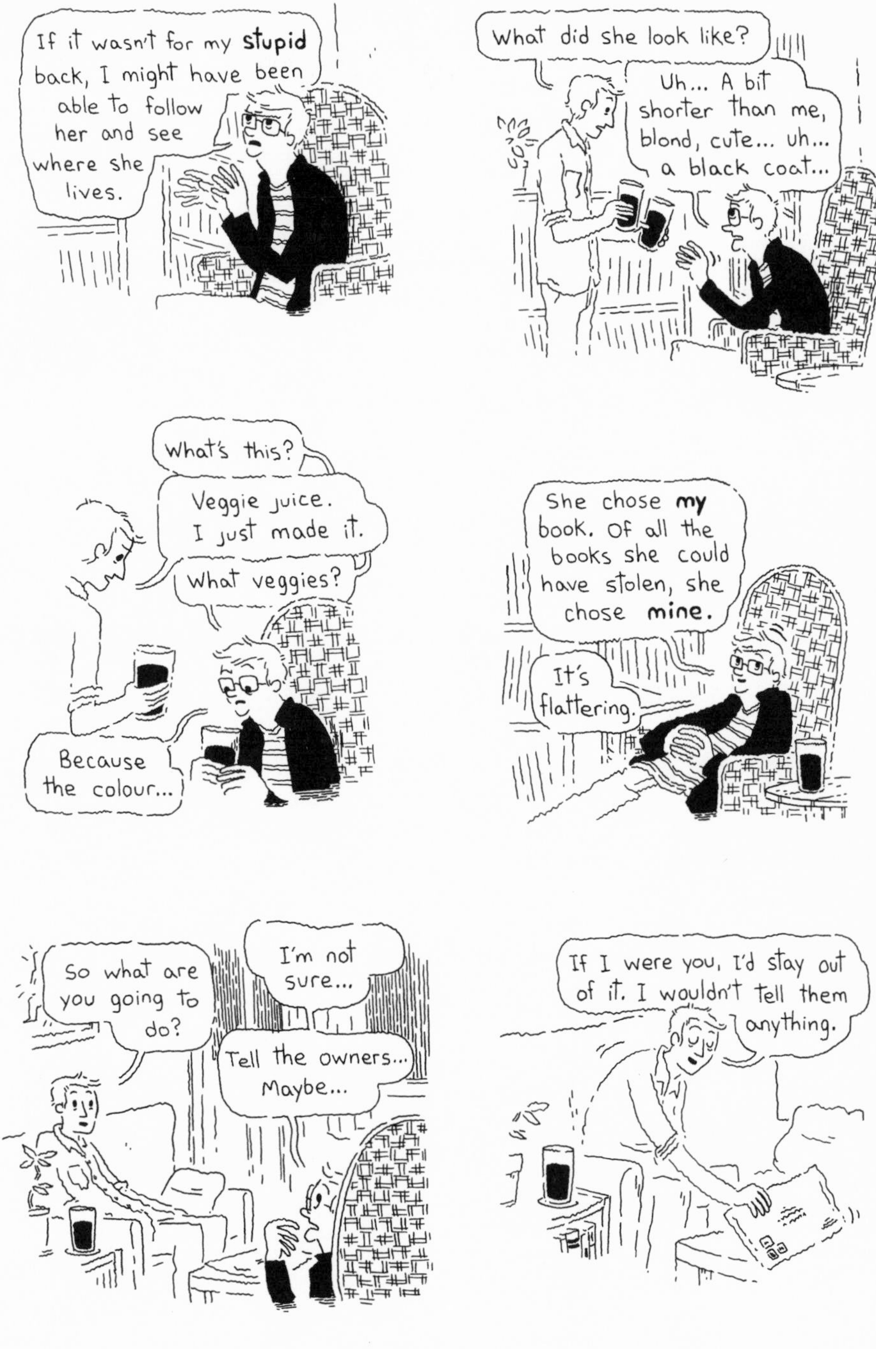
If it wasn't for my **stupid** back, I might have been able to follow her and see where she lives.
What did she look like?
Uh... A bit shorter than me, blond, cute... uh... a black coat...
What's this?
Veggie juice. I just made it.
What veggies?
Because the colour...
She chose **my** book. Of all the books she could have stolen, she chose **mine.**
It's flattering.
So what are you going to do?
I'm not sure...
Tell the owners... Maybe...
If I were you, I'd stay out of it. I wouldn't tell them anything.

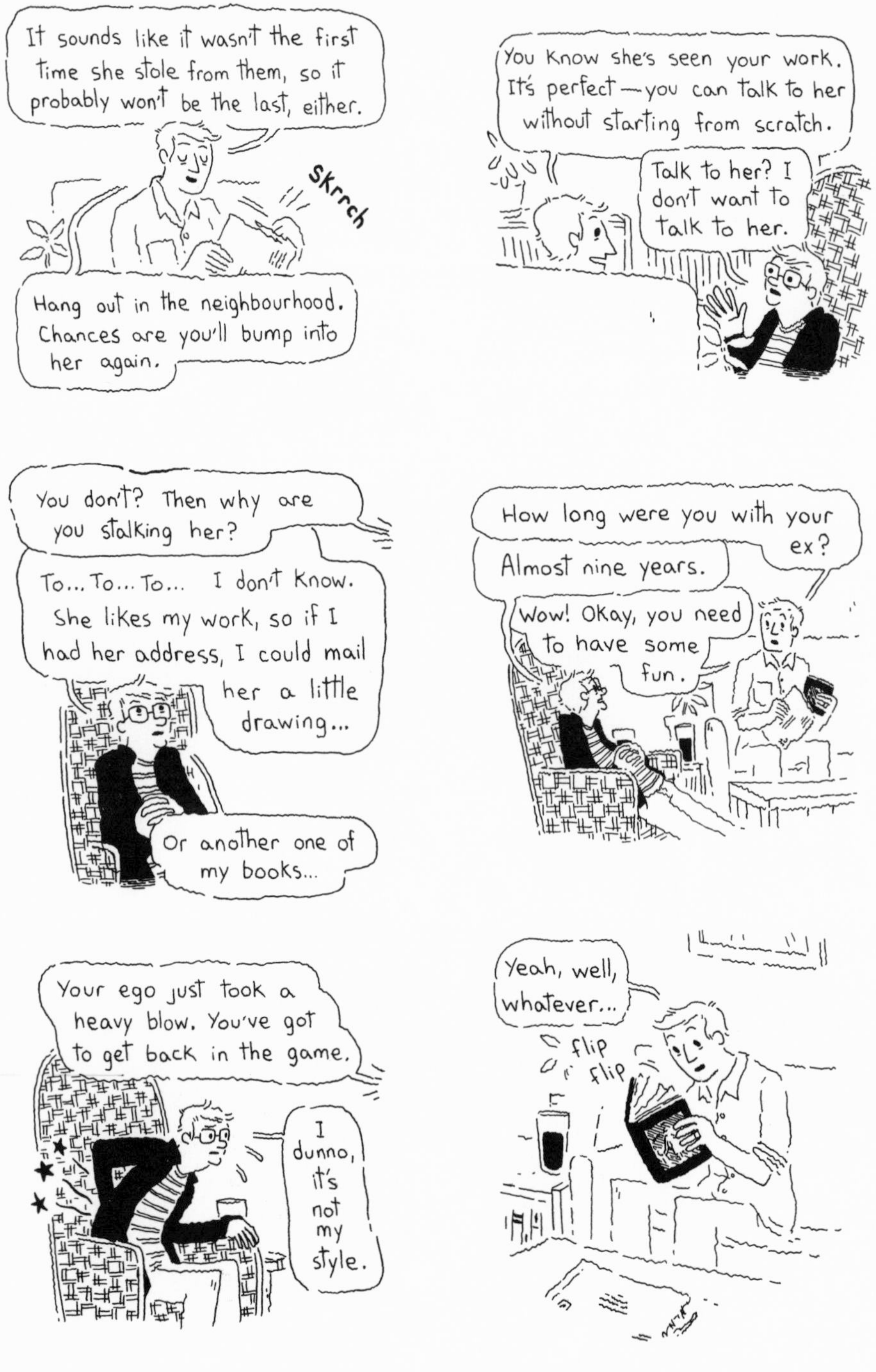
It sounds like it wasn't the first time she stole from them, so it probably won't be the last, either.
SKrrch
Hang out in the neighbourhood. Chances are you'll bump into her again.
You know she's seen your work. It's perfect—you can talk to her without starting from scratch.
Talk to her? I don't want to talk to her.
You don't? Then why are you stalking her?
To... To... To... I don't know. She likes my work, so if I had her address, I could mail her a little drawing...
Or another one of my books...
How long were you with your ex?
Almost nine years.
Wow! Okay, you need to have some fun.
Your ego just took a heavy blow. You've got to get back in the game.
I dunno, it's not my style.
Yeah, well, whatever...
flip
flip

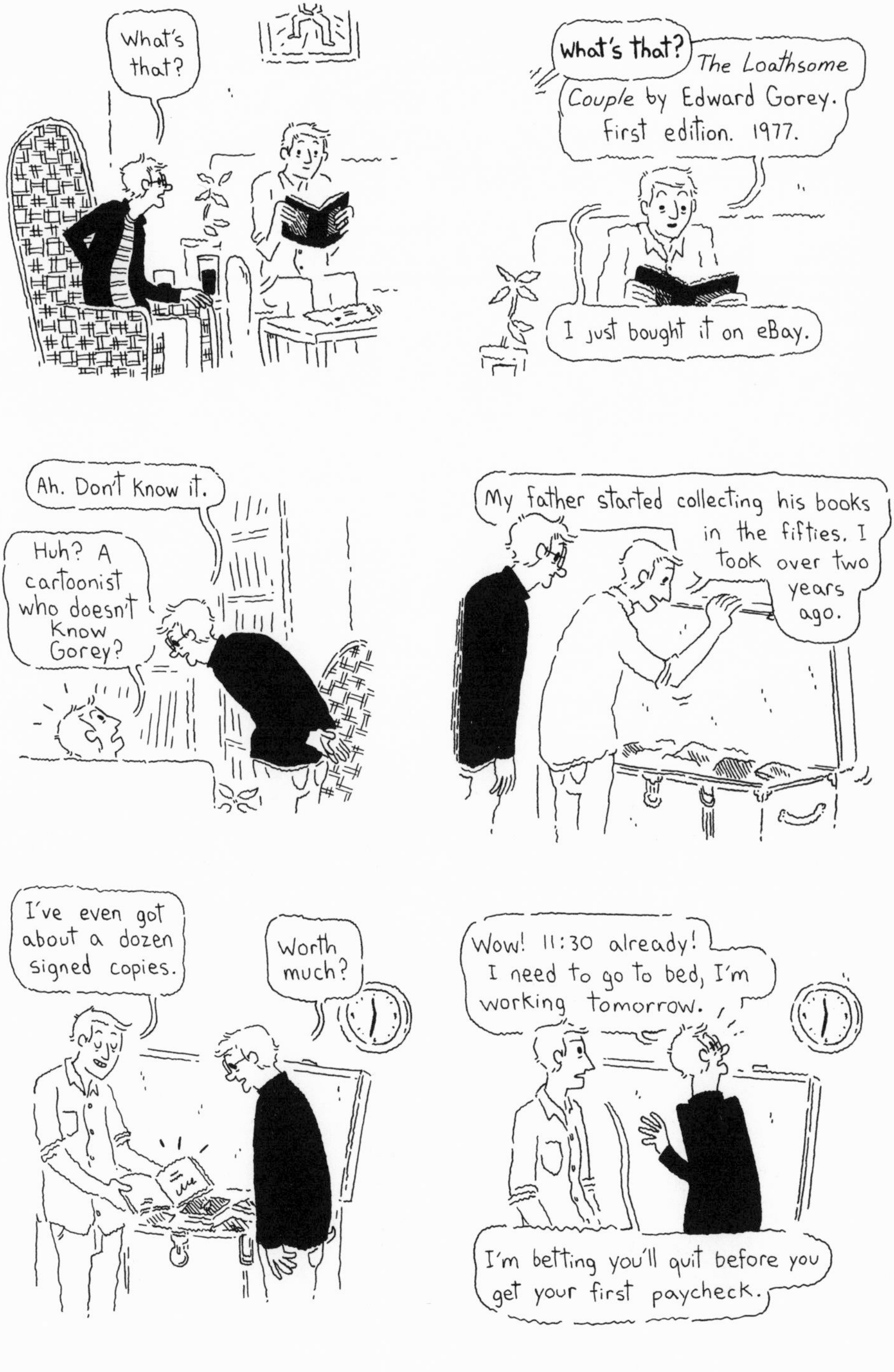
What's that?
What's that?
The Loathsome Couple by Edward Gorey. First edition. 1977.
I just bought it on eBay.
Ah. Don't know it.
Huh? A cartoonist who doesn't know Gorey?
My father started collecting his books in the fifties. I took over two years ago.
I've even got about a dozen signed copies.
Worth much?
Wow! 11:30 already! I need to go to bed, I'm working tomorrow.
I'm betting you'll quit before you get your first paycheck.

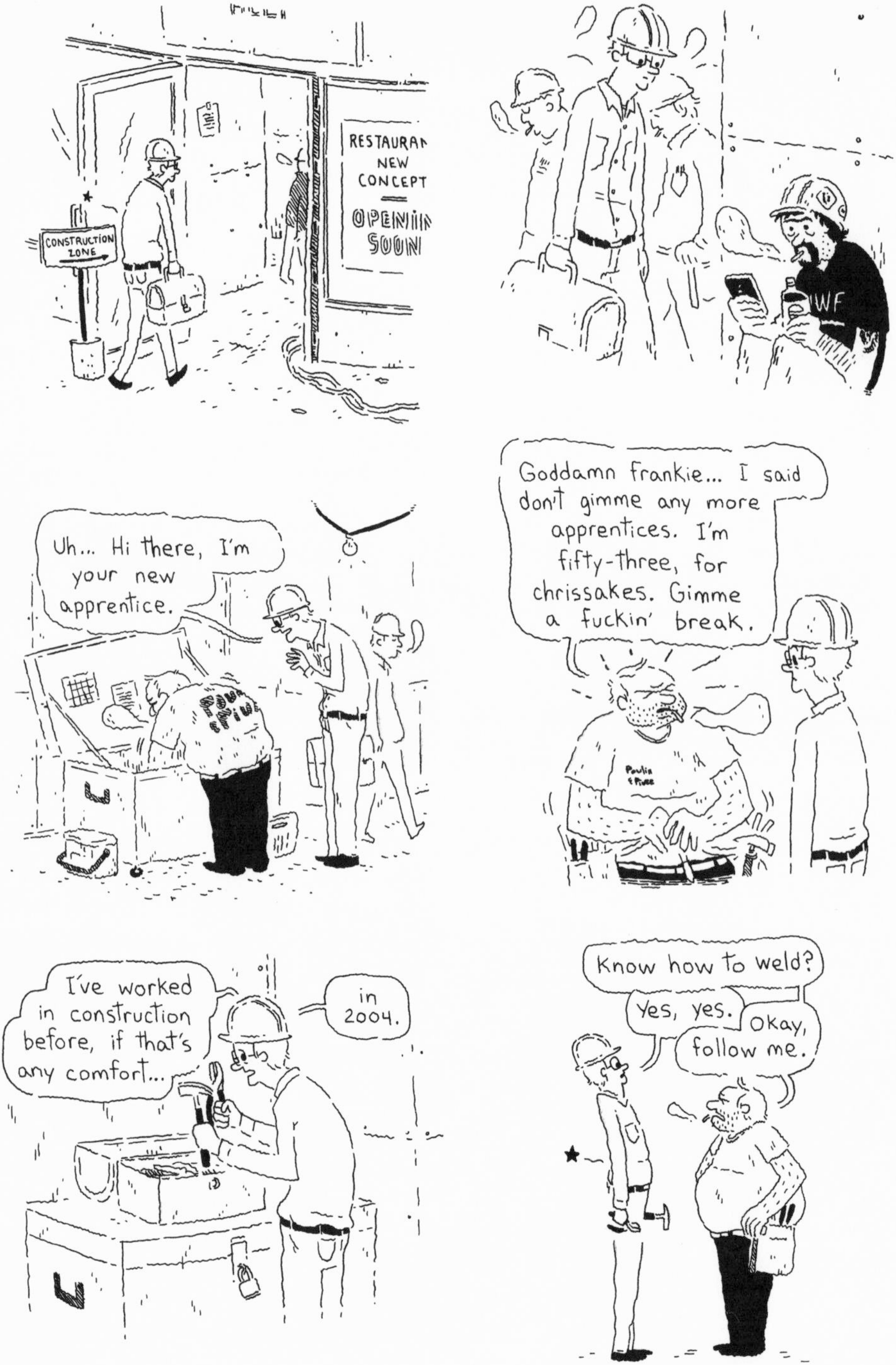
CONSTRUCTION ZONE
RESTAURAN
NEW
CONCEPT
OPENIN
SOON
Uh... Hi there, I'm your new apprentice.
Goddamn frankie... I said don't gimme any more apprentices. I'm fifty-three, for chrissakes. Gimme a fuckin' break.
I've worked in construction before, if that's any comfort...
in 2004.
Know how to weld?
Yes, yes.
Okay, follow me.

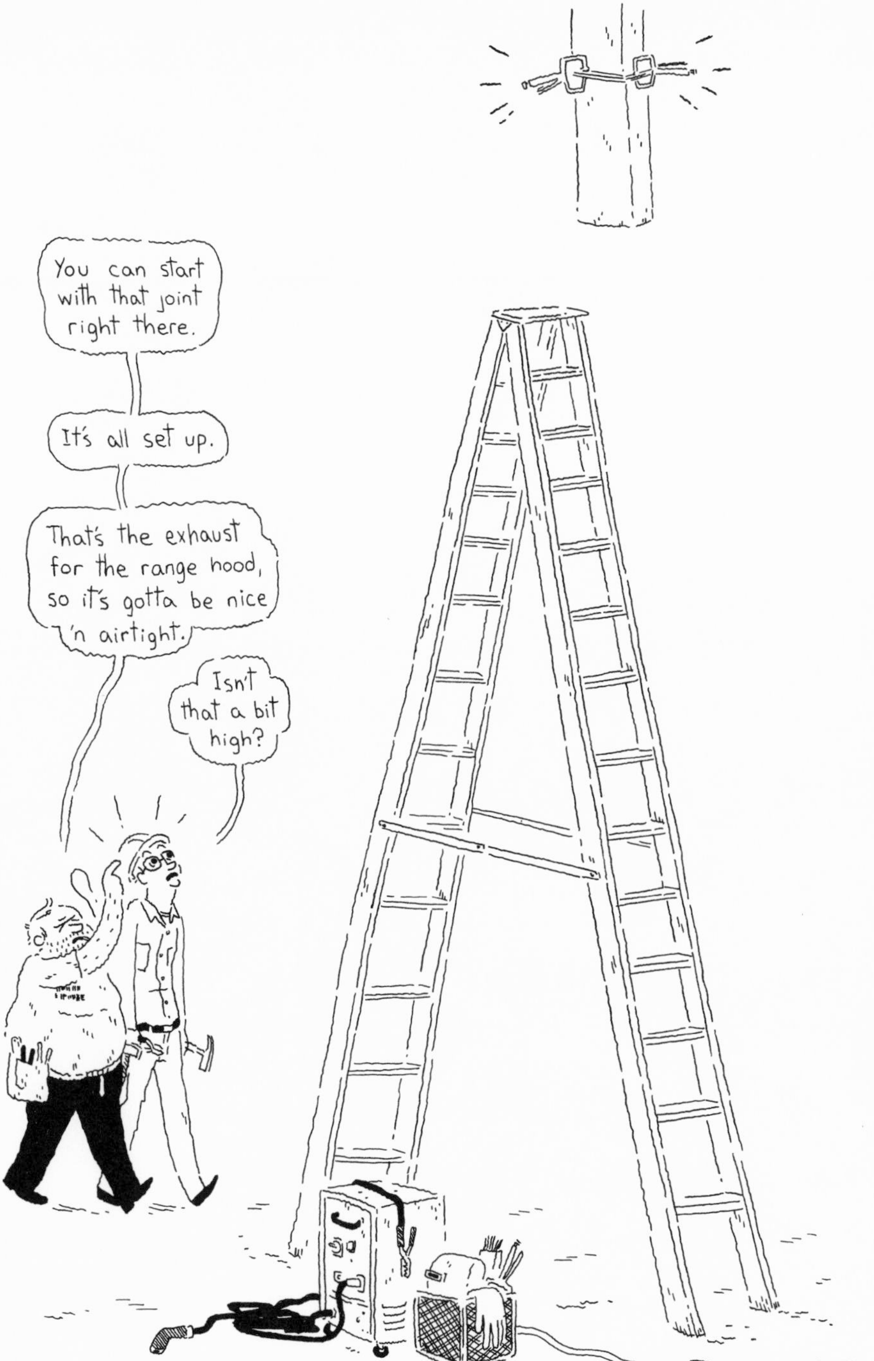
You can start with that joint right there.
It's all set up.
That's the exhaust for the range hood, so it's gotta be nice 'n airtight.
Isn't that a bit high?

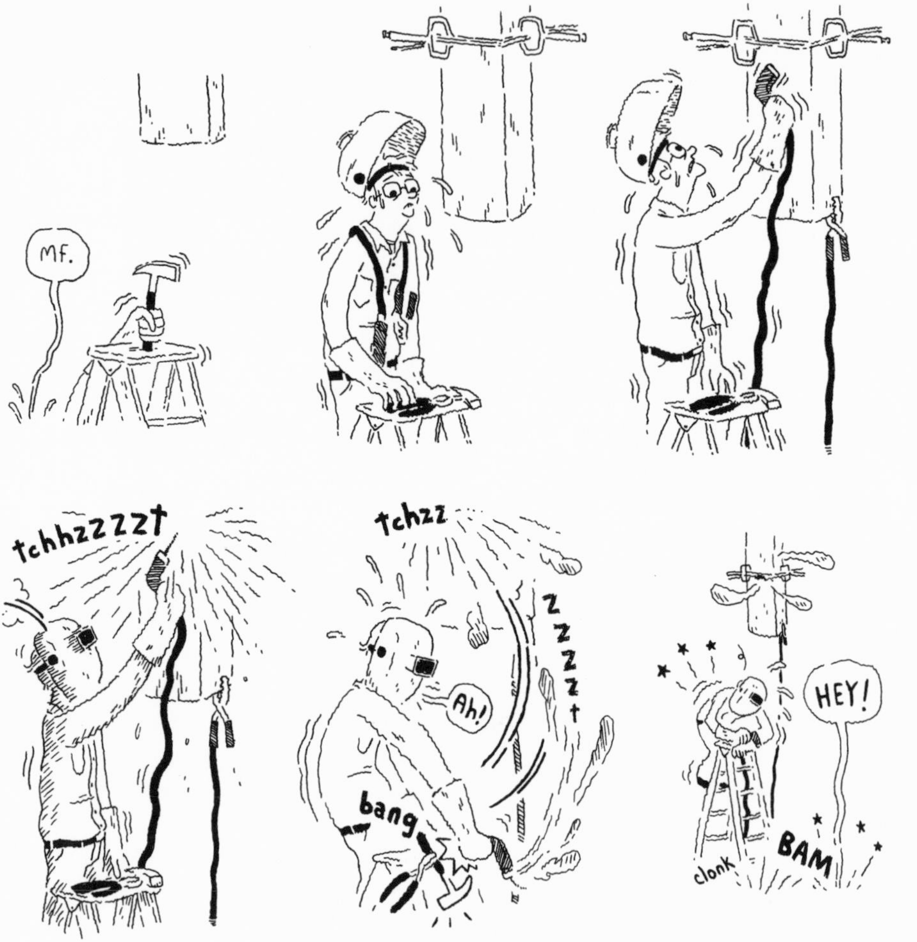
MF.
tchhzzzzt
tchzz
Ah!
zzzzt
bang
HEY!
clonk
BAM
S... Sorry.

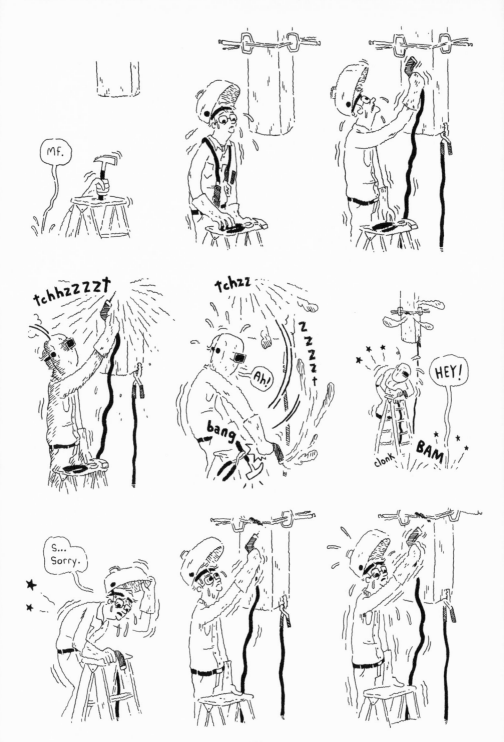

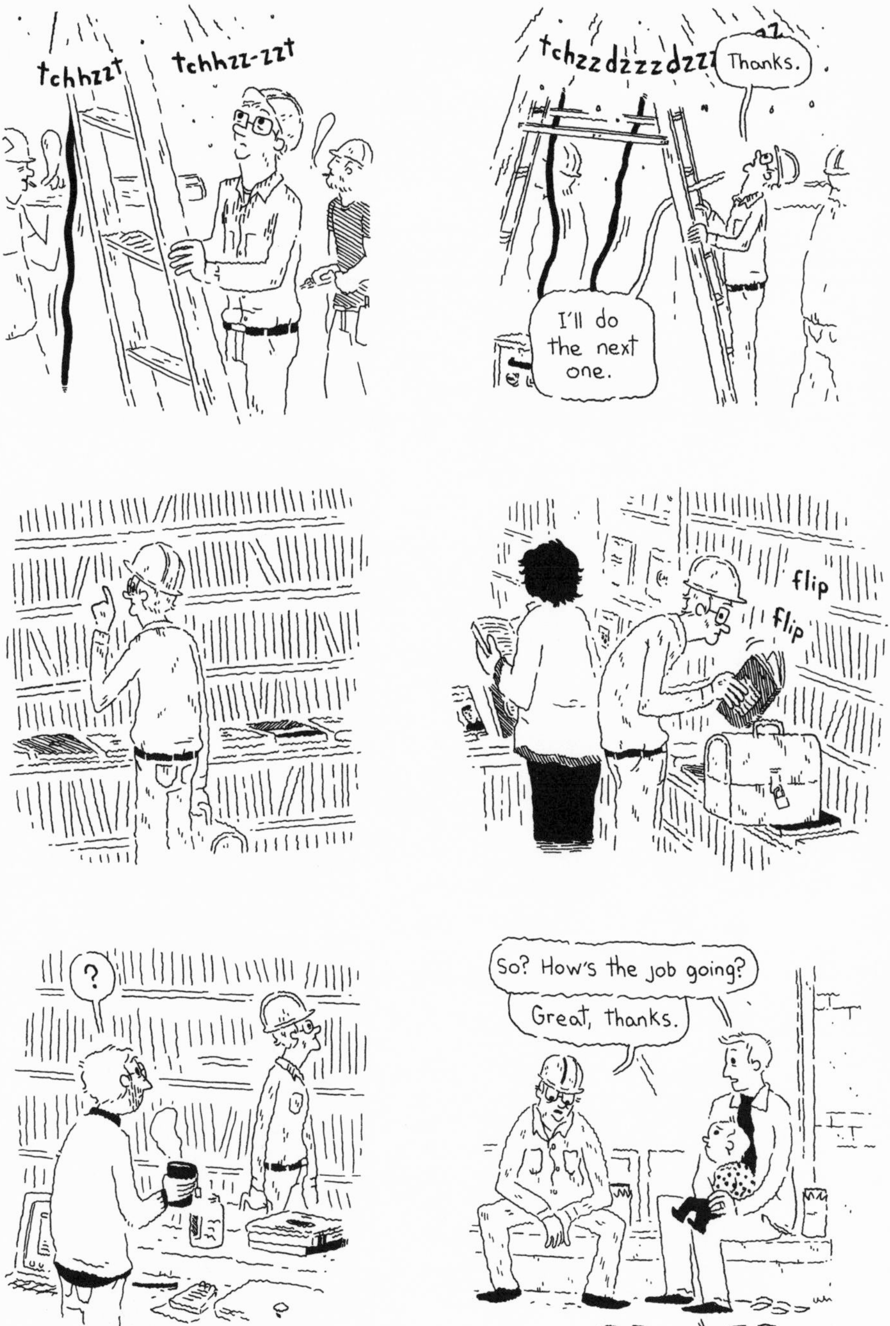
tchhzzt
tchhzz-zzt
tchzzdzzzdzzz
Thanks.
I'll do the next one.
flip
flip
?
So? How's the job going?
Great, thanks.

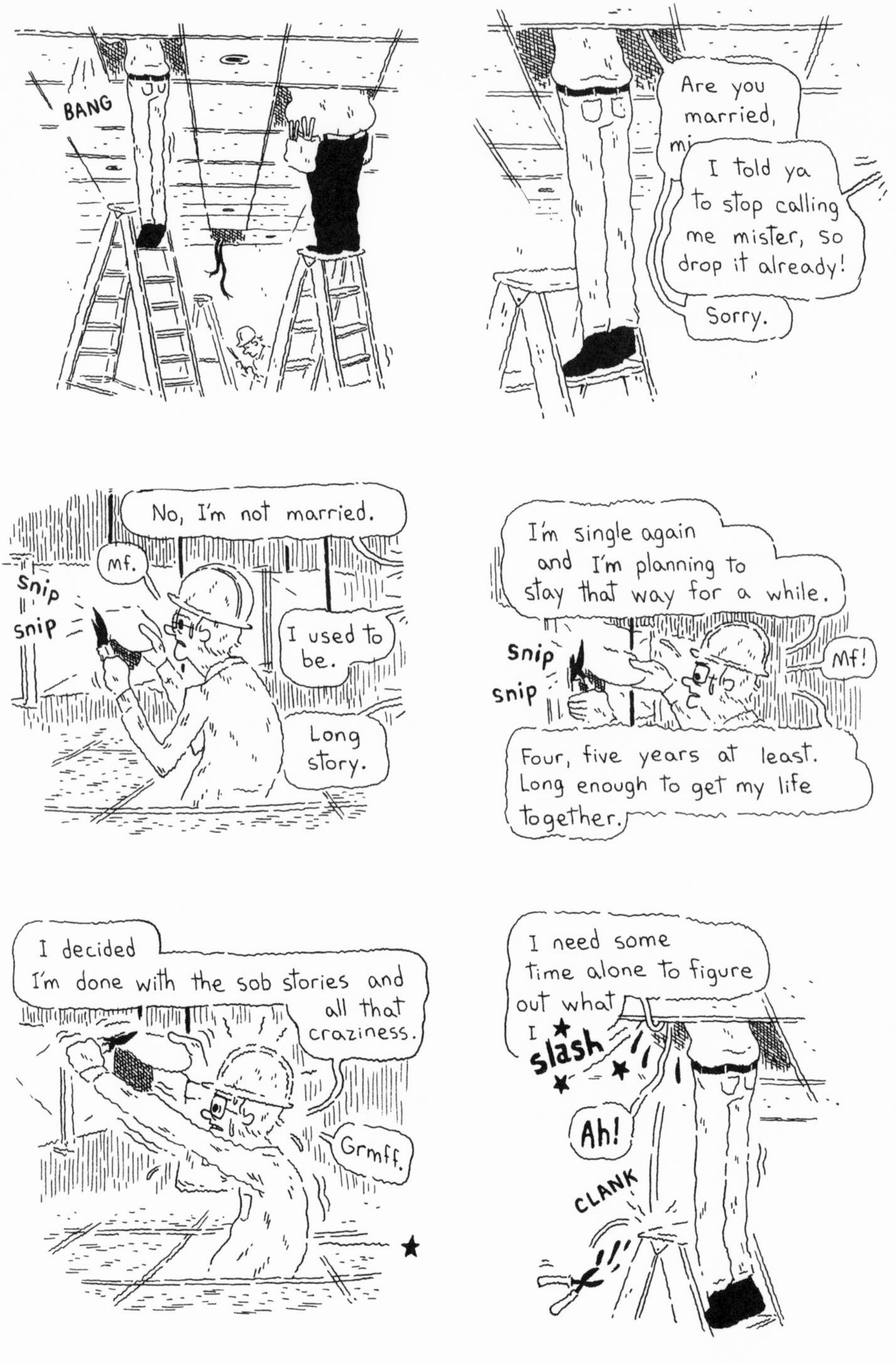
BANG
Are you married, mi
I told ya to stop calling me mister, so drop it already!
Sorry.
No, I'm not married.
Mf.
Snip
snip
I used to be.
Long story.
I'm single again and I'm planning to stay that way for a while.
Snip
snip
Mf!
Four, five years at least. Long enough to get my life together.
I decided I'm done with the sob stories and all that craziness.
Grmff.
I need some time alone to figure out what I
slash
Ah!
CLANK

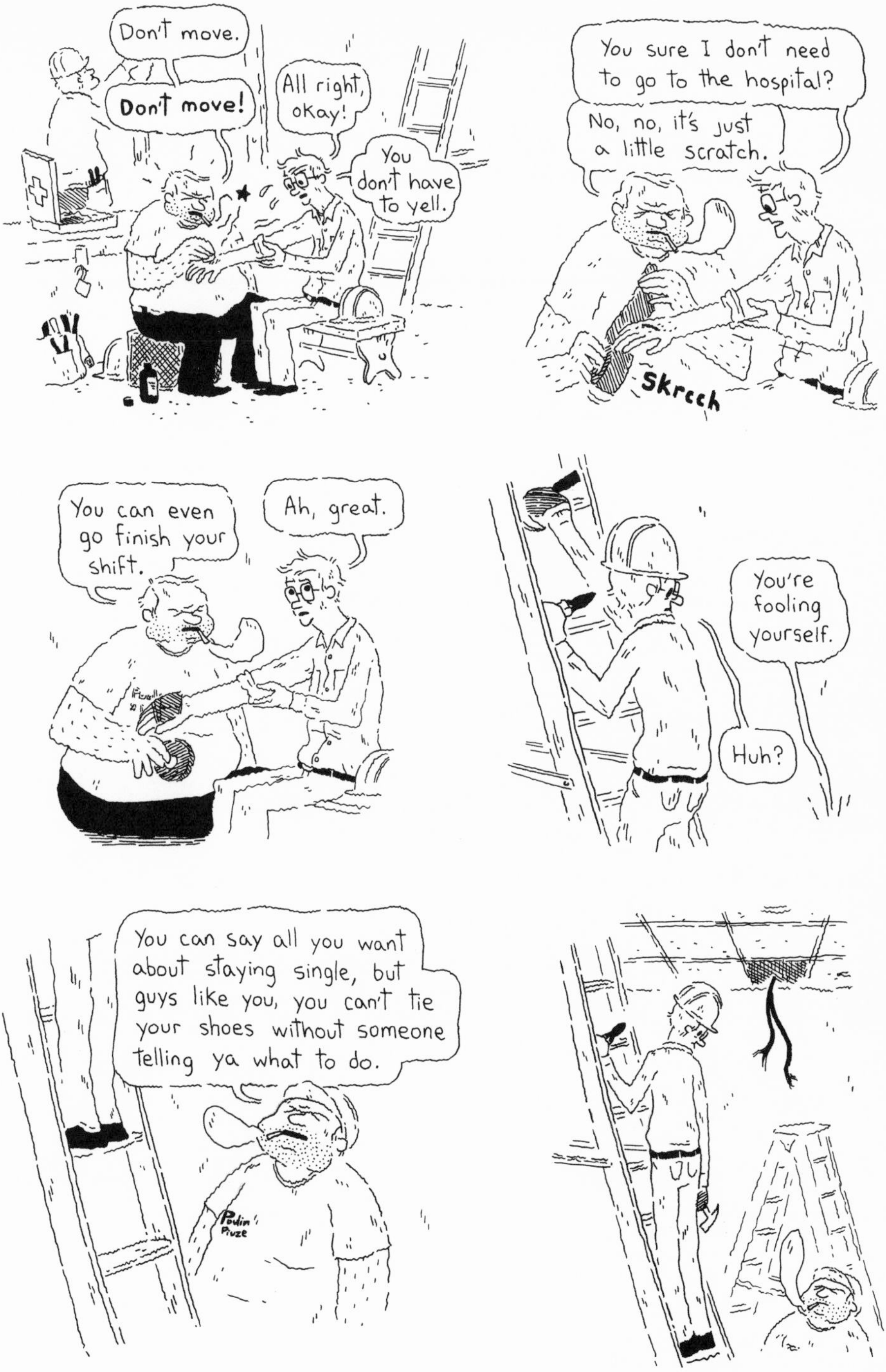
Don't move.
Don't move!
All right, okay!
You don't have to yell.
You sure I don't need to go to the hospital?
No, no, it's just a little scratch.
Skrcch
You can even go finish your shift.
Ah, great.
You're fooling yourself.
Huh?
You can say all you want about staying single, but guys like you, you can't tie your shoes without someone telling ya what to do.

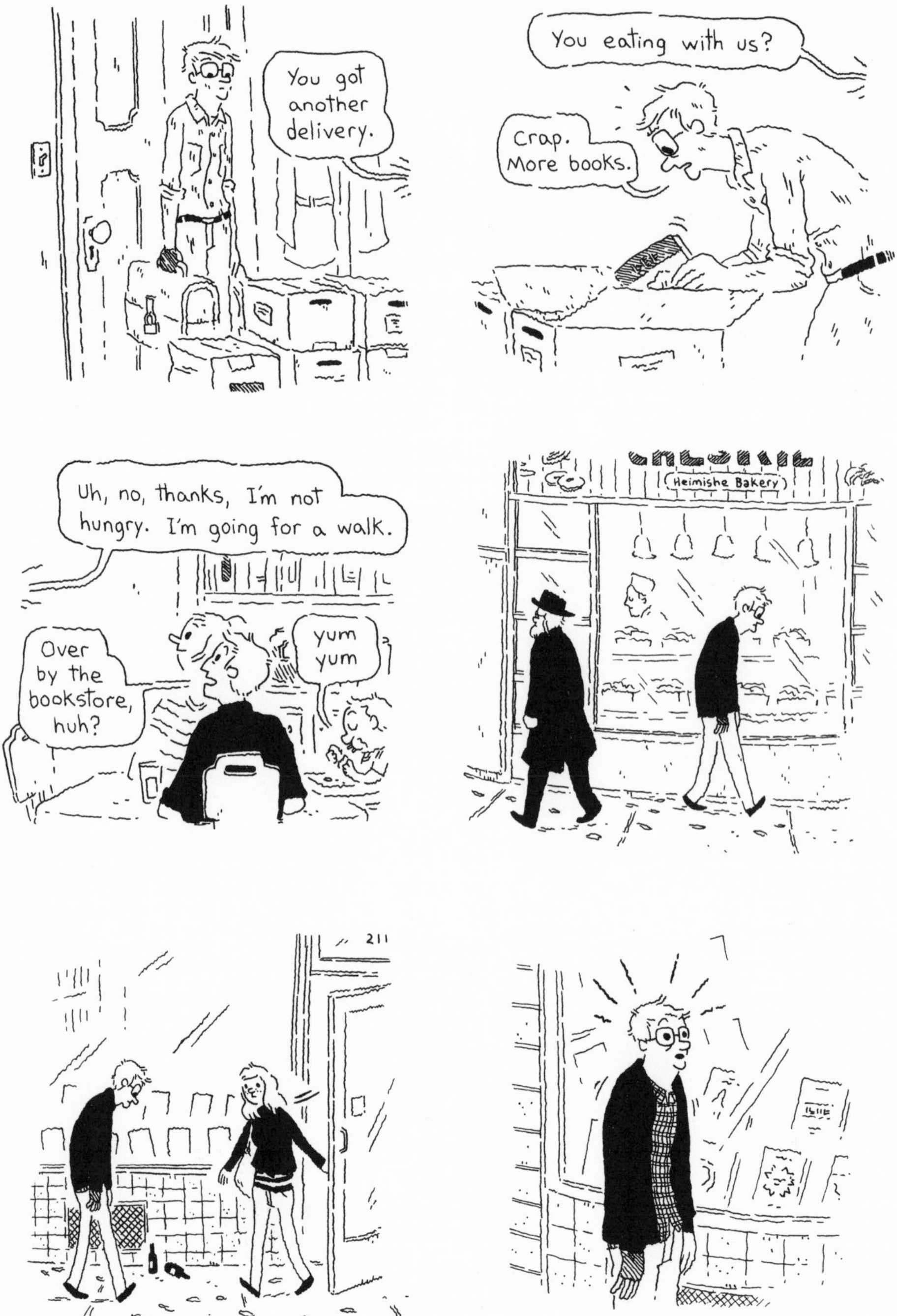
You got another delivery.
You eating with us?
Crap. More books.
Uh, no, thanks, I'm not hungry. I'm going for a walk.
Over by the bookstore, huh?
yum yum
Heimishe Bakery
211

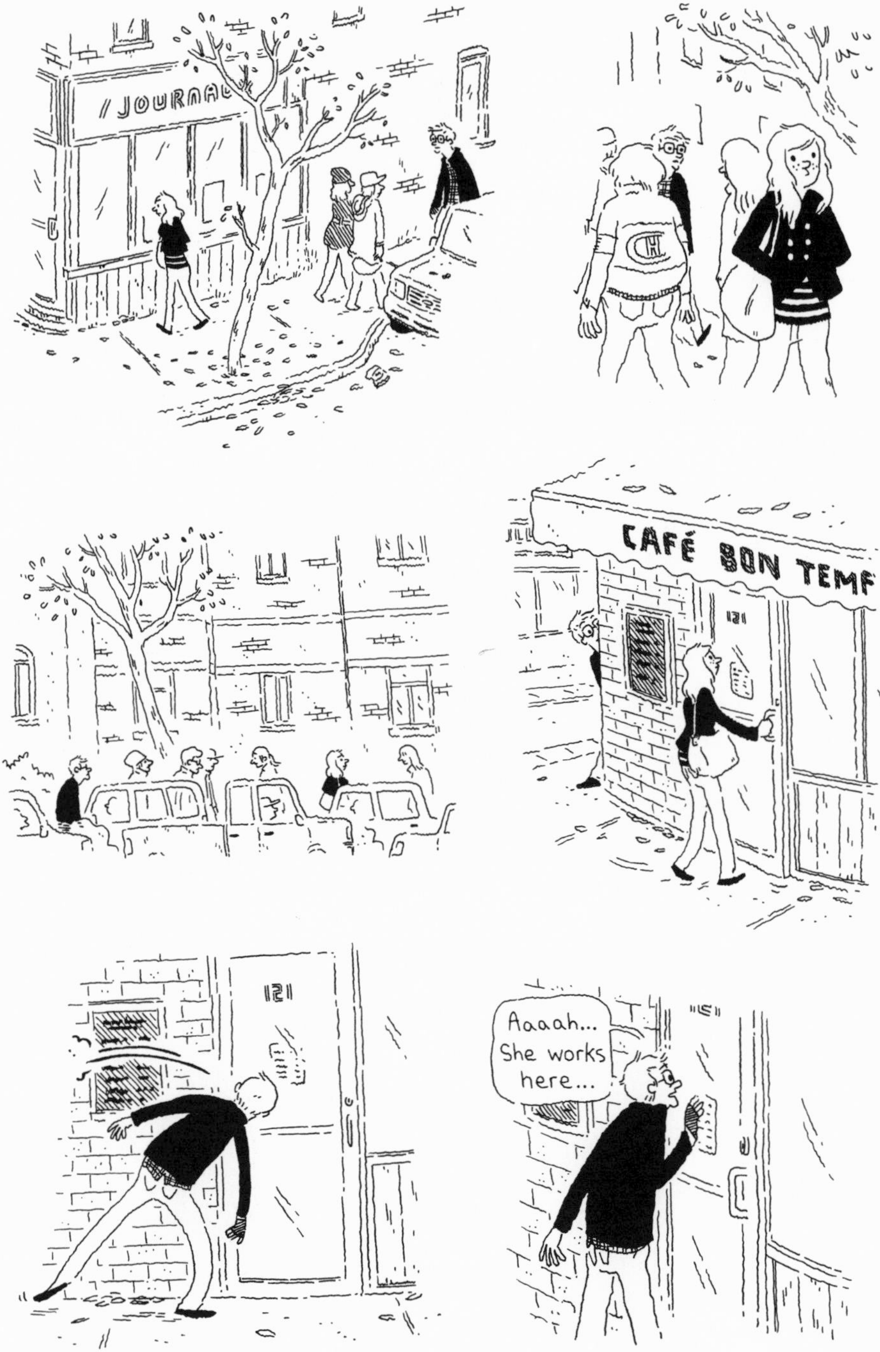
JOURNAL
CAFÉ BON TEMP
121
121
Aaaah... She works here...

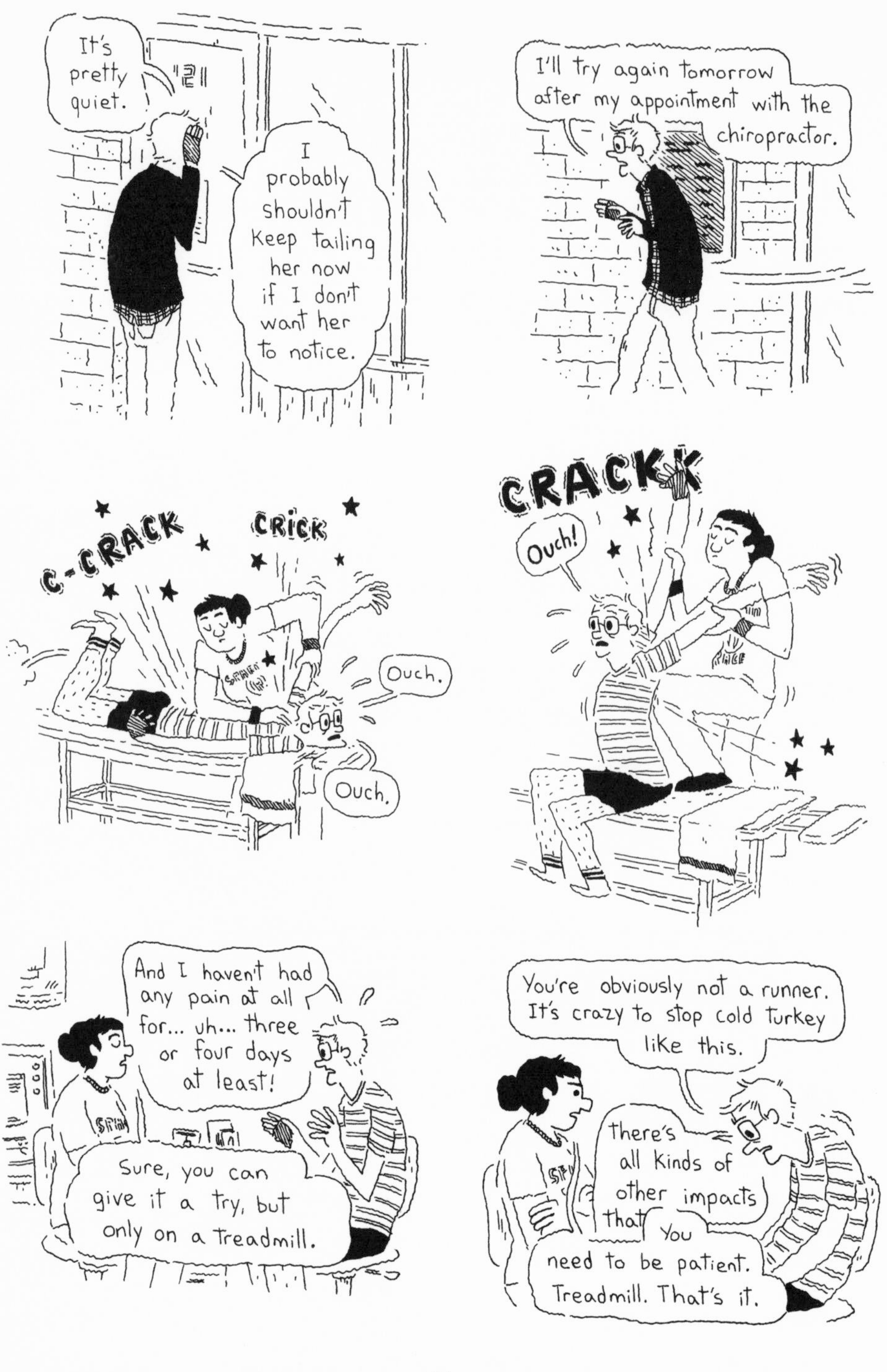

It's pretty quiet.
I probably shouldn't keep tailing her now if I don't want her to notice.
I'll try again tomorrow after my appointment with the chiropractor.
C-CRACK
CRICK
Ouch.
Ouch.
CRACKK
Ouch!
And I haven't had any pain at all for... uh... three or four days at least!
Sure, you can give it a try, but only on a treadmill.
You're obviously not a runner. It's crazy to stop cold turkey like this.
there's all kinds of other impacts that
You need to be patient. Treadmill. That's it.

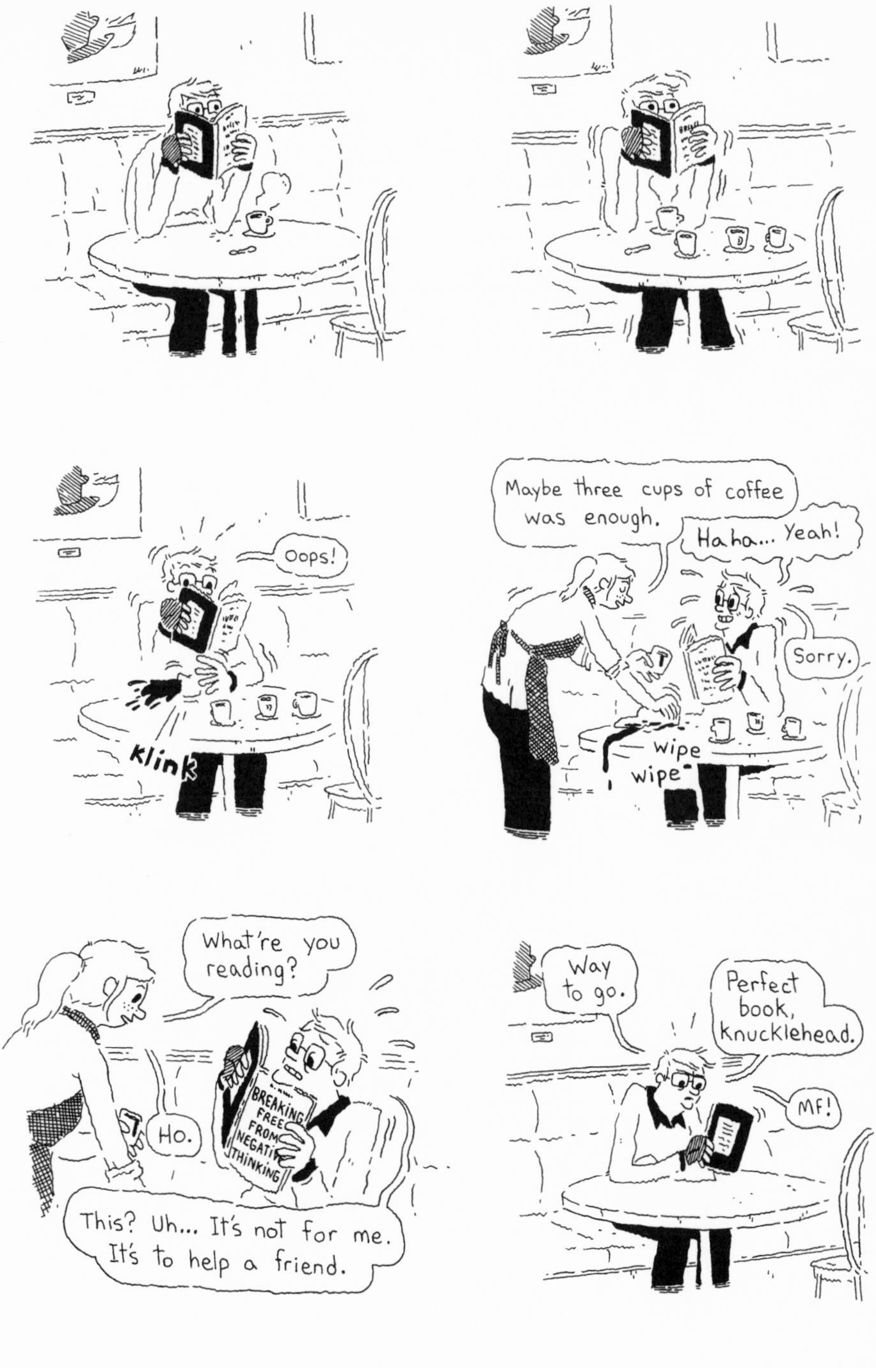
Oops!
klink
Maybe three cups of coffee was enough.
Haha... Yeah!
Sorry.
wipe
wipe
What're you reading?
Ho.
This? Uh... It's not for me. It's to help a friend.
BREAKING FREE FROM NEGATIVE THINKING
Way to go.
Perfect book, knucklehead.
MF!

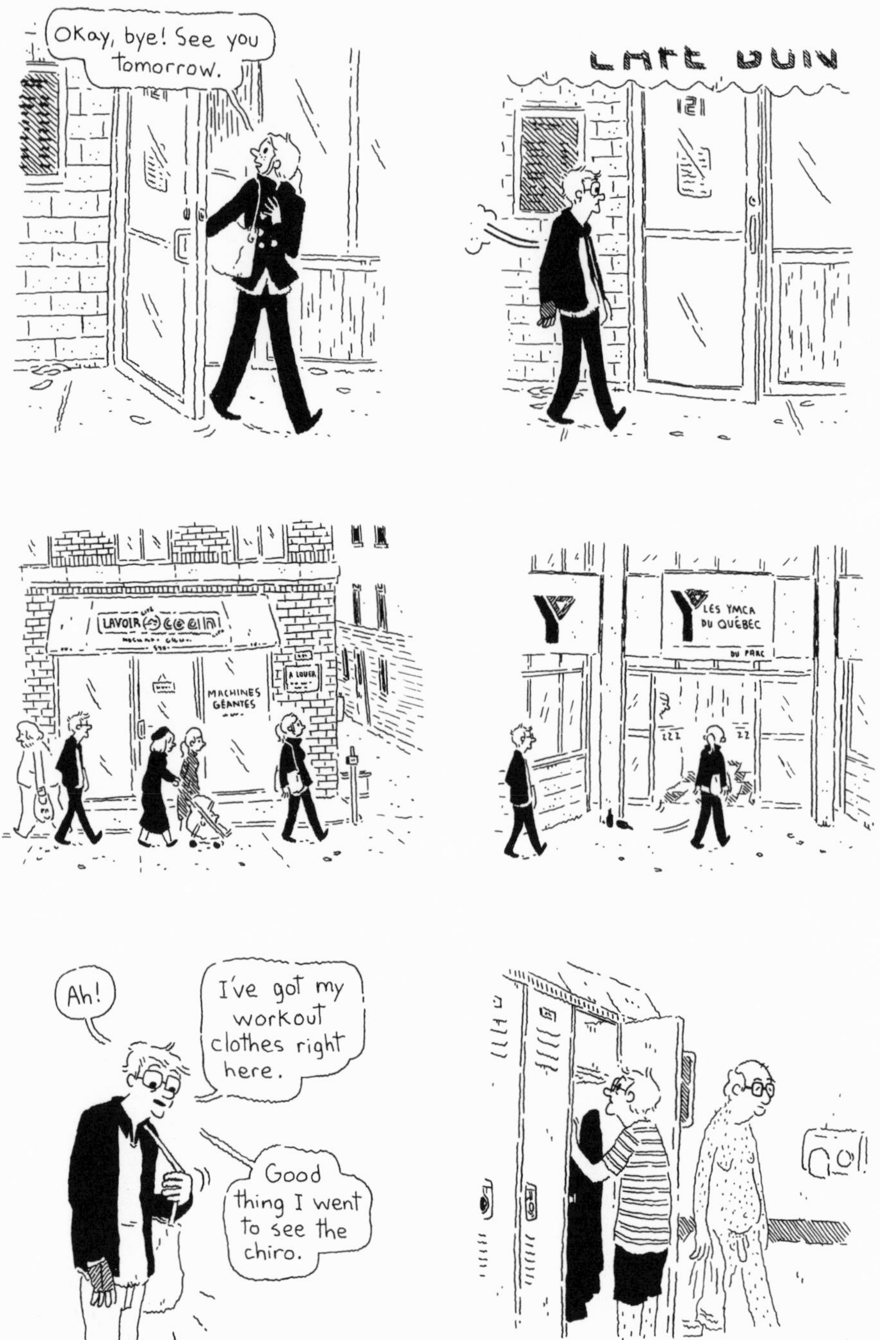
Okay, bye! See you tomorrow.
121
LAVOIR
MACHINES GÉANTES
À LOUER
LES YMCA DU QUÉBEC
DU PARC
Ah!
I've got my workout clothes right here.
Good thing I went to see the chiro.

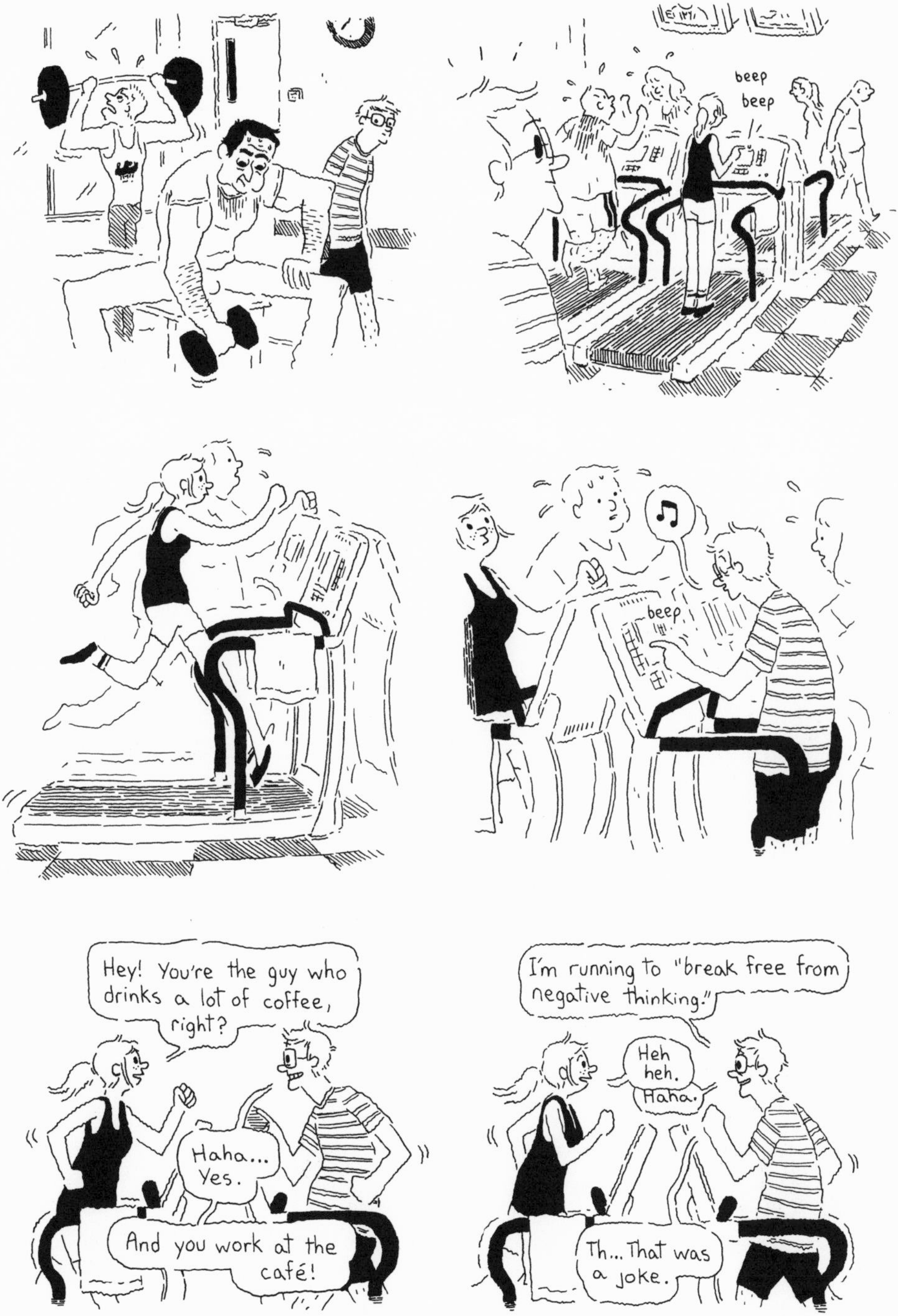
beep
beep
beep
Hey! You're the guy who drinks a lot of coffee, right?
Haha... Yes.
And you work at the café!
I'm running to "break free from negative thinking."
Heh heh.
Haha.
Th... That was a joke.

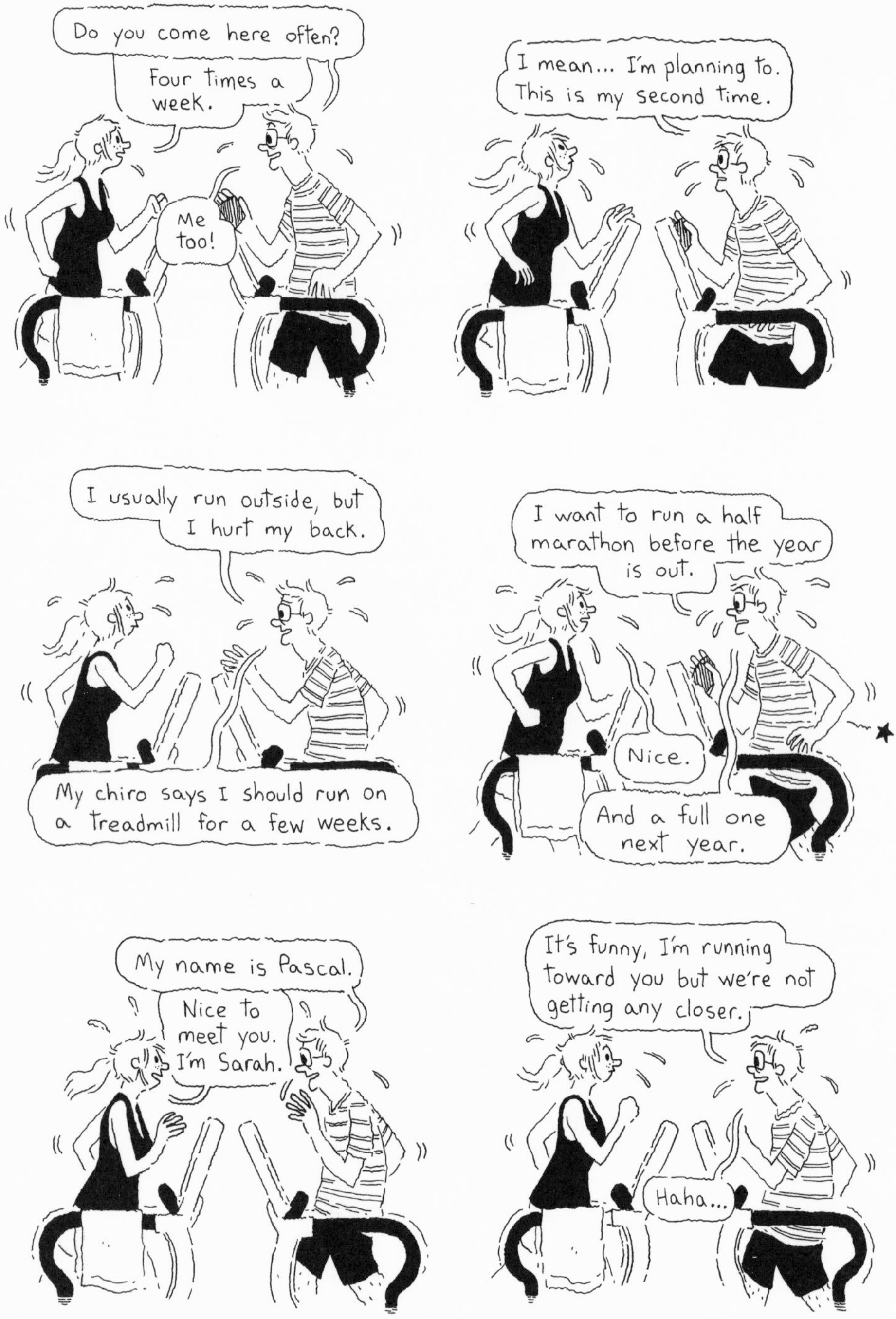

Do you come here often?
Four times a week.
Me too!
I mean... I'm planning to. This is my second time.
I usually run outside, but I hurt my back.
My chiro says I should run on a treadmill for a few weeks.
I want to run a half marathon before the year is out.
Nice.
And a full one next year.
My name is Pascal.
Nice to meet you. I'm Sarah.
It's funny, I'm running toward you but we're not getting any closer.
Haha...

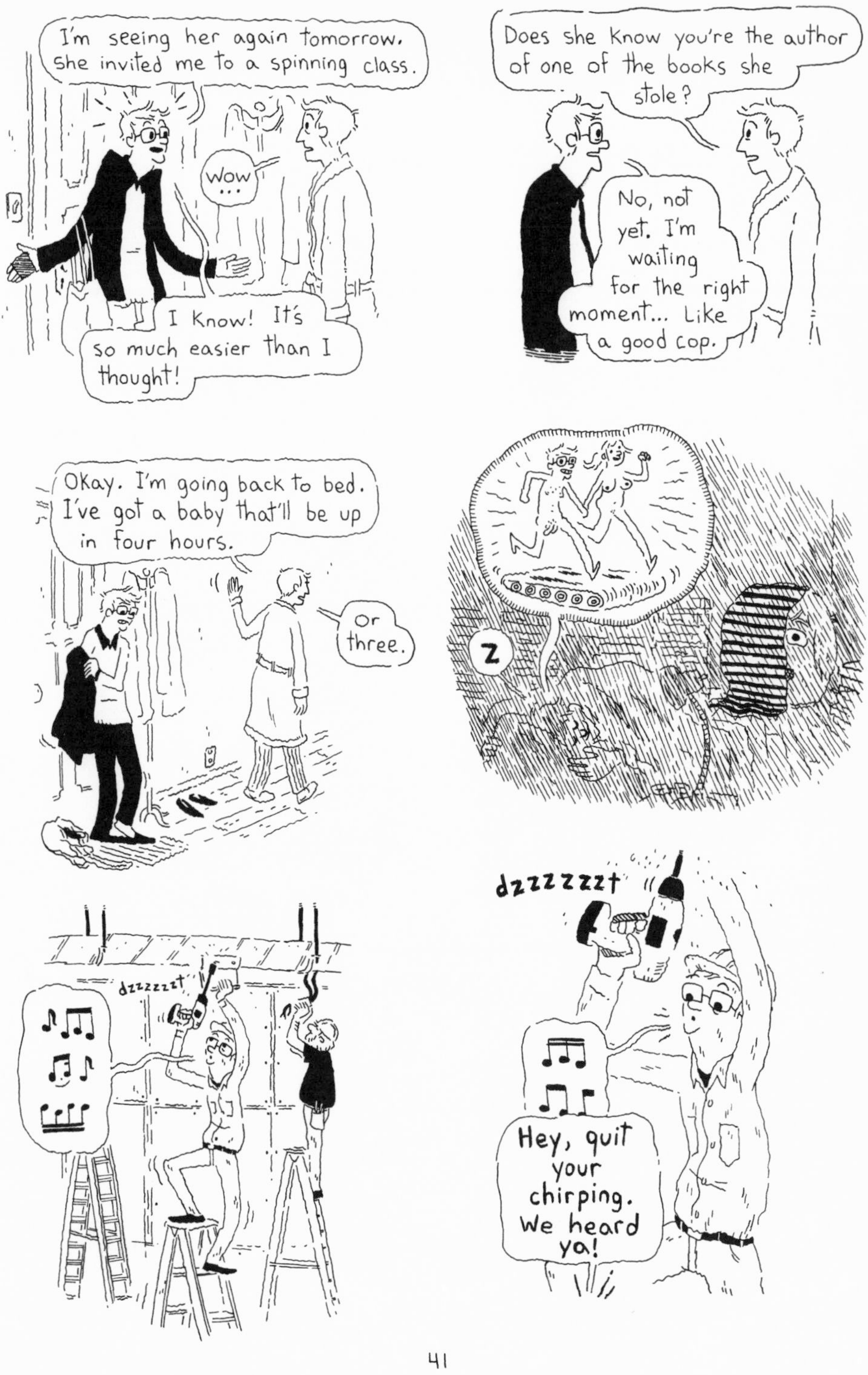
I'm seeing her again tomorrow. She invited me to a spinning class.
Wow...
I know! It's so much easier than I thought!
Does she know you're the author of one of the books she stole?
No, not yet. I'm waiting for the right moment... Like a good cop.
Okay. I'm going back to bed. I've got a baby that'll be up in four hours.
Or three.
Z
dzzzzzt
dzzzzzzt
Hey, quit your chirping. We heard ya!

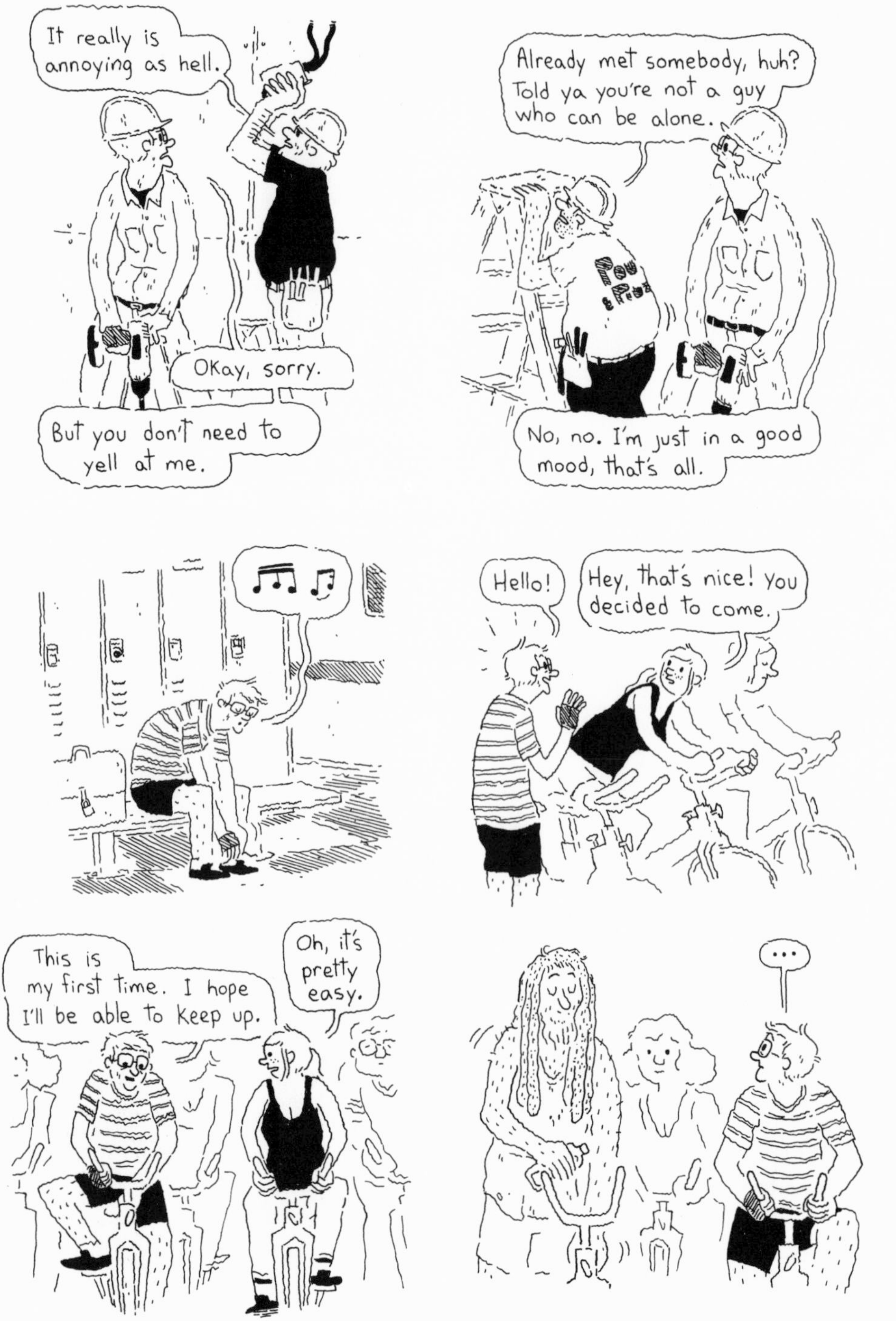
It really is annoying as hell.
Okay, sorry.
But you don't need to yell at me.
Already met somebody, huh? Told ya you're not a guy who can be alone.
No, no. I'm just in a good mood, that's all.
Hello!
Hey, that's nice! You decided to come.
This is my first time. I hope I'll be able to keep up.
Oh, it's pretty easy.
...

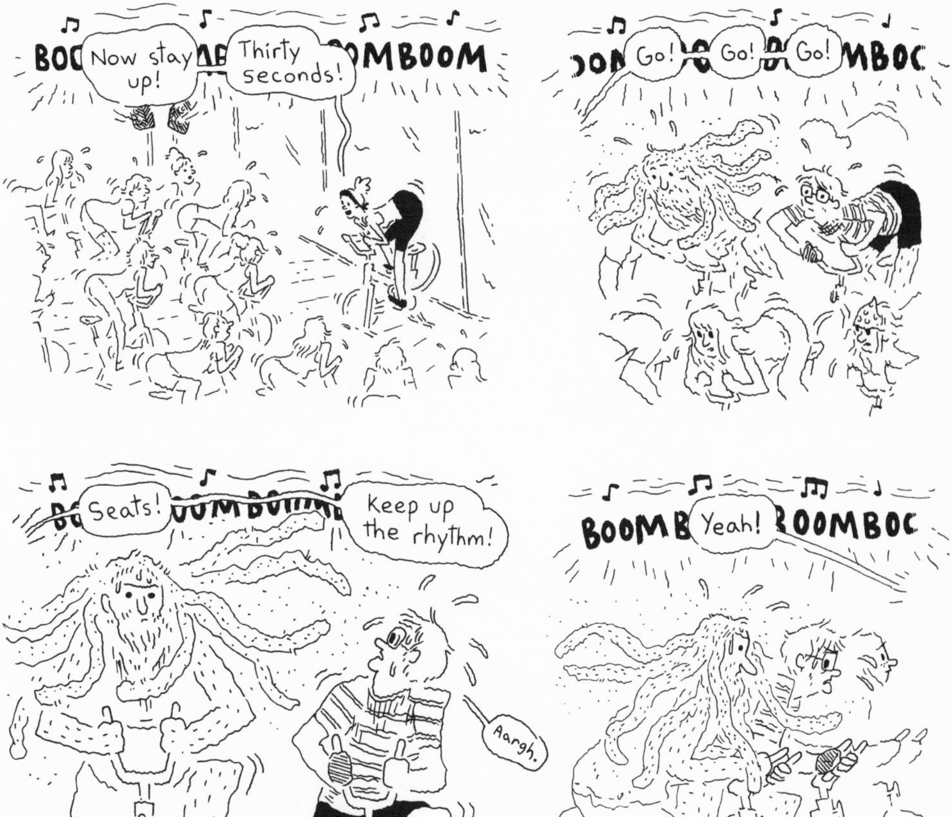
BOO
Now stay up!
Thirty seconds!
OMBOOM
Go!
Go!
Go!
MBOC
Seats!
Keep up the rhythm!
Aargh.
BOOMB
Yeah!
OOMBOC
Yeah, that was fun. I really liked it.
That's great!
Okay, well, see you around sometime.
So... uh...
W... Uh... Hold on! Are you d... doing anything... now?
Are... Are you busy?

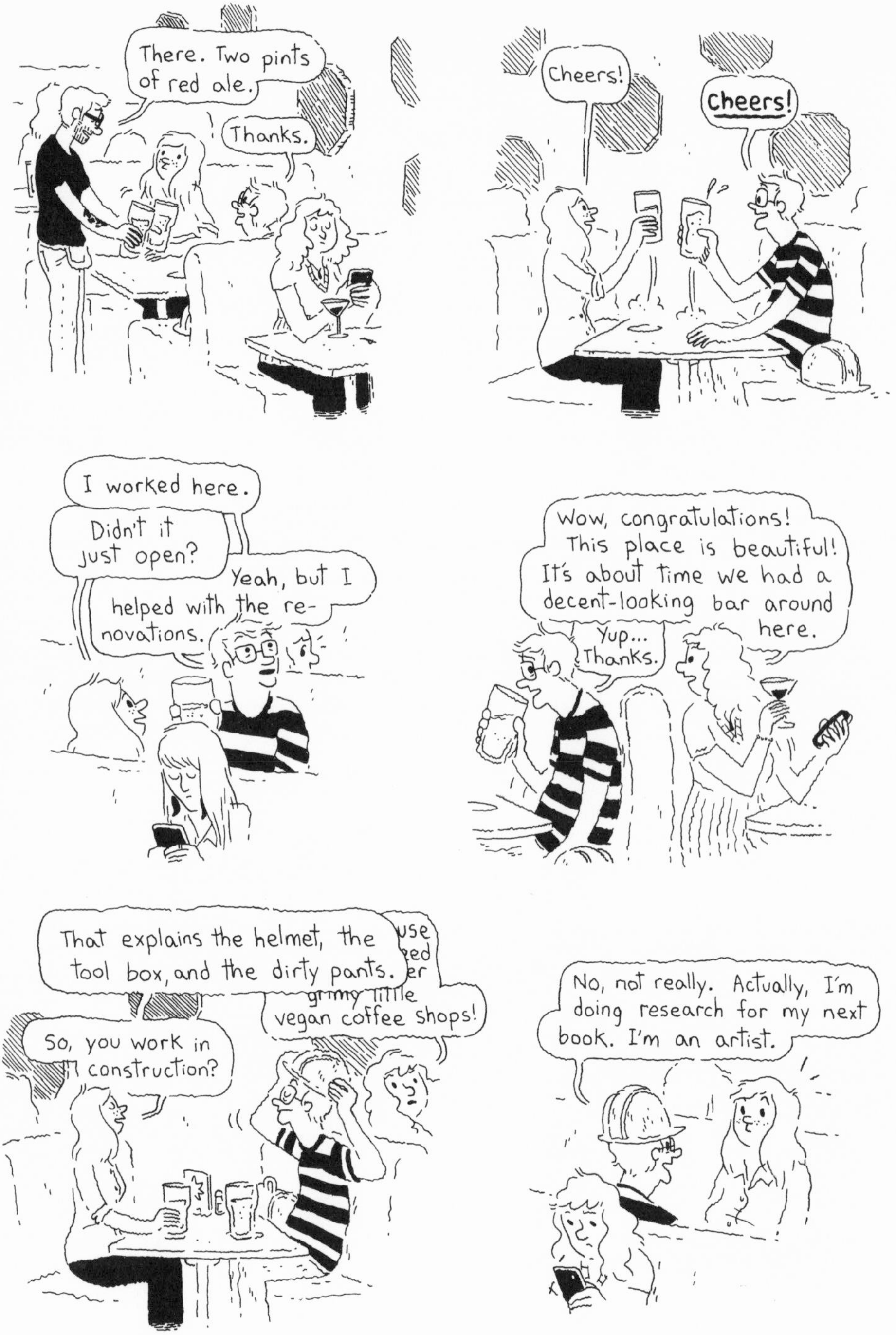
There. Two pints of red ale.
Thanks.
Cheers!
Cheers!
I worked here.
Didn't it just open?
Yeah, but I helped with the re-novations.
Wow, congratulations! This place is beautiful! It's about time we had a decent-looking bar around here.
Yup... Thanks.
That explains the helmet, the tool box, and the dirty pants.
grimy little vegan coffee shops!
So, you work in construction?
No, not really. Actually, I'm doing research for my next book. I'm an artist.

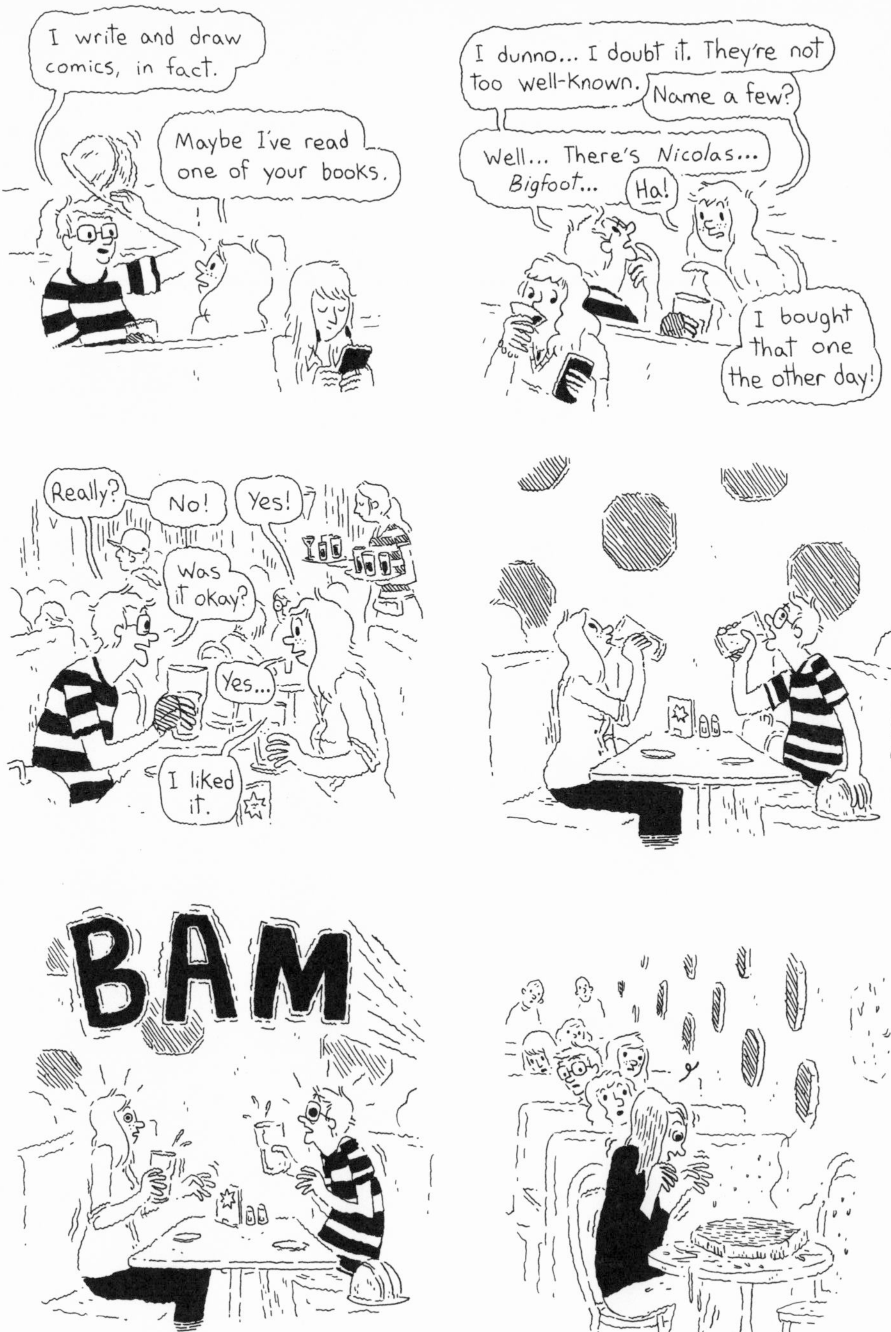
I write and draw comics, in fact.
Maybe I've read one of your books.
I dunno... I doubt it. They're not too well-Known.
Name a few?
Well... There's *Nicolas*... *Bigfoot*...
Ha!
I bought that one the other day!
Really?
No!
Yes!
Was it okay?
Yes...
I liked it.
BAM

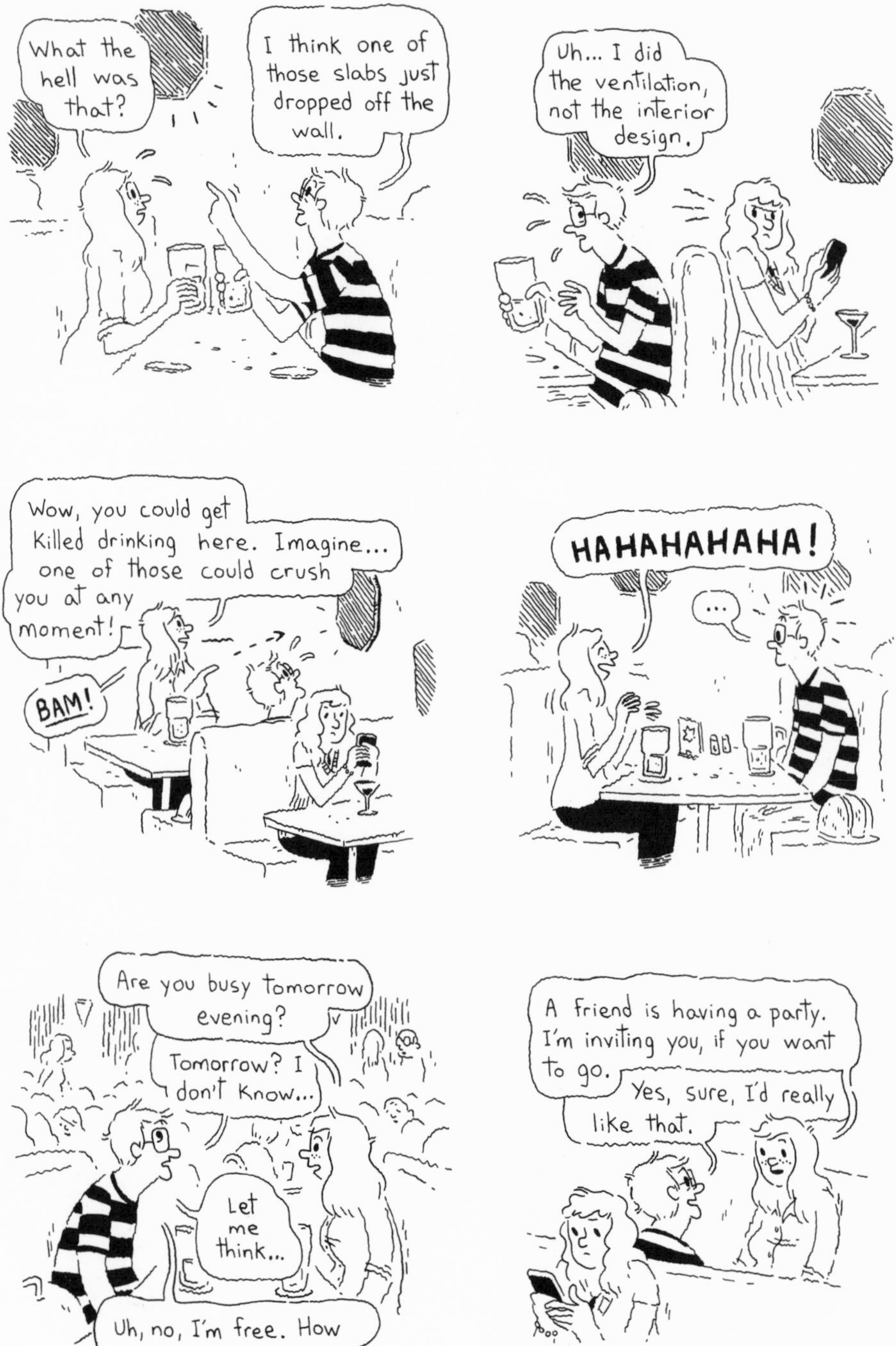
What the hell was that?
I think one of those slabs just dropped off the wall.
Uh... I did the ventilation, not the interior design.
Wow, you could get killed drinking here. Imagine... one of those could crush you at any moment!
BAM!
HAHAHAHAHA!
...
Are you busy tomorrow evening?
Tomorrow? I don't know...
Let me think...
Uh, no, I'm free. How come?
A friend is having a party. I'm inviting you, if you want to go.
Yes, sure, I'd really like that.

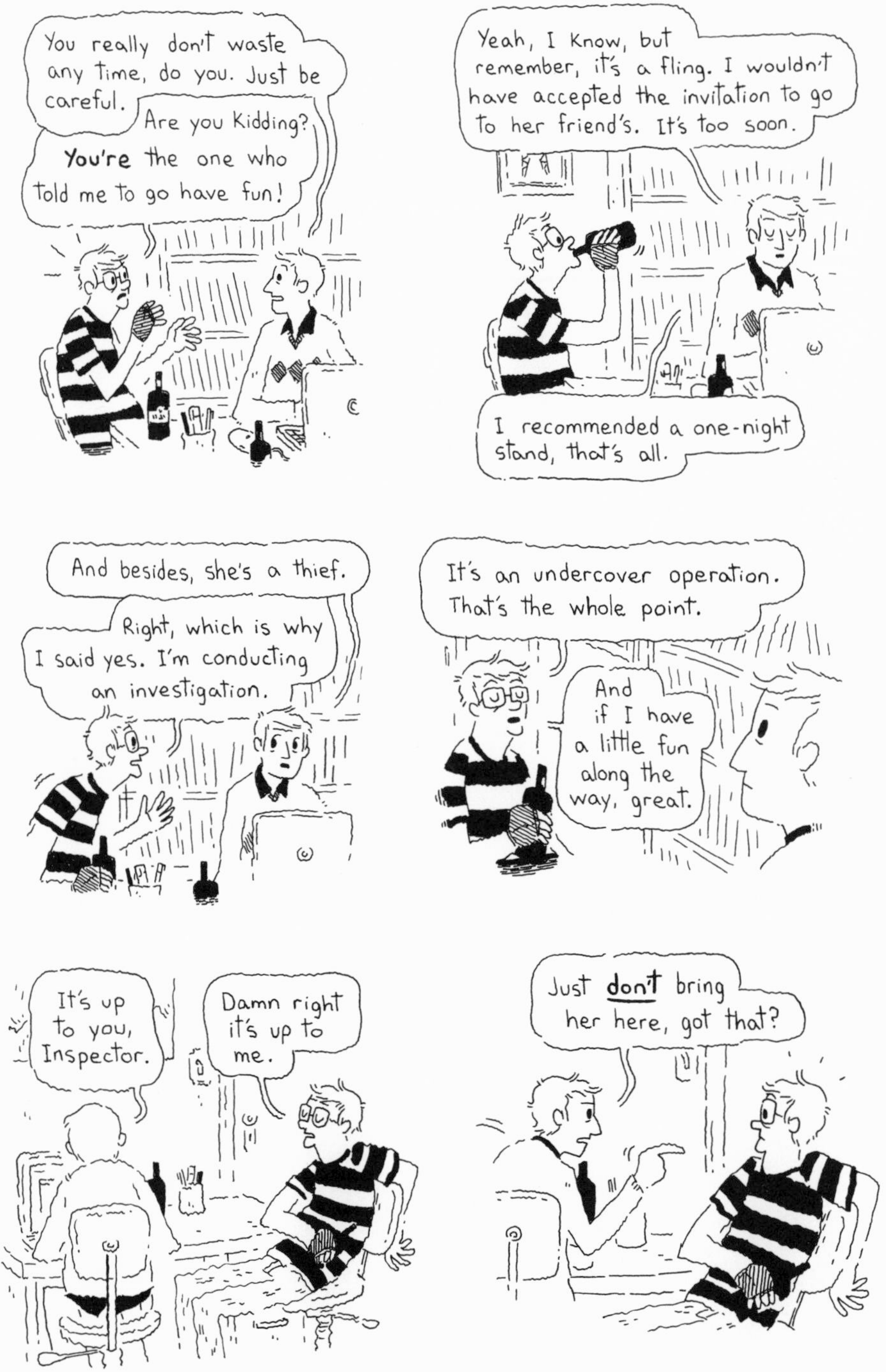
You really don't waste any time, do you. Just be careful.
Are you kidding? **You're** the one who told me to go have fun!
Yeah, I know, but remember, it's a fling. I wouldn't have accepted the invitation to go to her friend's. It's too soon.
I recommended a one-night stand, that's all.
And besides, she's a thief.
Right, which is why I said yes. I'm conducting an investigation.
It's an undercover operation. That's the whole point.
And if I have a little fun along the way, great.
It's up to you, Inspector.
Damn right it's up to me.
Just don't bring her here, got that?

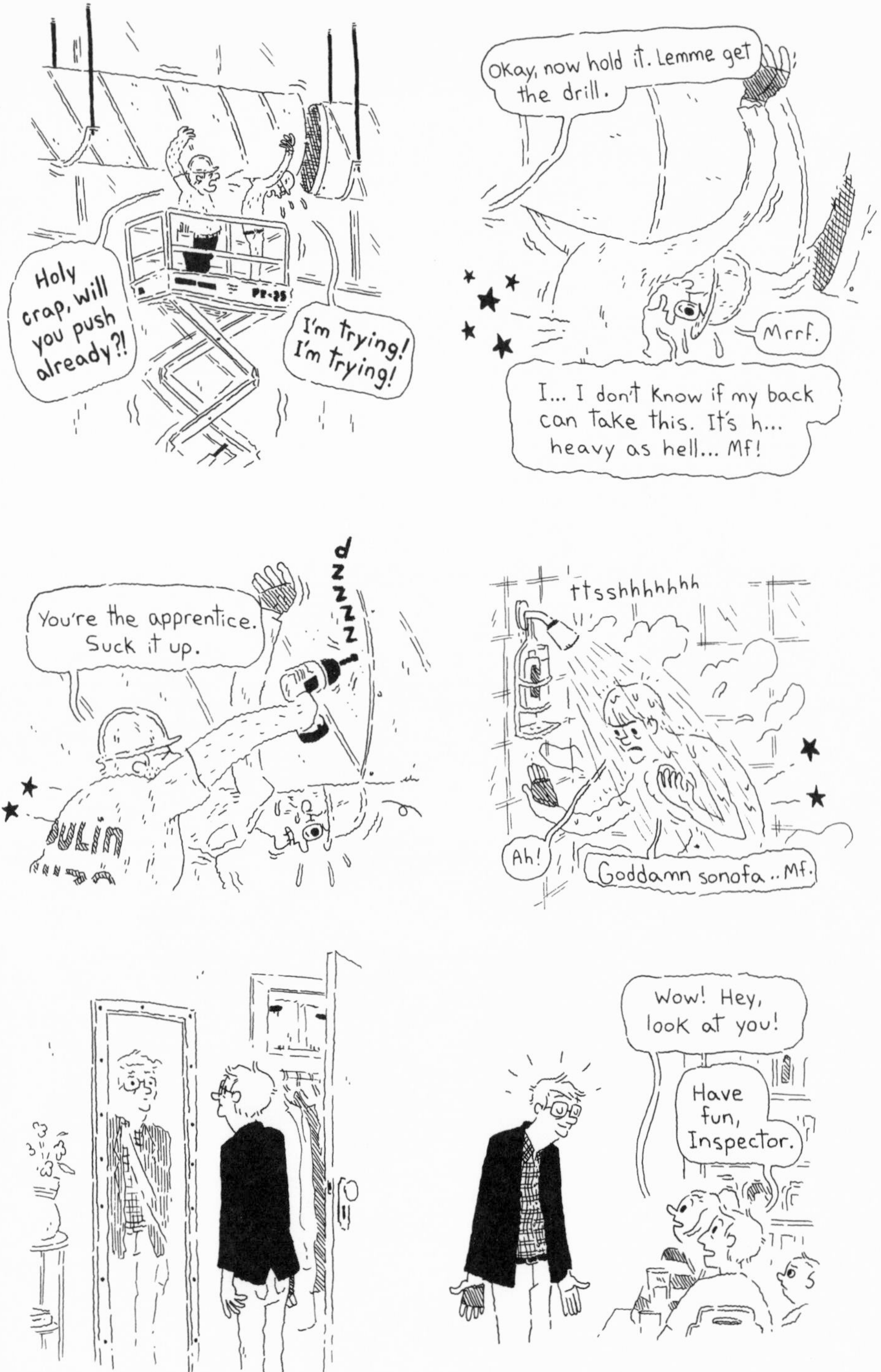
Holy crap, will you push already?!
I'm trying! I'm trying!
Okay, now hold it. Lemme get the drill.
Mrrf.
I... I don't know if my back can take this. It's h... heavy as hell... Mf!
You're the apprentice. Suck it up.
dzzzz
ttsshhhhhhh
Ah!
Goddamn sonofa.. Mf.
Wow! Hey, look at you!
Have fun, Inspector.

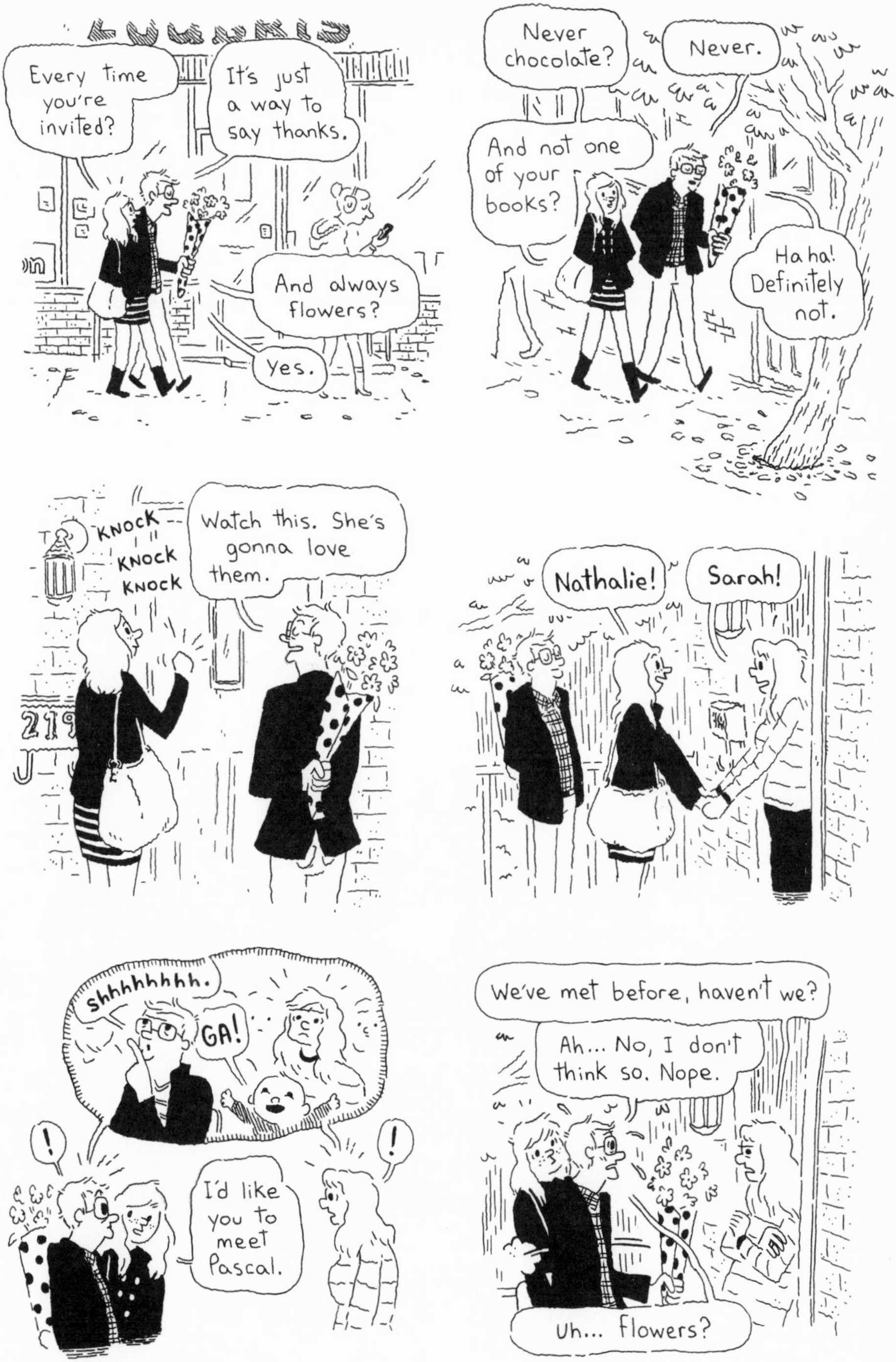
Every time you're invited?
It's just a way to say thanks.
And always flowers?
Yes.
Never chocolate?
Never.
And not one of your books?
Ha ha! Definitely not.
KNOCK KNOCK KNOCK
Watch this. She's gonna love them.
Nathalie!
Sarah!
shhhhhhhh.
GA!
!
!
I'd like you to meet Pascal.
We've met before, haven't we?
Ah... No, I don't think so. Nope.
Uh... flowers?

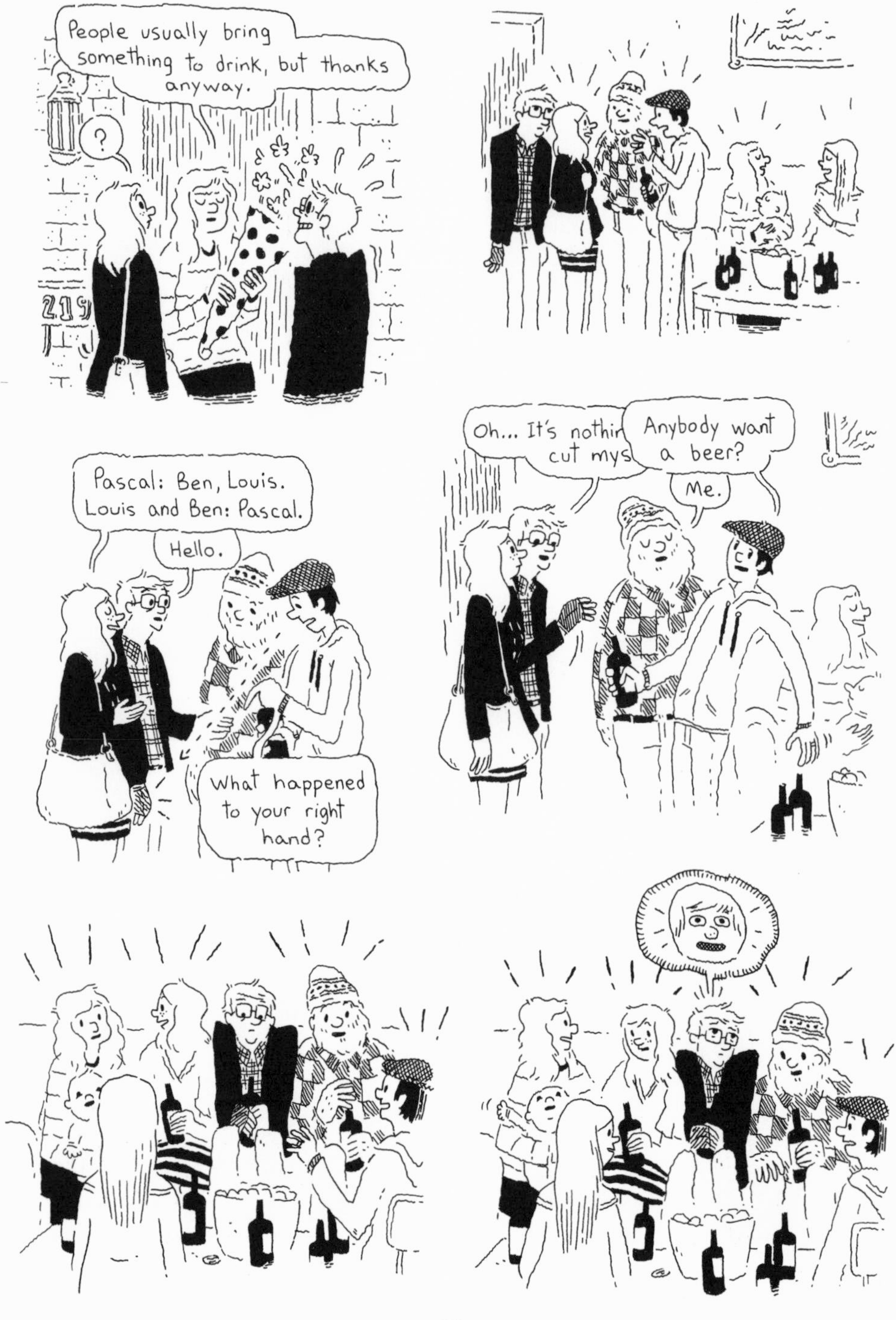

People usually bring something to drink, but thanks anyway.
?
219
Pascal: Ben, Louis. Louis and Ben: Pascal.
Hello.
What happened to your right hand?
Oh... It's nothir cut mys
Anybody want a beer?
Me.

The perfect family...

I'm just about ready to leave.

Great, so am I.

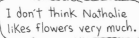

I don't think Nathalie likes flowers very much.

Ha ha.

Yeah, that wasn't the reaction I was expecting.

Whew, I drank too much.

I'm gonna head straight home. My shift starts early tomorrow morning.

O.... Okay?

Uh... Okay.

I've just come out of a l... long relationship. I need to... uh... take things slow.

Get to bed early, wake up early, go easy on the b... booze.

That's... uh... That's it... But I'm... uh... I'm over it... I'm ready to...

...

Uh...

...

...well, meet some... uh... a.... a gi... woman... Ha ha!

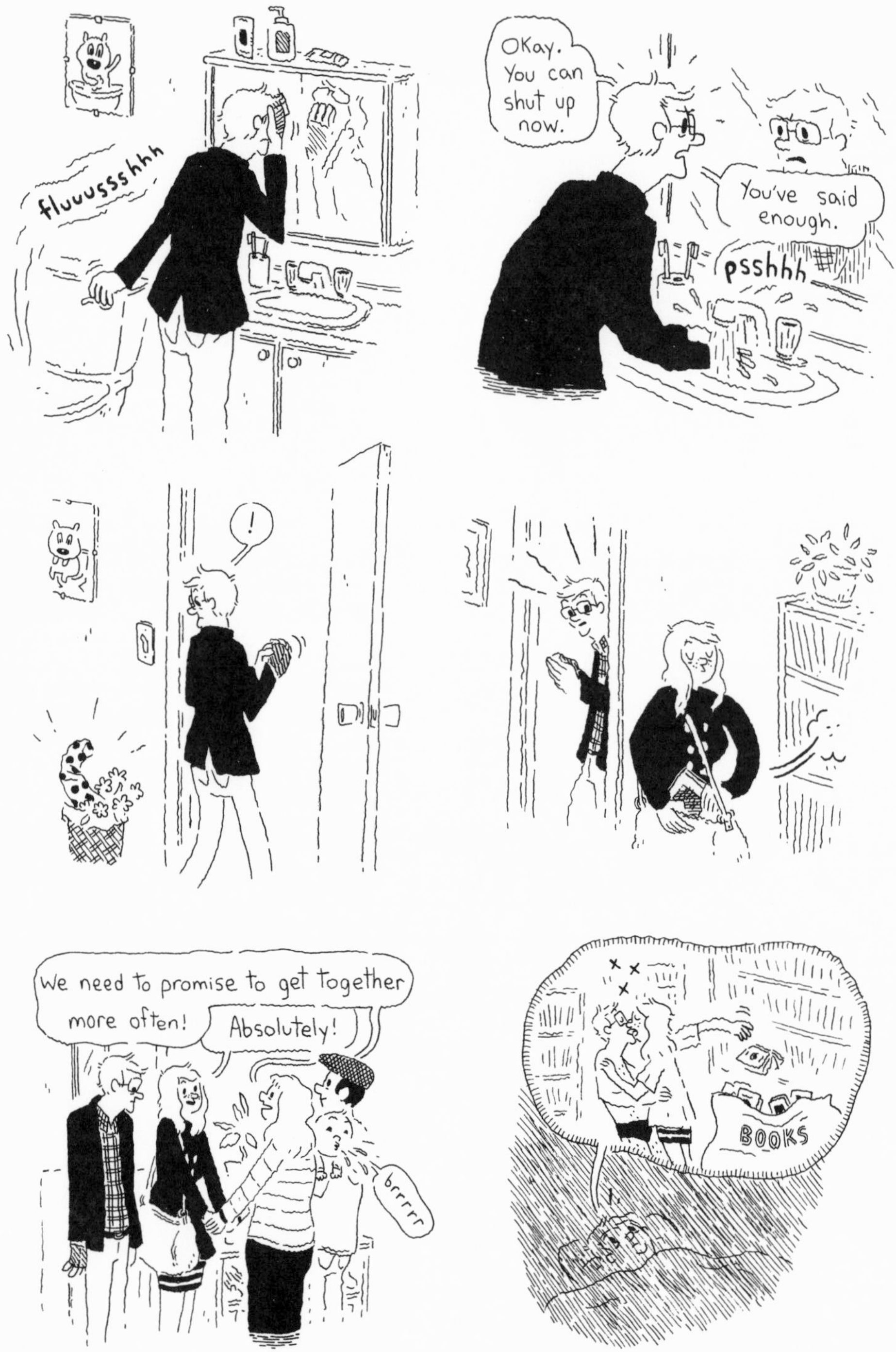
fluuussshhh
OKay. You can shut up now.
You've said enough.
psshhh
!
We need to promise to get together more often!
Absolutely!
brrrrr
BOOKS

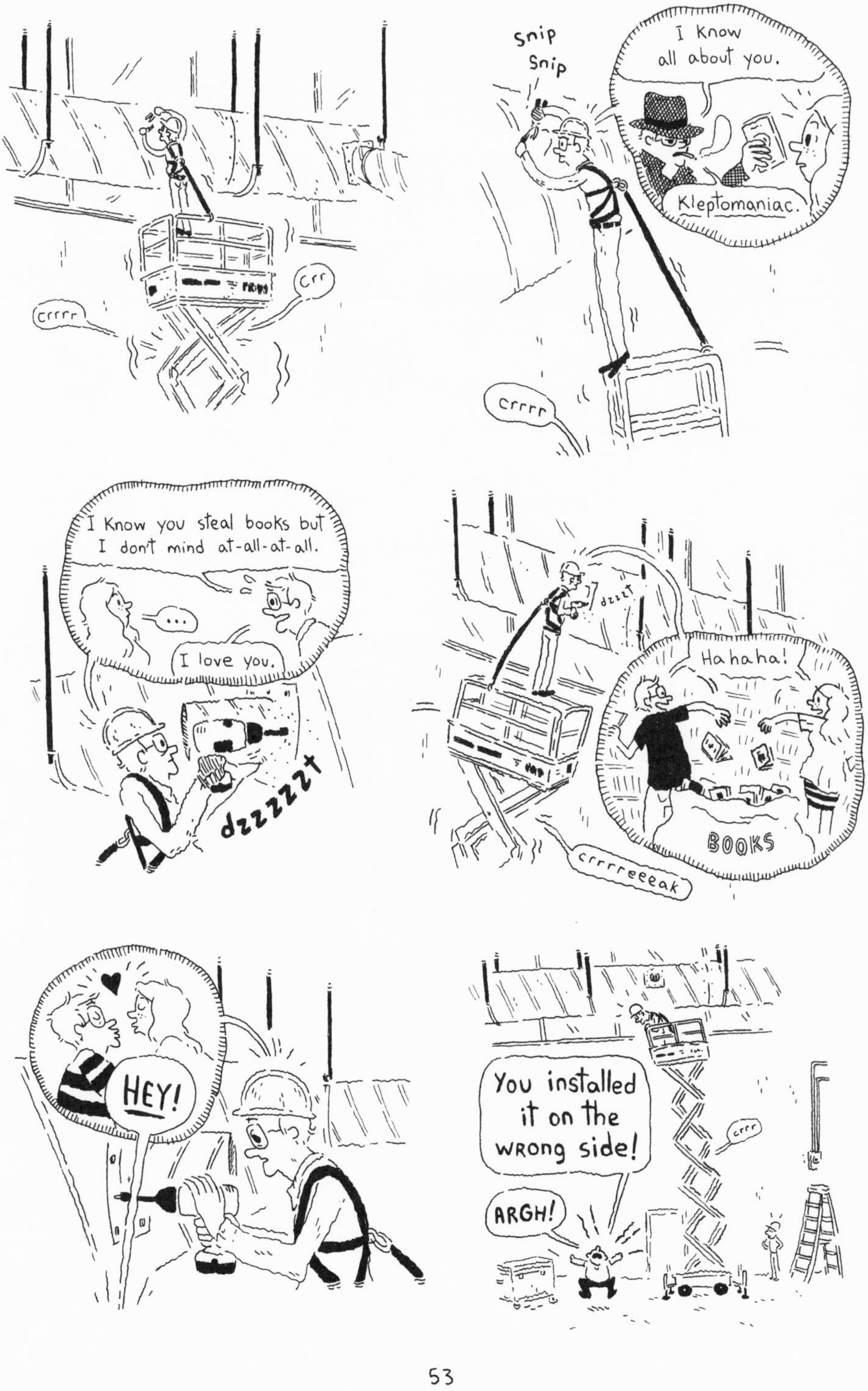
crrrr
crr
Snip
Snip
I know all about you.
Kleptomaniac.
crrrr
I know you steal books but I don't mind at-all-at-all.
...
I love you.
dzzzzzt
dzzzt
Hahaha!
BOOKS
crrrreeeak
HEY!
You installed it on the wrong side!
ARGH!
crrr

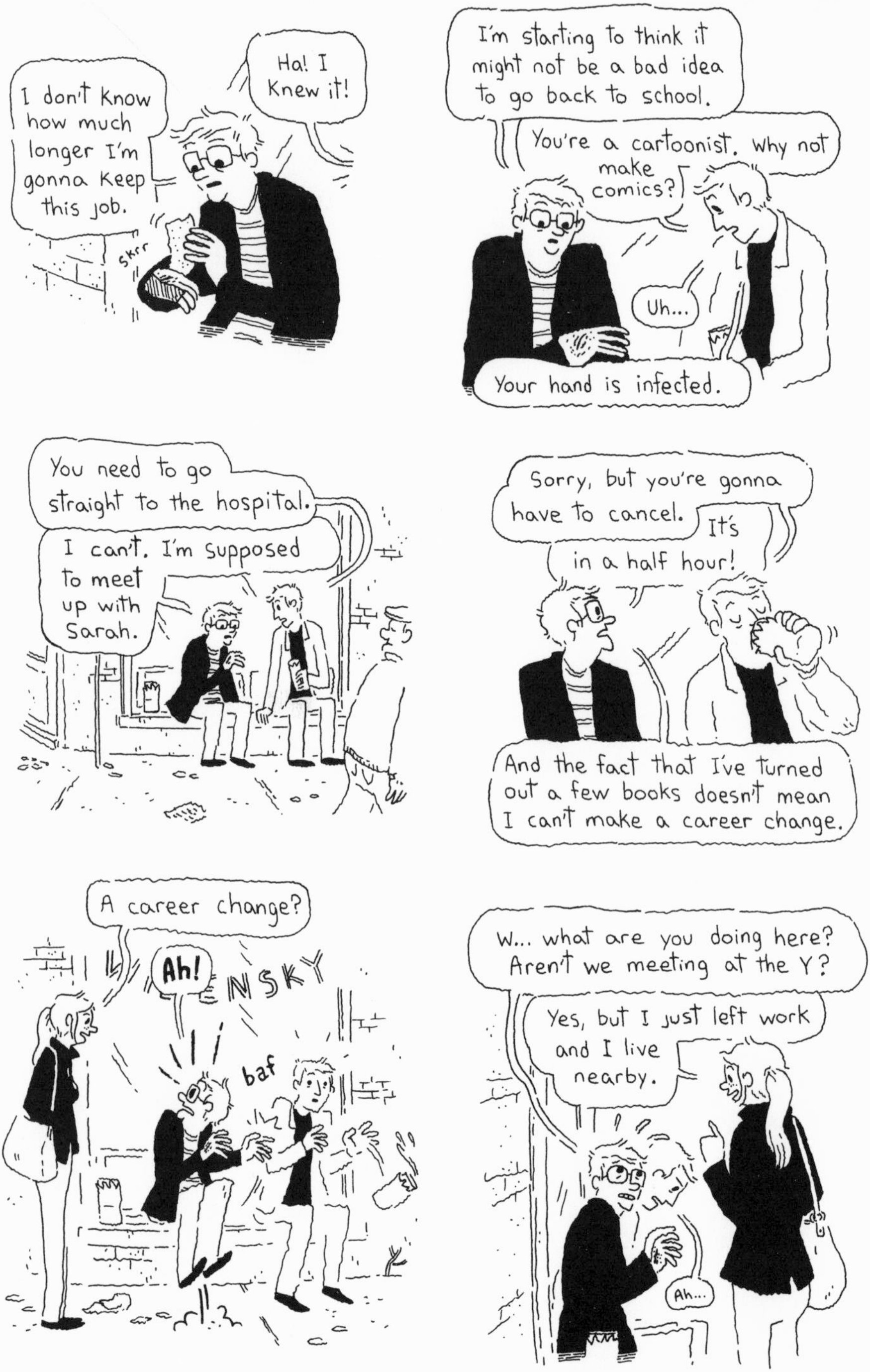
Ha! I Knew it!
I don't Know how much longer I'm gonna Keep this job.
Skrr
I'm starting to think it might not be a bad idea to go back to school.
You're a cartoonist. Why not make comics?
Uh...
Your hand is infected.
You need to go straight to the hospital.
I can't. I'm supposed to meet up with Sarah.
Sorry, but you're gonna have to cancel.
It's in a half hour!
And the fact that I've turned out a few books doesn't mean I can't make a career change.
A career change?
Ah!
NSKY
baf
W... what are you doing here? Aren't we meeting at the Y?
Yes, but I just left work and I live nearby.
Ah...

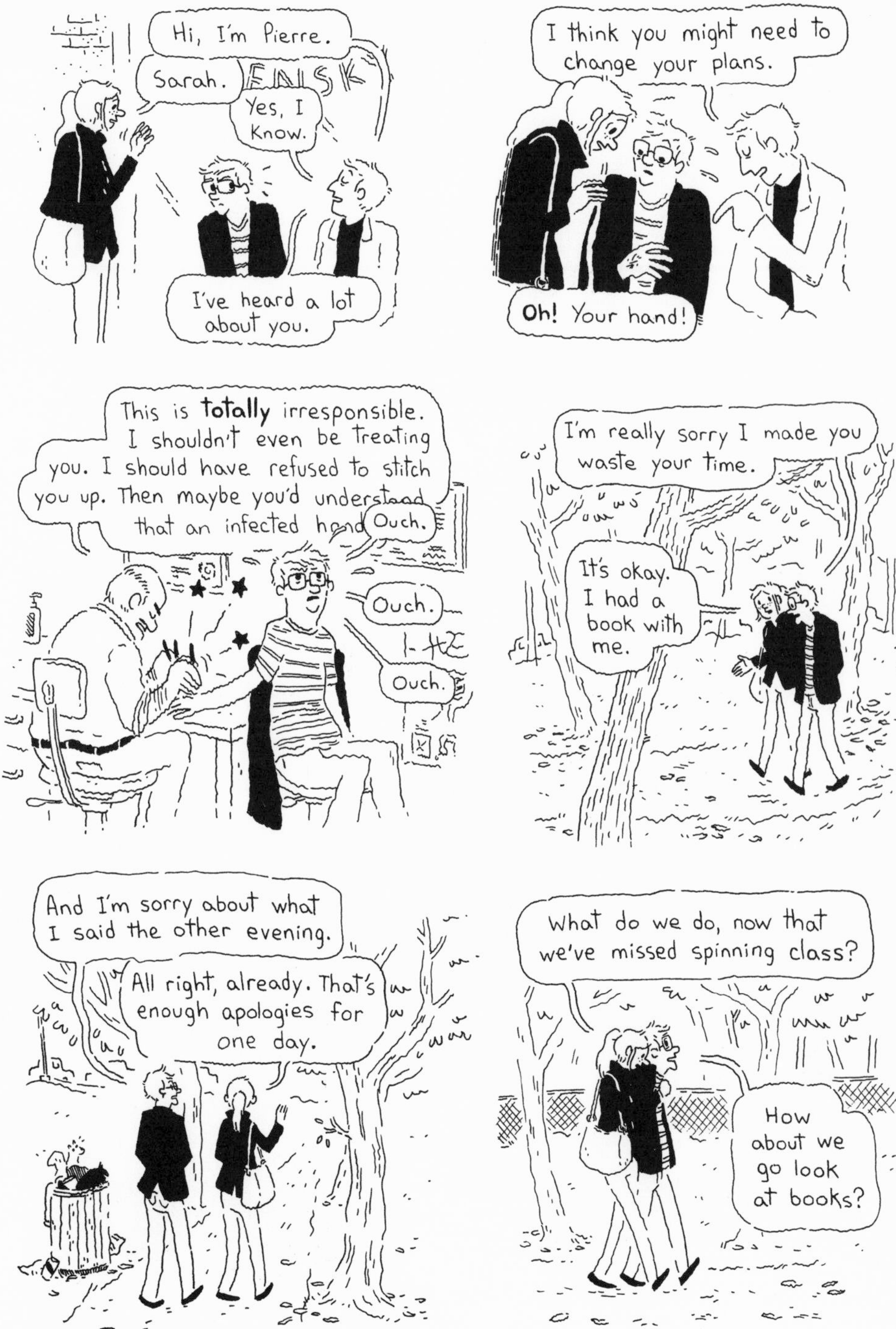
Hi, I'm Pierre.
Sarah.
Yes, I Know.
I've heard a lot about you.
I think you might need to change your plans.
Oh! Your hand!
This is **totally** irresponsible. I shouldn't even be treating you. I should have refused to stitch you up. Then maybe you'd understand that an infected hand
Ouch.
Ouch.
Ouch.
I'm really sorry I made you waste your time.
It's okay. I had a book with me.
And I'm sorry about what I said the other evening.
All right, already. That's enough apologies for one day.
What do we do, now that we've missed spinning class?
How about we go look at books?

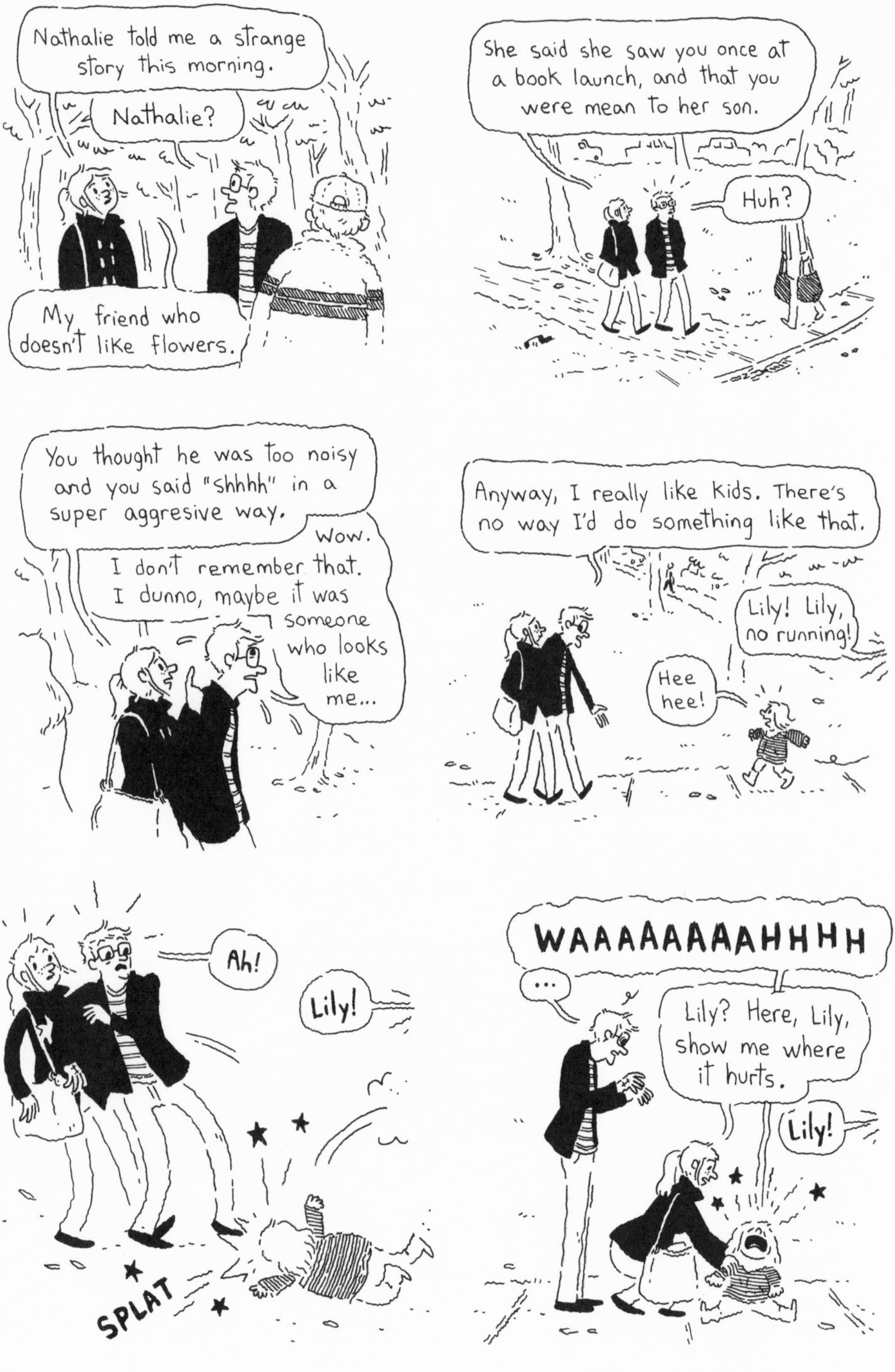
Nathalie told me a strange story this morning.
Nathalie?
My friend who doesn't like flowers.
She said she saw you once at a book launch, and that you were mean to her son.
Huh?
You thought he was too noisy and you said "shhhh" in a super aggresive way.
Wow. I don't remember that. I dunno, maybe it was someone who looks like me...
Anyway, I really like kids. There's no way I'd do something like that.
Lily! Lily, no running!
Hee hee!
Ah!
Lily!
SPLAT
WAAAAAAAAHHHH
...
Lily? Here, Lily, show me where it hurts.
Lily!

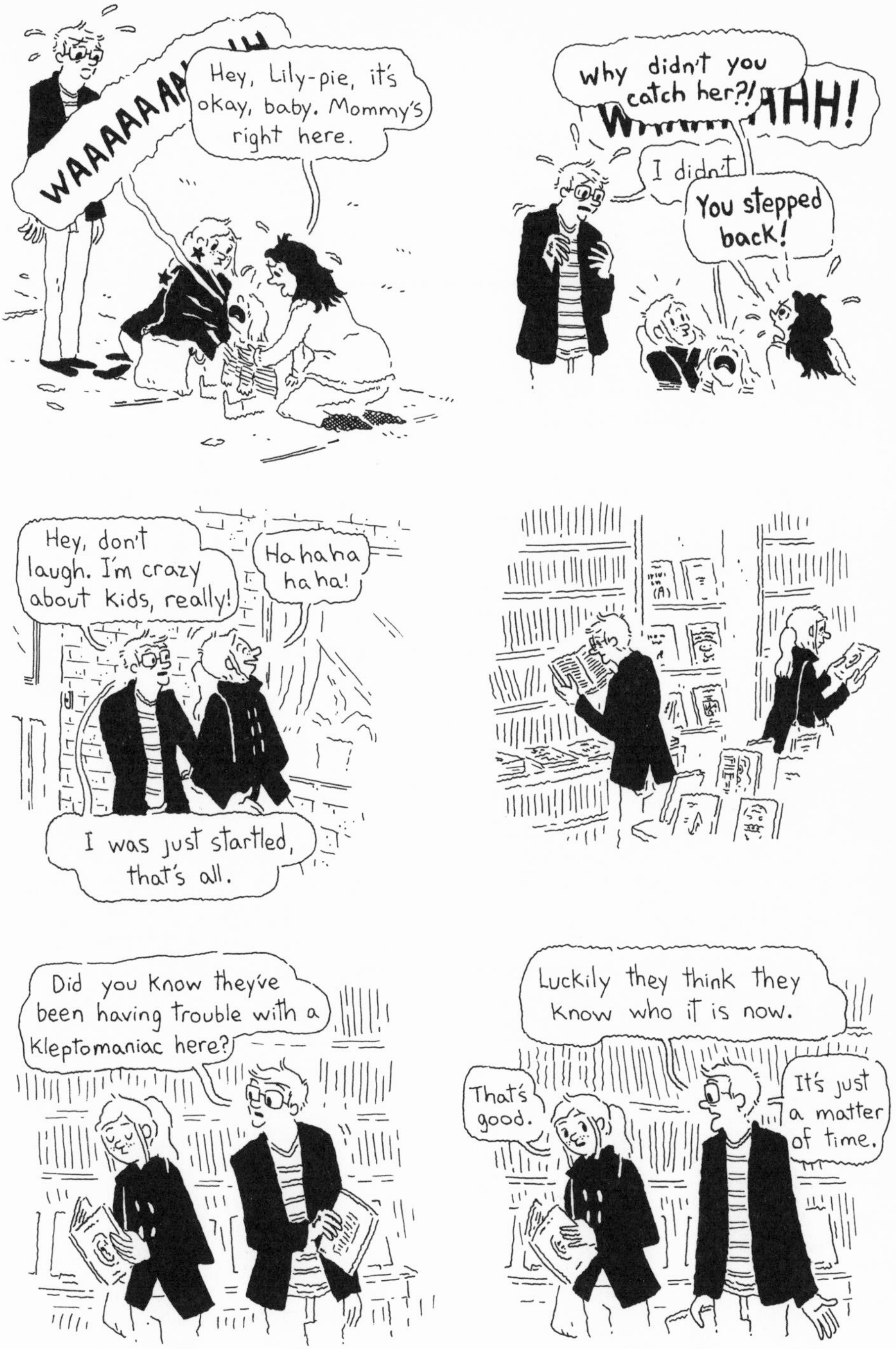
WAAAAAAA
Hey, Lily-pie, it's okay, baby. Mommy's right here.
Why didn't you catch her?!
I didn
You stepped back!
Hey, don't laugh. I'm crazy about kids, really!
Ha ha ha ha ha!
I was just startled, that's all.
Did you know they've been having trouble with a kleptomaniac here?
Luckily they think they know who it is now.
That's good.
It's just a matter of time.

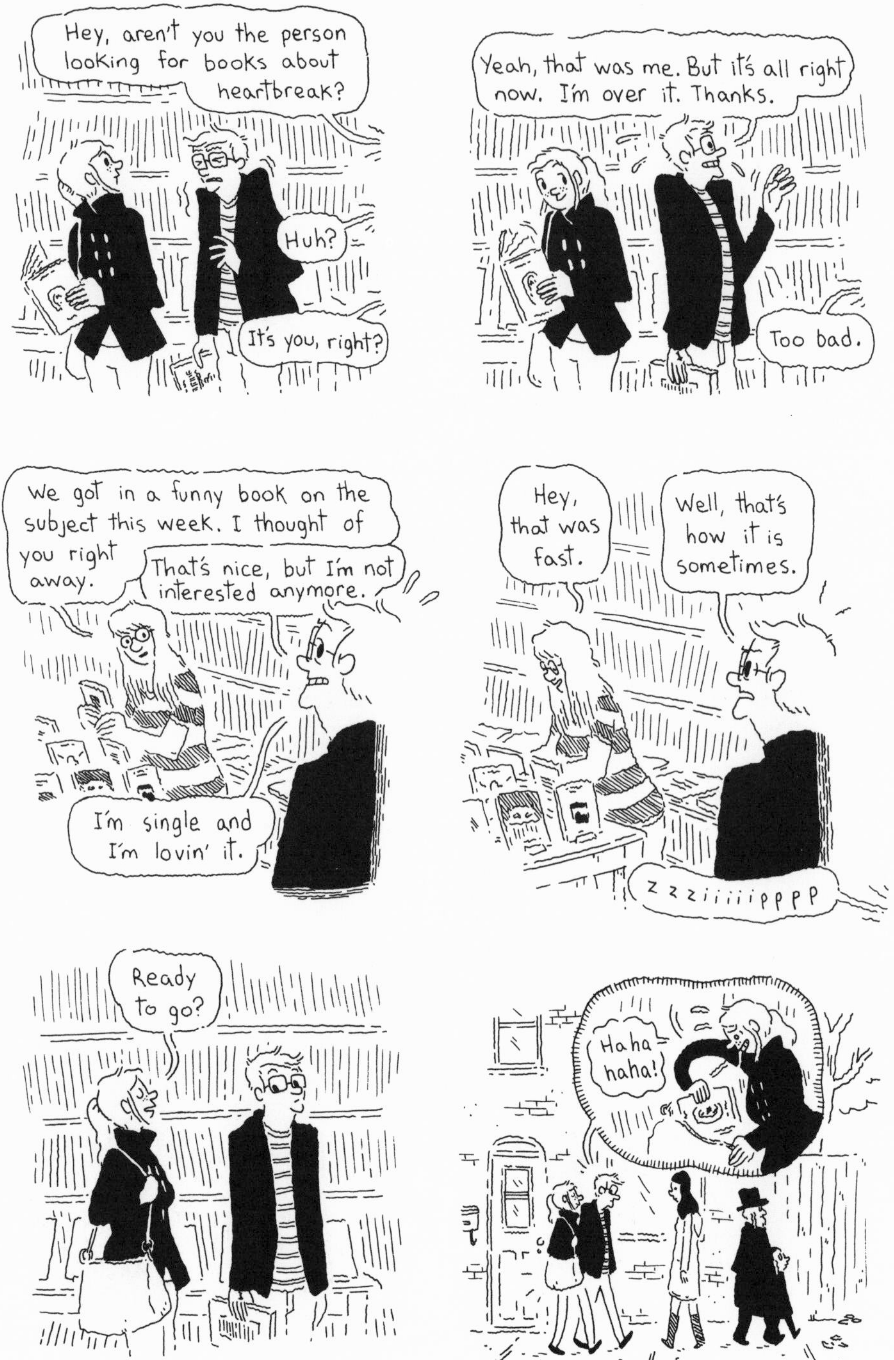
Hey, aren't you the person looking for books about heartbreak?
Huh?
It's you, right?
Yeah, that was me. But it's all right now. I'm over it. Thanks.
Too bad.
We got in a funny book on the subject this week. I thought of you right away.
That's nice, but I'm not interested anymore.
I'm single and I'm lovin' it.
Hey, that was fast.
Well, that's how it is sometimes.
zzziiiiipppp
Ready to go?
Haha haha!

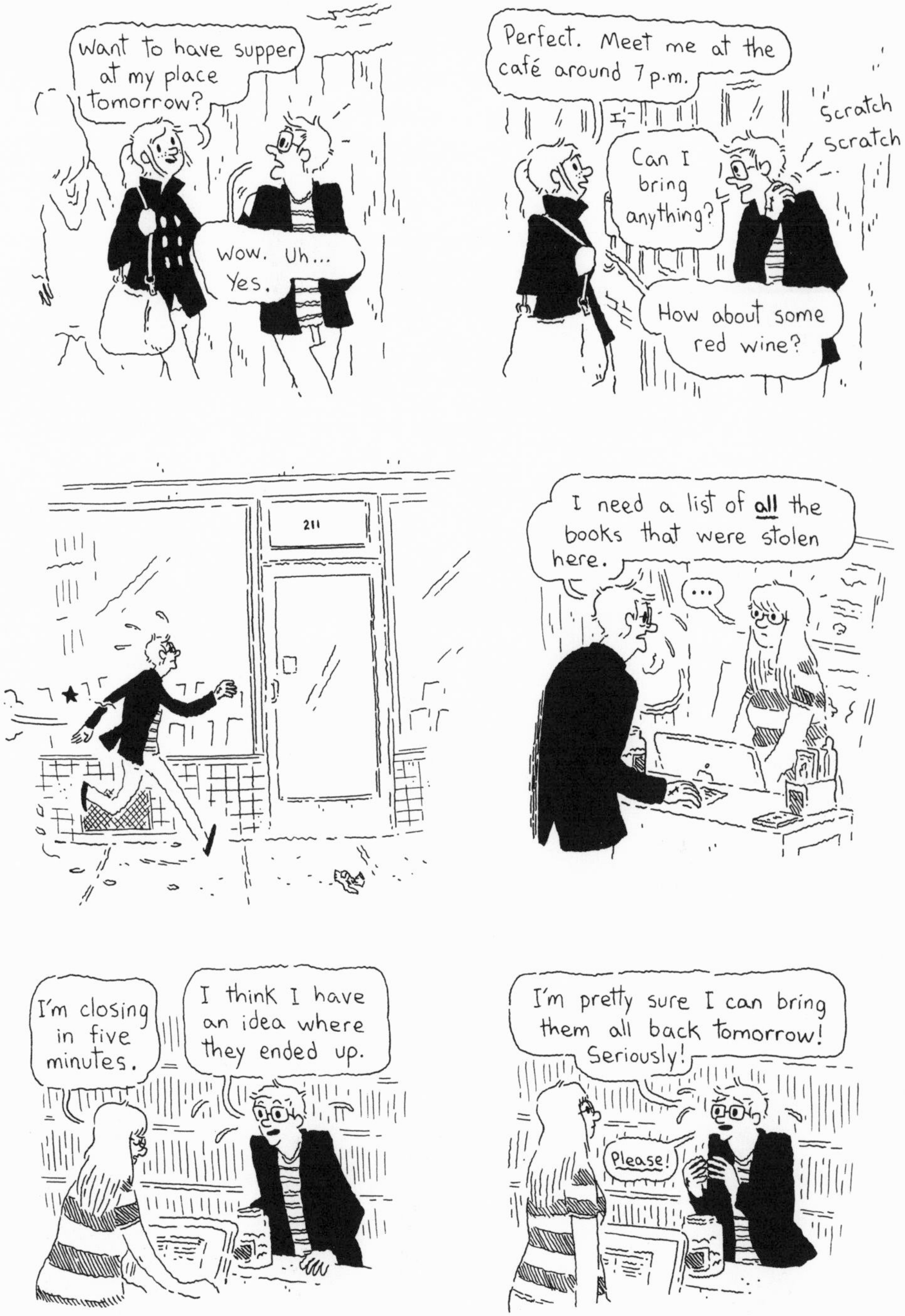
Want to have supper at my place tomorrow?
Wow. Uh... Yes.
Perfect. Meet me at the café around 7 p.m.
Can I bring anything?
Scratch Scratch
How about some red wine?
211
I need a list of **all** the books that were stolen here.
...
I'm closing in five minutes.
I think I have an idea where they ended up.
I'm pretty sure I can bring them all back tomorrow! Seriously!
Please!

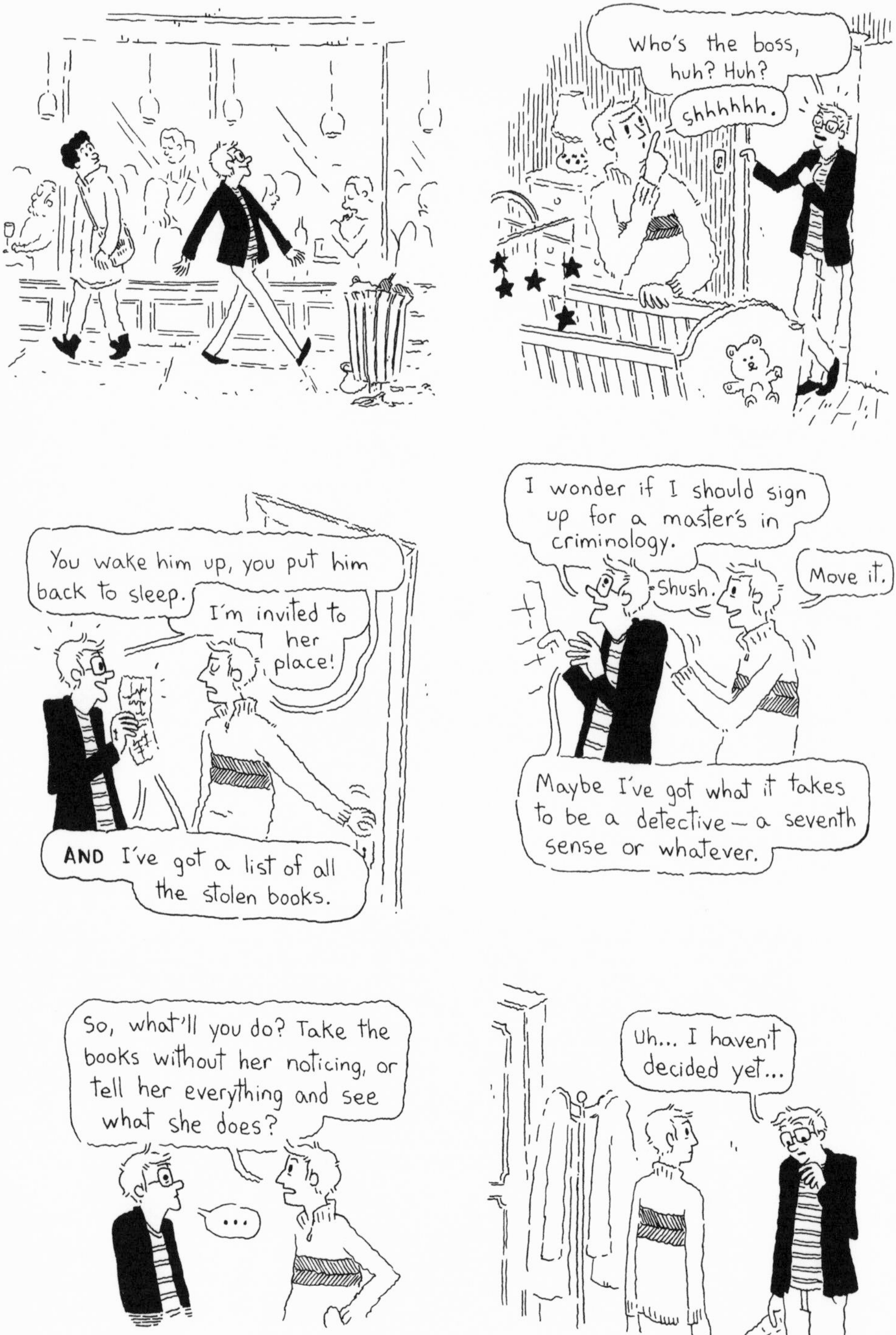

Who's the boss, huh? Huh?
shhhhhh.
You wake him up, you put him back to sleep.
I'm invited to her place!
AND I've got a list of all the stolen books.
I wonder if I should sign up for a master's in criminology.
Shush.
Move it.
Maybe I've got what it takes to be a detective – a seventh sense or whatever.
So, what'll you do? Take the books without her noticing, or tell her everything and see what she does?
...
Uh... I haven't decided yet...

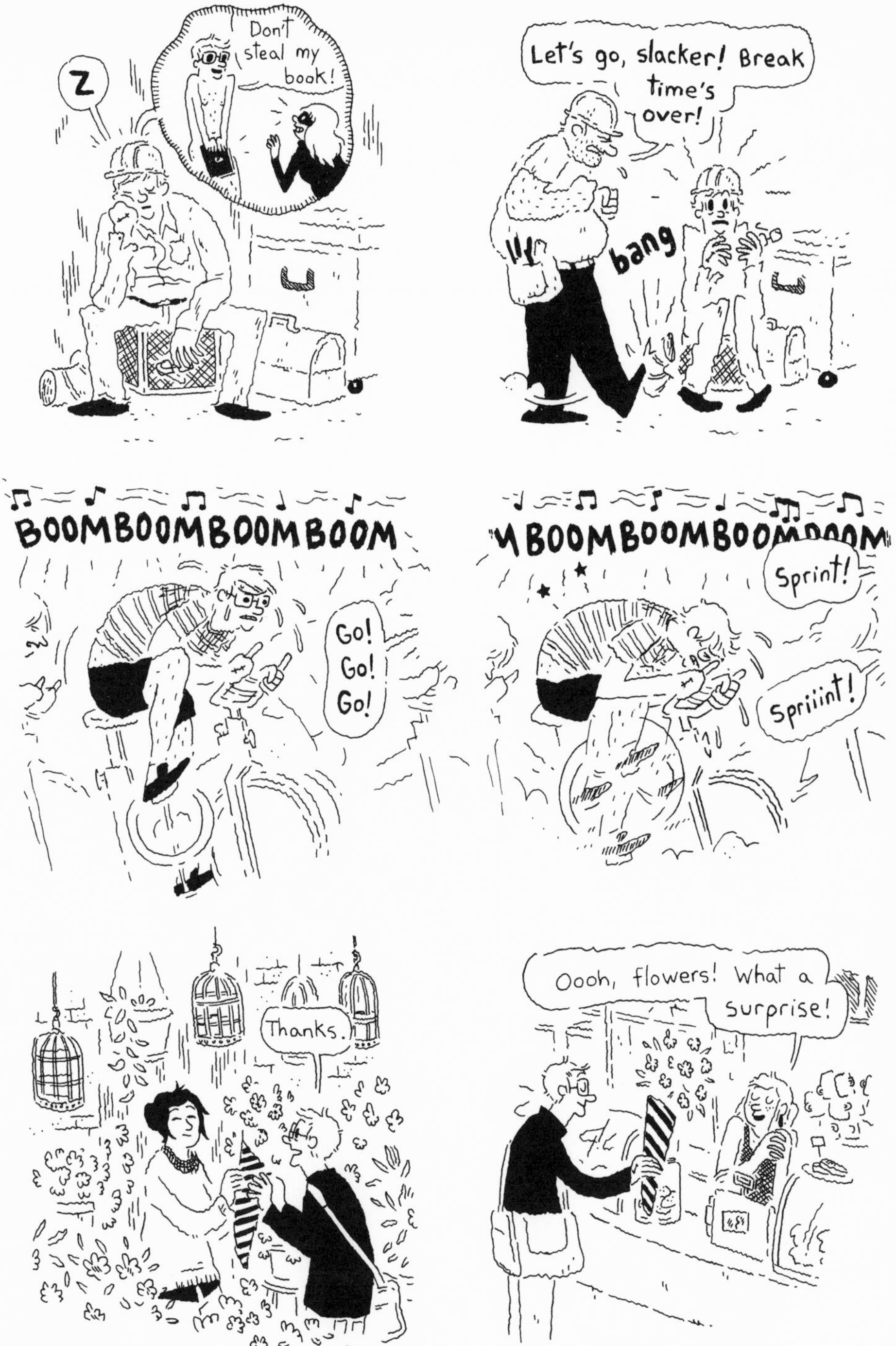
Z
Don't steal my book!
Let's go, slacker! Break time's over!
bang
BOOMBOOMBOOMBOOM
Go! Go! Go!
BOOMBOOMBOO
Sprint!
Spriiint!
Thanks.
Oooh, flowers! What a surprise!

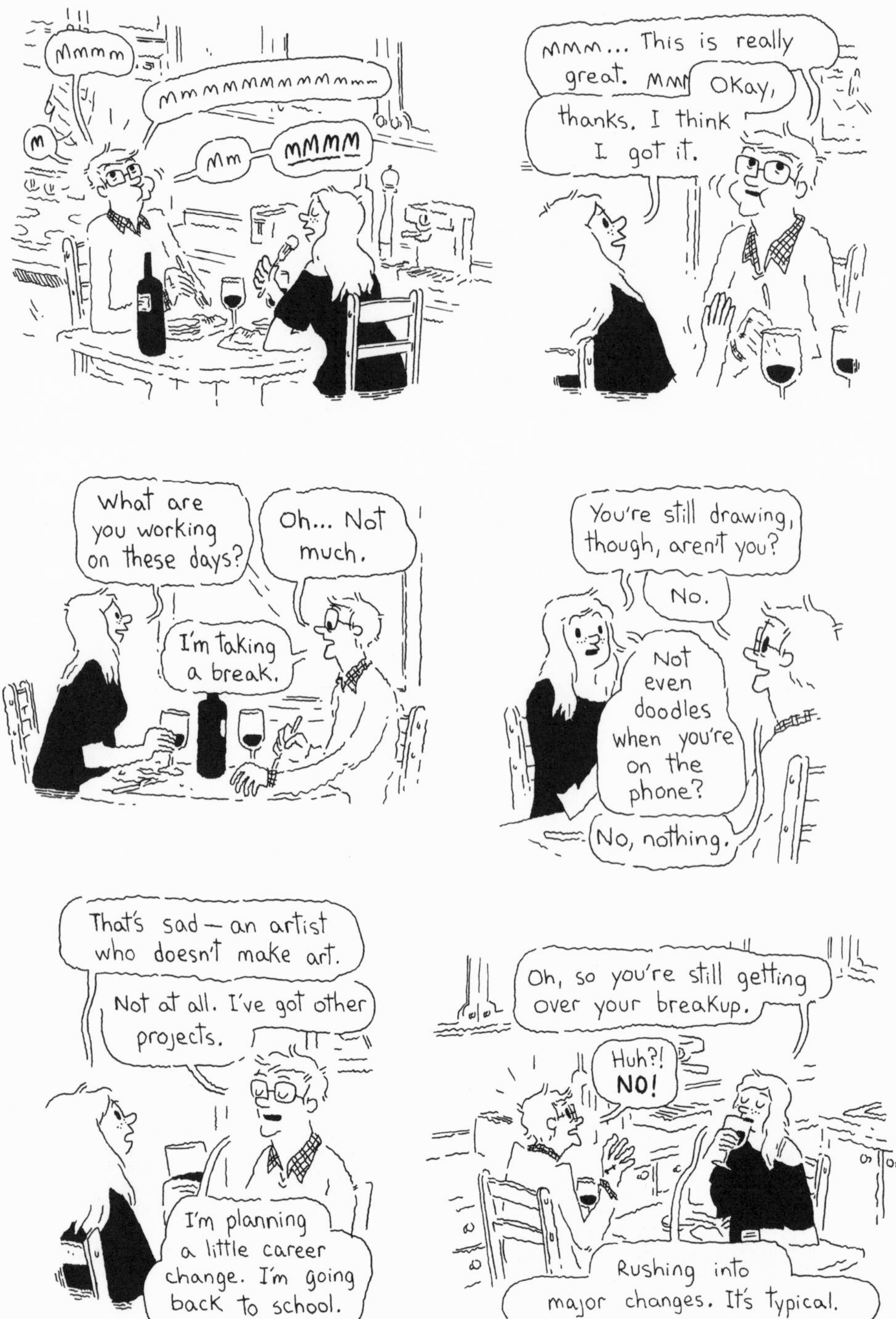
Mmmm
M
Mmmmmmmmmmmmmm
Mm
MMMM
MMM... This is really great. MMM
Okay, thanks. I think I got it.
What are you working on these days?
Oh... Not much.
I'm taking a break.
You're still drawing, though, aren't you?
No.
Not even doodles when you're on the phone?
No, nothing.
That's sad — an artist who doesn't make art.
Not at all. I've got other projects.
I'm planning a little career change. I'm going back to school.
Oh, so you're still getting over your breakup.
Huh?! NO!
Rushing into major changes. It's typical.

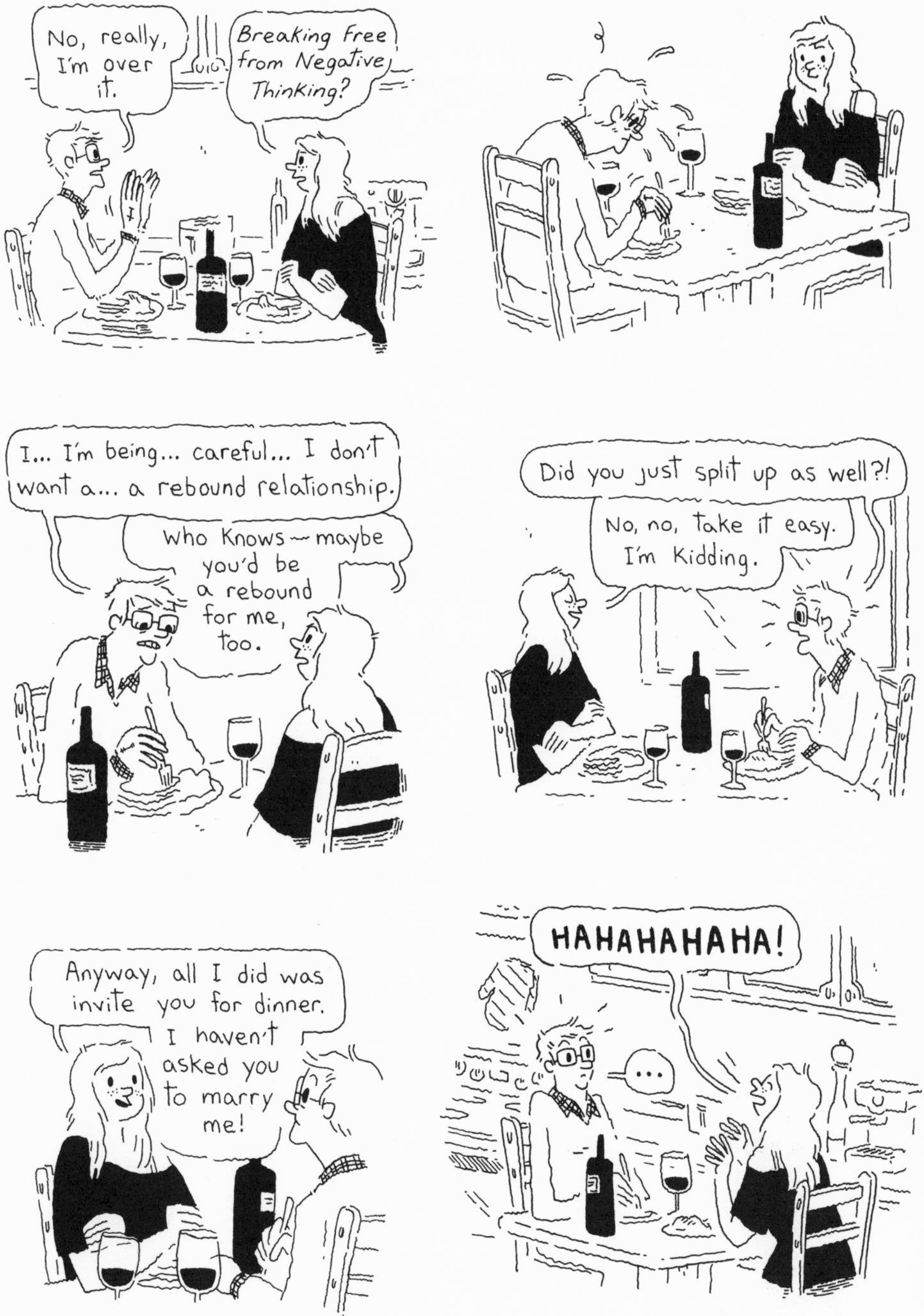
No, really, I'm over it.
Breaking free from Negative Thinking?
I... I'm being... careful... I don't want a... a rebound relationship.
Who knows — maybe you'd be a rebound for me, too.
Did you just split up as well?!
No, no, take it easy. I'm kidding.
Anyway, all I did was invite you for dinner.
I haven't asked you to marry me!
HAHAHAHAHA!
...

Wow! You've got books stashed everywhere!

Yeah. I used to buy books all the time.

But I don't have any space left for them. I have stacks of boxes in my cupboards. I could sell some, but I keep hoping I'll find a bigger apartment that's not too expensive.

I had almost as many when I lived in Quebec City.

And now it looks like my ex wants to get rid of them all as fast as possible. There's a delivery guy who brings me at least 300 books a week!

I only have a small room, so I don't know where to put them.

I swear, sometimes I feel like they're literally crushing me. Don't you?

No, it's the opposite. They make me feel safe.

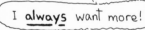

I **always** want more!

Oh well, that's great. I've just found a taker for all my books!

Ha ha!

clap

Oh, my phone. Sorry, I need to get that. I'm expecting an important call.

Yes, yes! No, I was in the living room, mom. Yes, of course, all alone...

Okay...

Make it quick...

C'mon!...

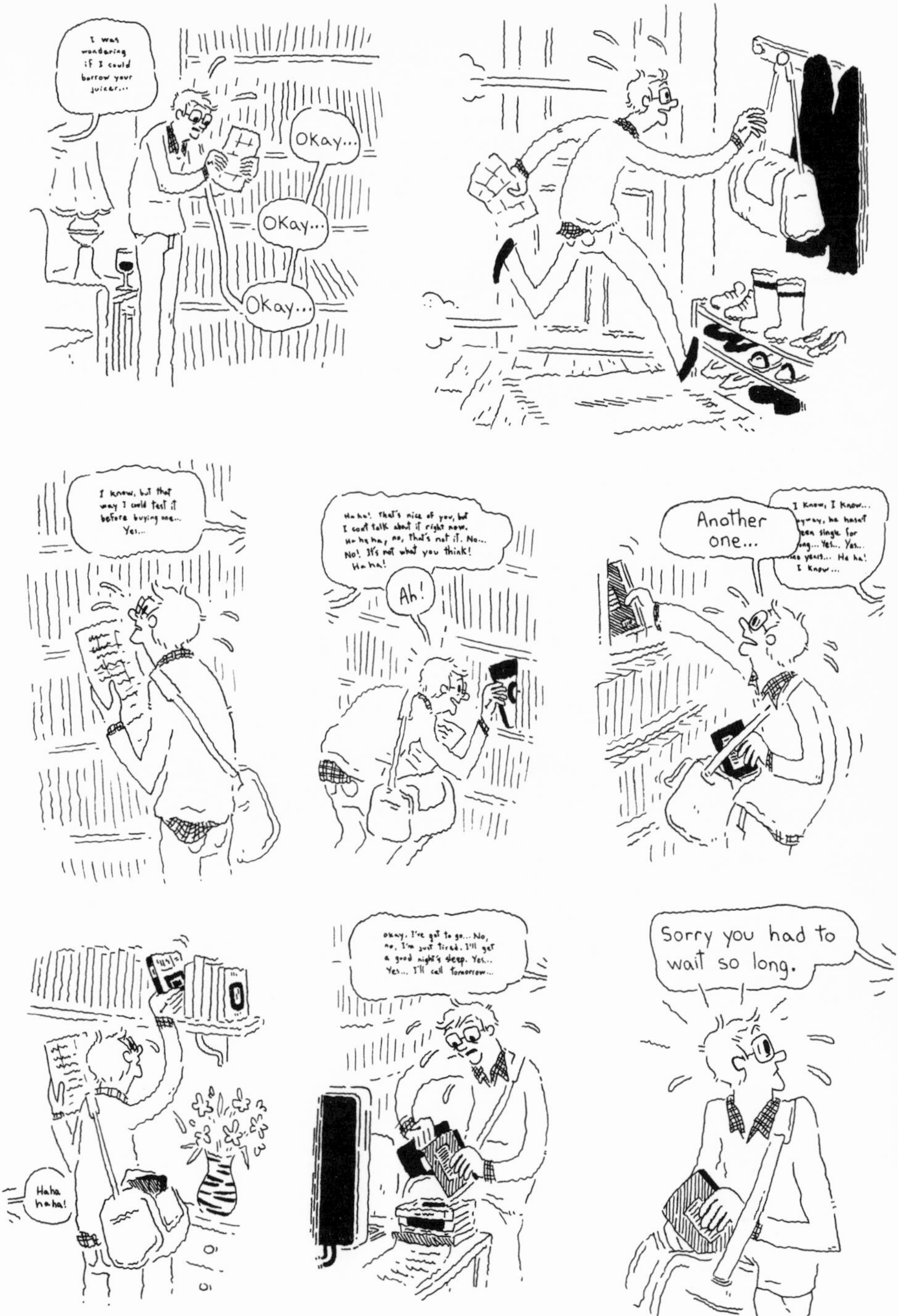

I was wondering if I could borrow your juicer...
Okay...
Okay...
Okay...
I know, but that way I could test it before buying one... Yes...
Ha ha! That's nice of you, but I can't talk about it right now. Ha ha ha, no, that's not it. No... No! It's not what you think! Ha ha!
Ah!
Another one...
I know, I know... ...yway, he hasn't ...een single for ...ng... Yes... Yes... ...o years... Ha ha! I know...
Haha haha!
Okay, I've got to go... No, no, I'm just tired. I'll get a good night's sleep. Yes... Yes... I'll call tomorrow...
Sorry you had to wait so long.

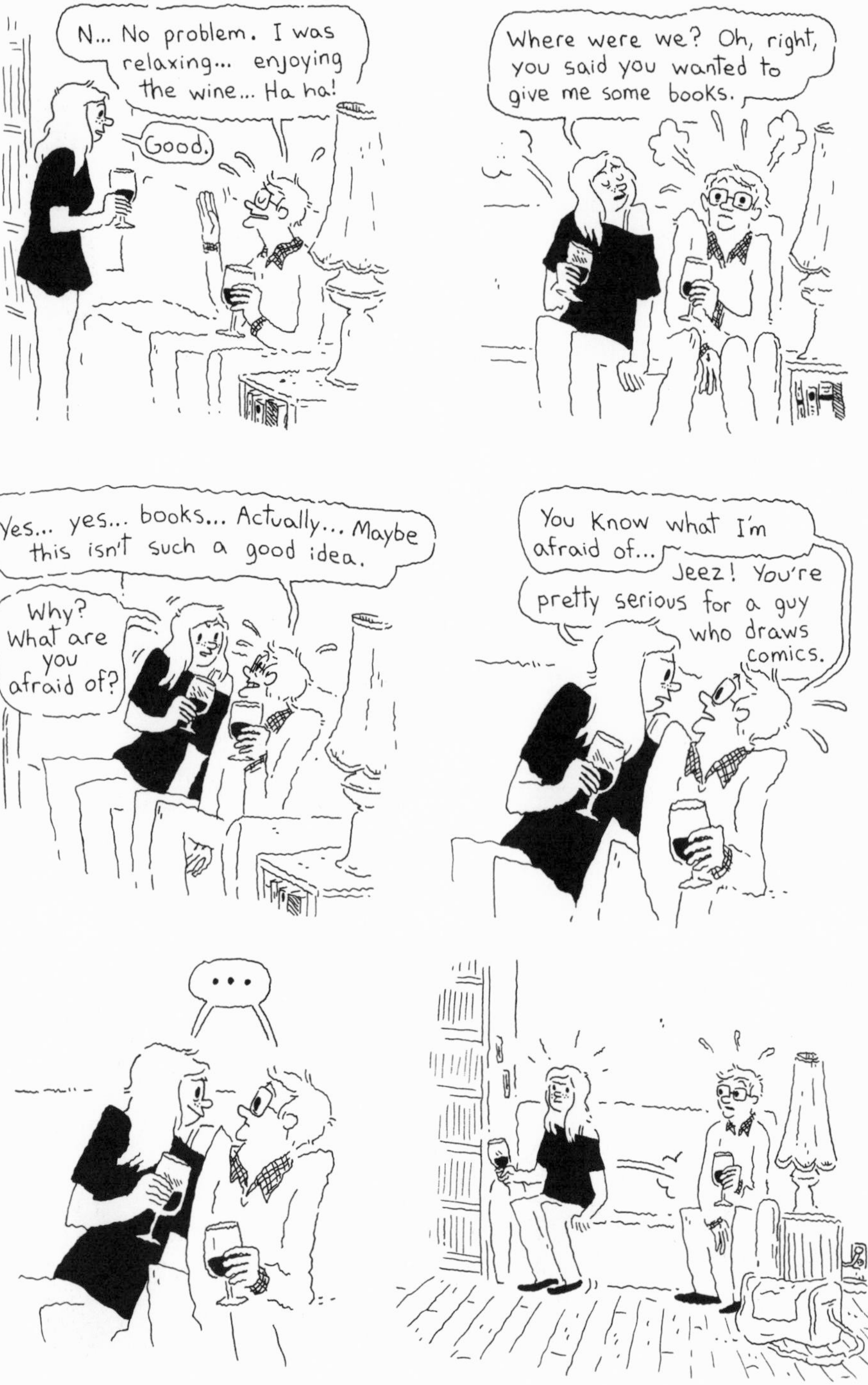

N... No problem. I was relaxing... enjoying the wine... Ha ha!
Good.
Where were we? Oh, right, you said you wanted to give me some books.
Yes... yes... books... Actually... Maybe this isn't such a good idea.
Why? What are you afraid of?
You know what I'm afraid of...
Jeez! You're pretty serious for a guy who draws comics.
...

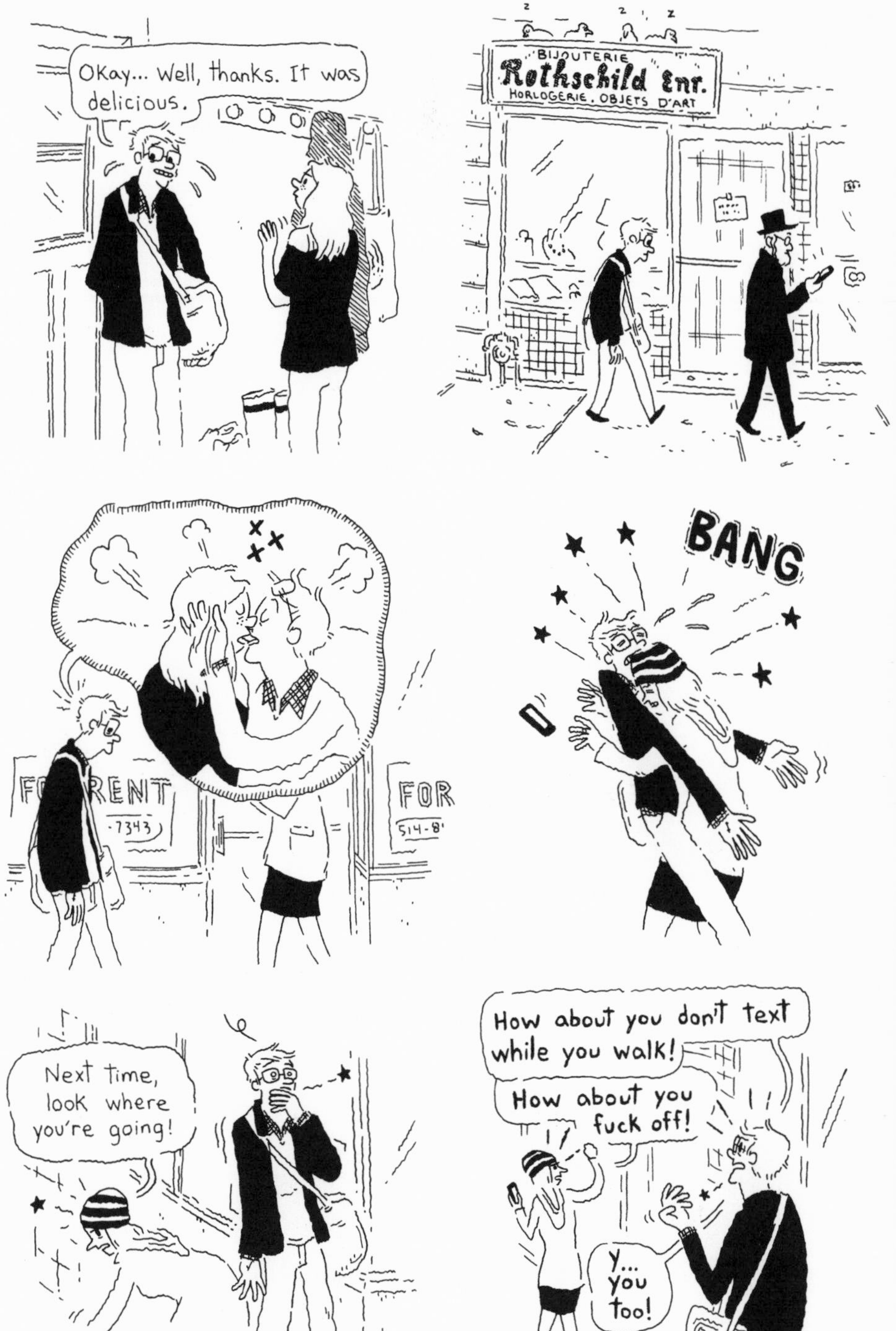
Okay... Well, thanks. It was delicious.
BIJOUTERIE
Rothschild Enr.
HORLOGERIE. OBJETS D'ART
FOR RENT
-7343
FOR
514-8
BANG
Next time, look where you're going!
How about you don't text while you walk!
How about you fuck off!
Y... you too!

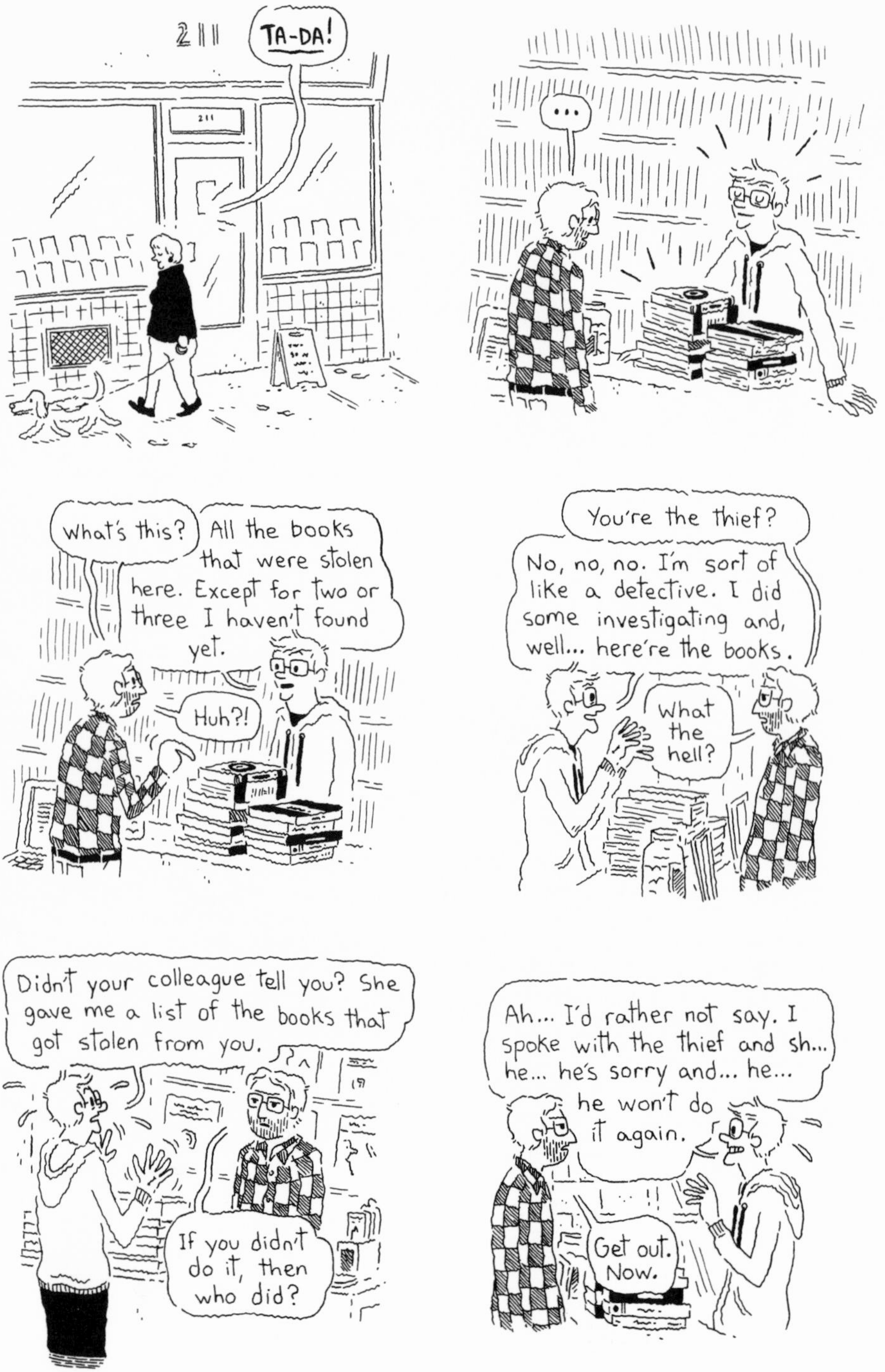
211
TA-DA!
211
...
What's this?
All the books that were stolen here. Except for two or three I haven't found yet.
Huh?!
You're the thief?
No, no, no. I'm sort of like a detective. I did some investigating and, well... here're the books.
What the hell?
Didn't your colleague tell you? She gave me a list of the books that got stolen from you.
If you didn't do it, then who did?
Ah... I'd rather not say. I spoke with the thief and sh... he... he's sorry and... he... he won't do it again.
Get out. Now.

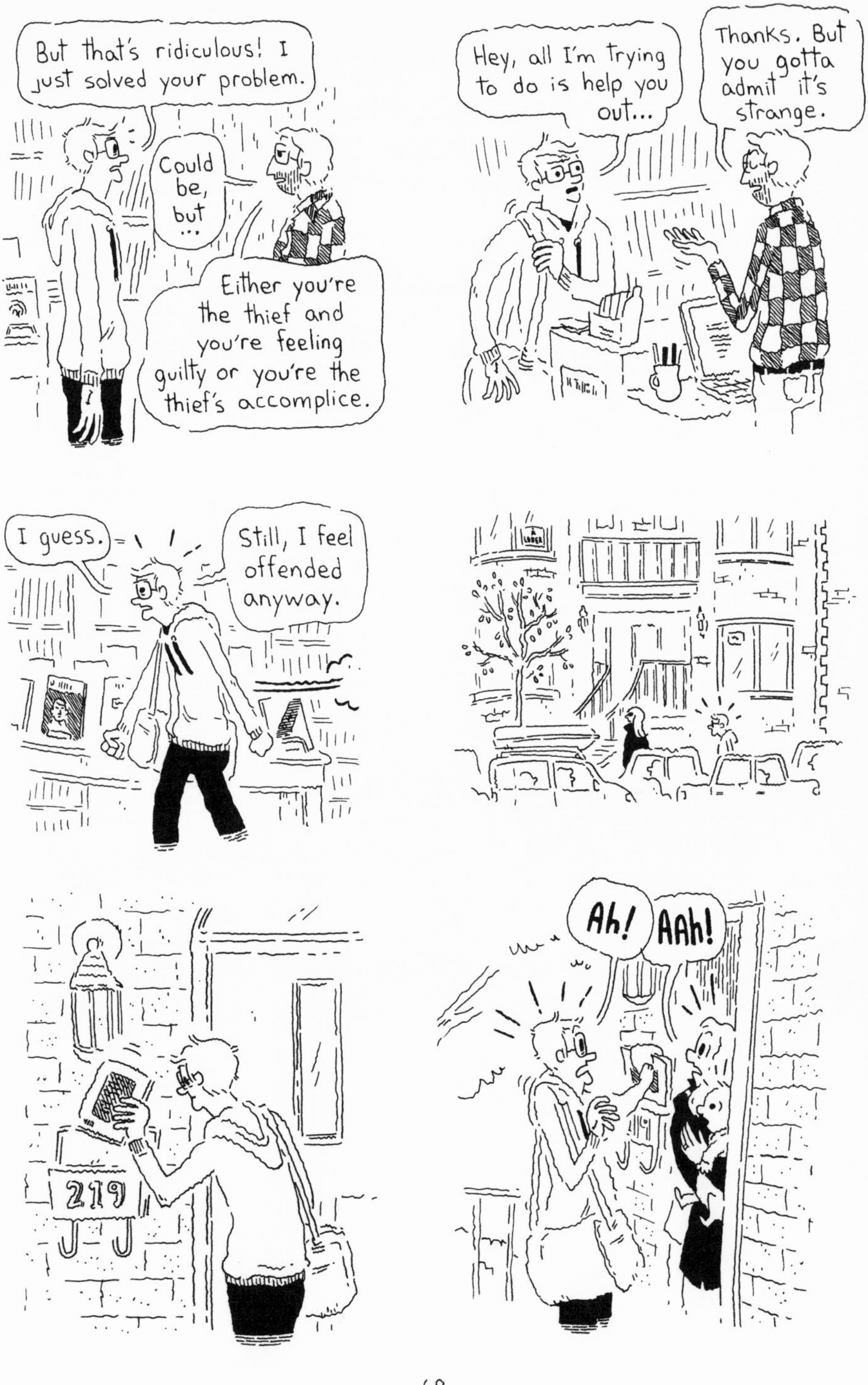
But that's ridiculous! I just solved your problem.
Could be, but ...
Either you're the thief and you're feeling guilty or you're the thief's accomplice.
Hey, all I'm trying to do is help you out...
Thanks. But you gotta admit it's strange.
I guess.
Still, I feel offended anyway.
219
Ah!
AAh!

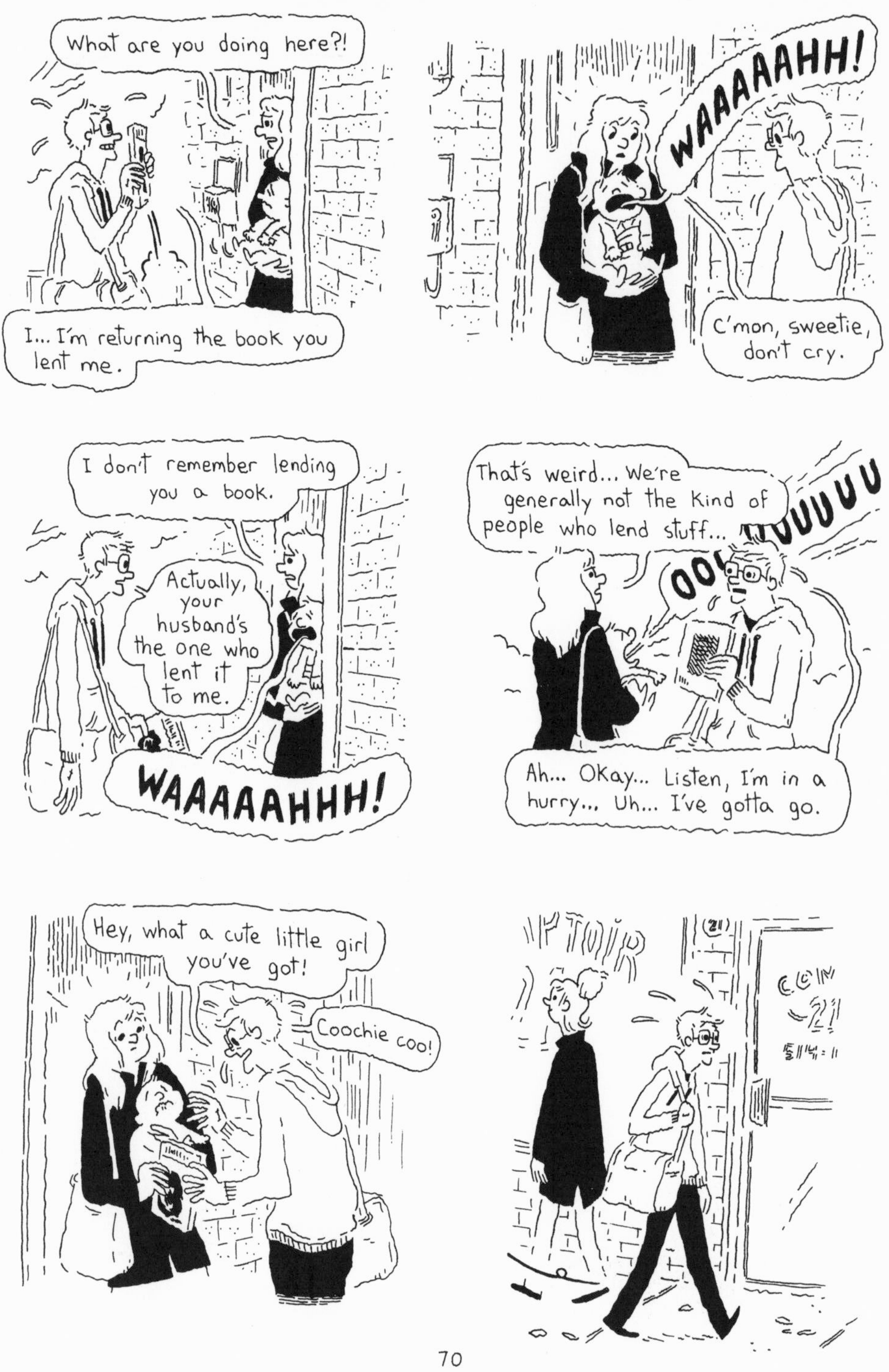
What are you doing here?!
I... I'm returning the book you lent me.
WAAAAAHH!
C'mon, sweetie, don't cry.
I don't remember lending you a book.
Actually, your husband's the one who lent it to me.
WAAAAAHHH!
That's weird... We're generally not the kind of people who lend stuff...
Ah... Okay... Listen, I'm in a hurry... Uh... I've gotta go.
Hey, what a cute little girl you've got!
Coochie coo!

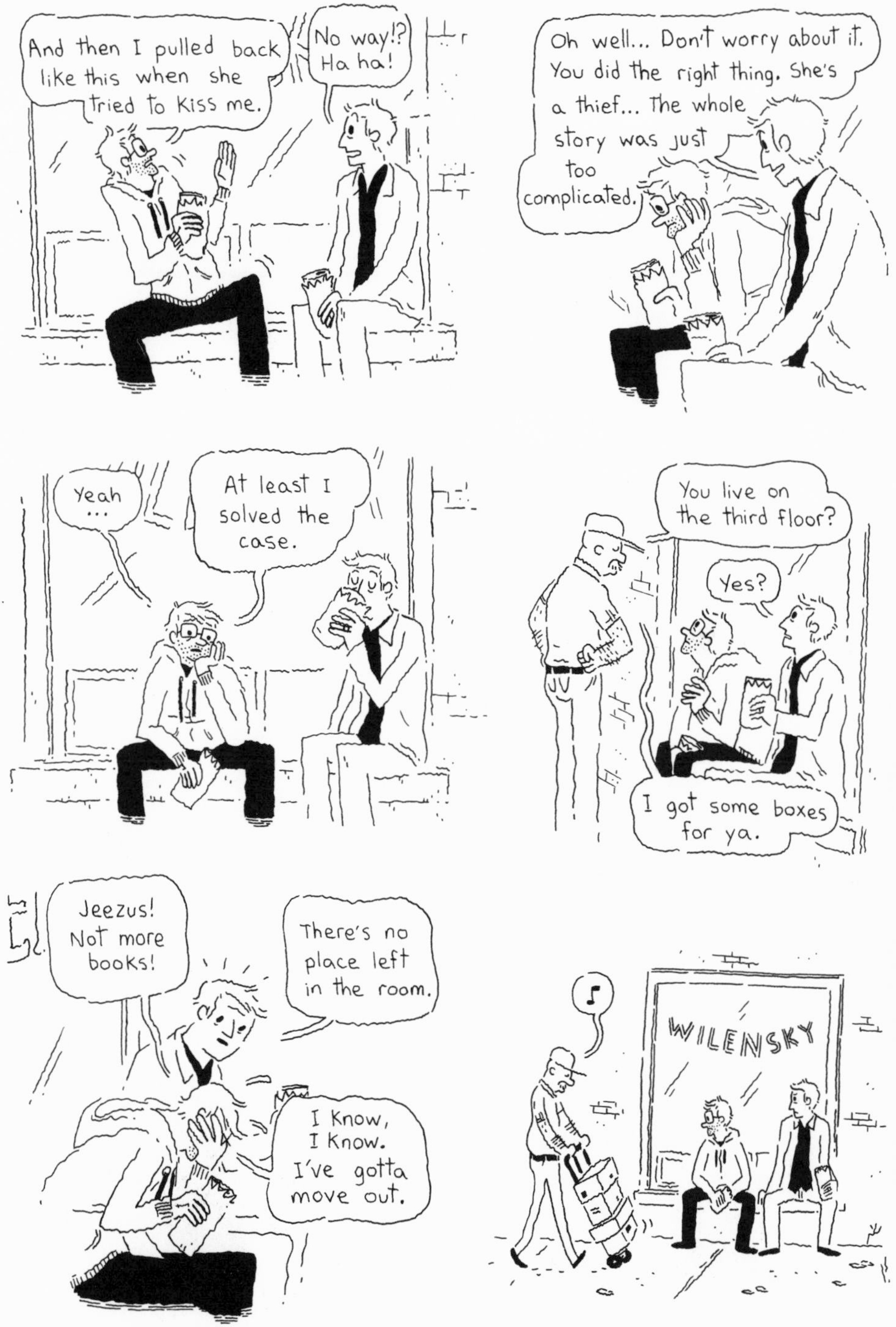

And then I pulled back like this when she tried to kiss me.
No way!? Ha ha!
Oh well... Don't worry about it. You did the right thing. She's a thief... The whole story was just too complicated.
Yeah ...
At least I solved the case.
You live on the third floor?
Yes?
I got some boxes for ya.
Jeezus! Not more books!
There's no place left in the room.
I know, I know. I've gotta move out.
WILENSKY

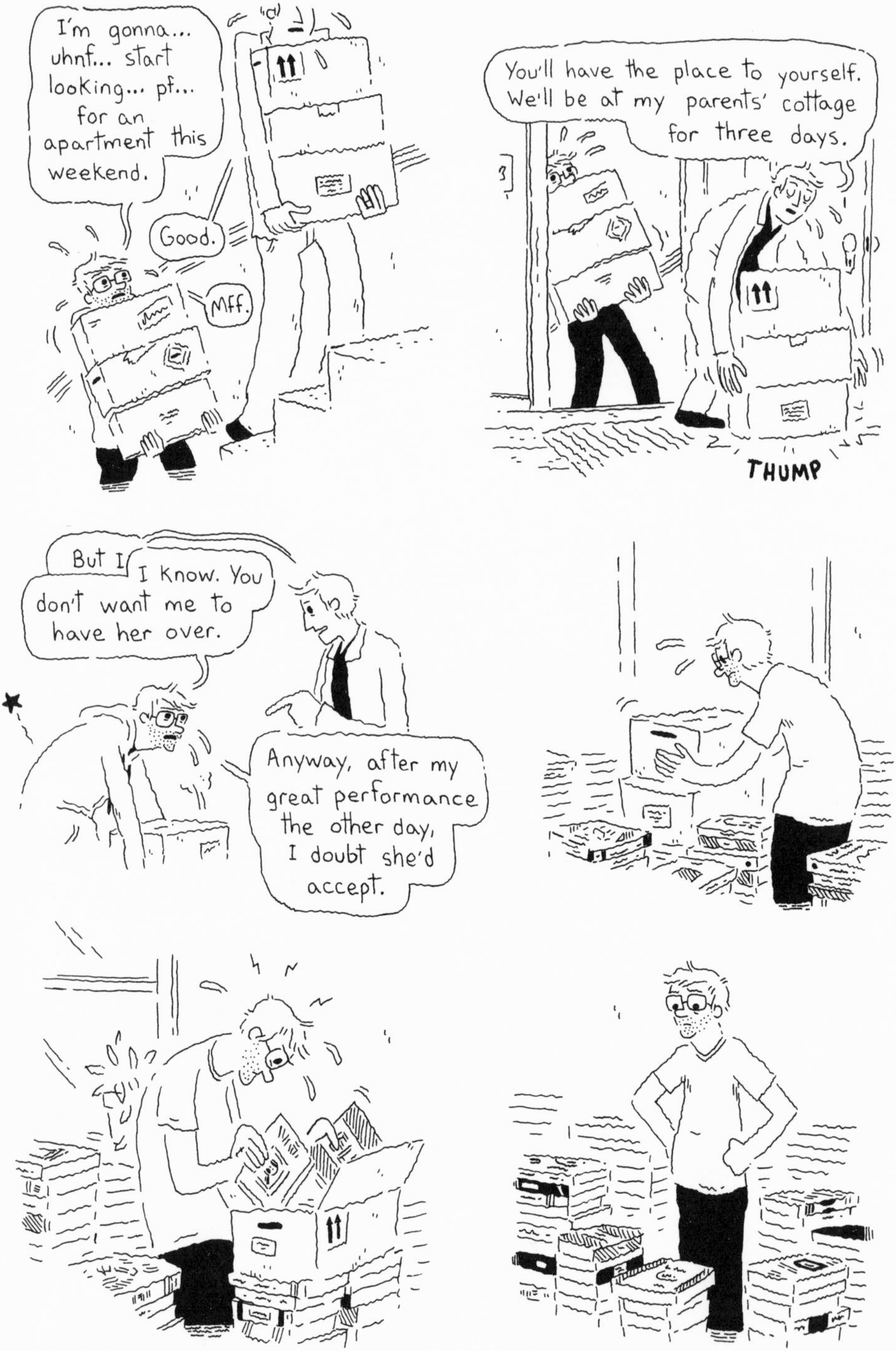
I'm gonna... uhnf... start looking... pf... for an apartment this weekend.
Good.
Mff.
You'll have the place to yourself. We'll be at my parents' cottage for three days.
THUMP
But I
I know. You don't want me to have her over.
Anyway, after my great performance the other day, I doubt she'd accept.

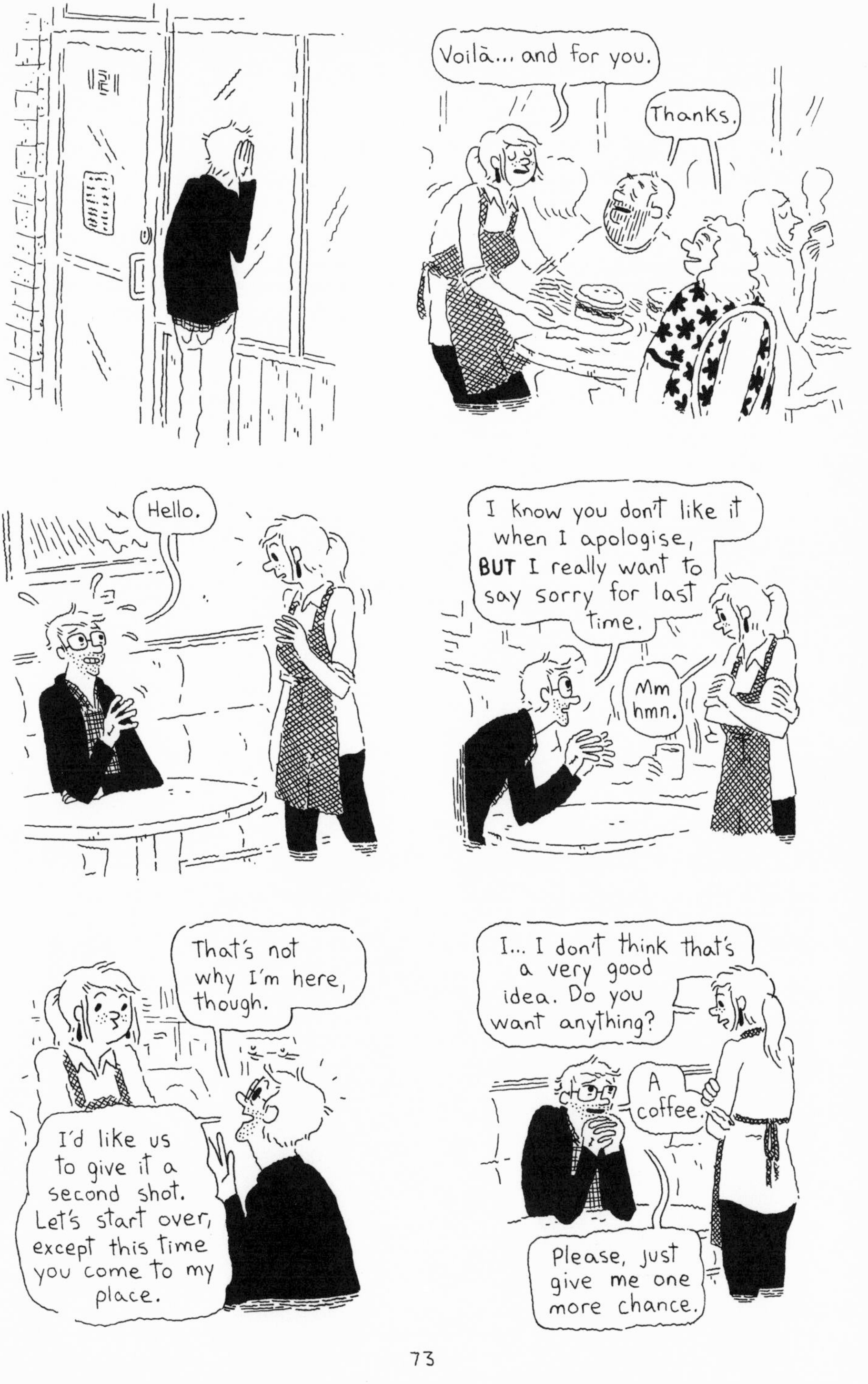
Voilà... and for you.
Thanks.
Hello.
I know you don't like it when I apologise, BUT I really want to say sorry for last time.
Mm hmn.
That's not why I'm here, though.
I'd like us to give it a second shot. Let's start over, except this time you come to my place.
I... I don't think that's a very good idea. Do you want anything?
A coffee.
Please, just give me one more chance.

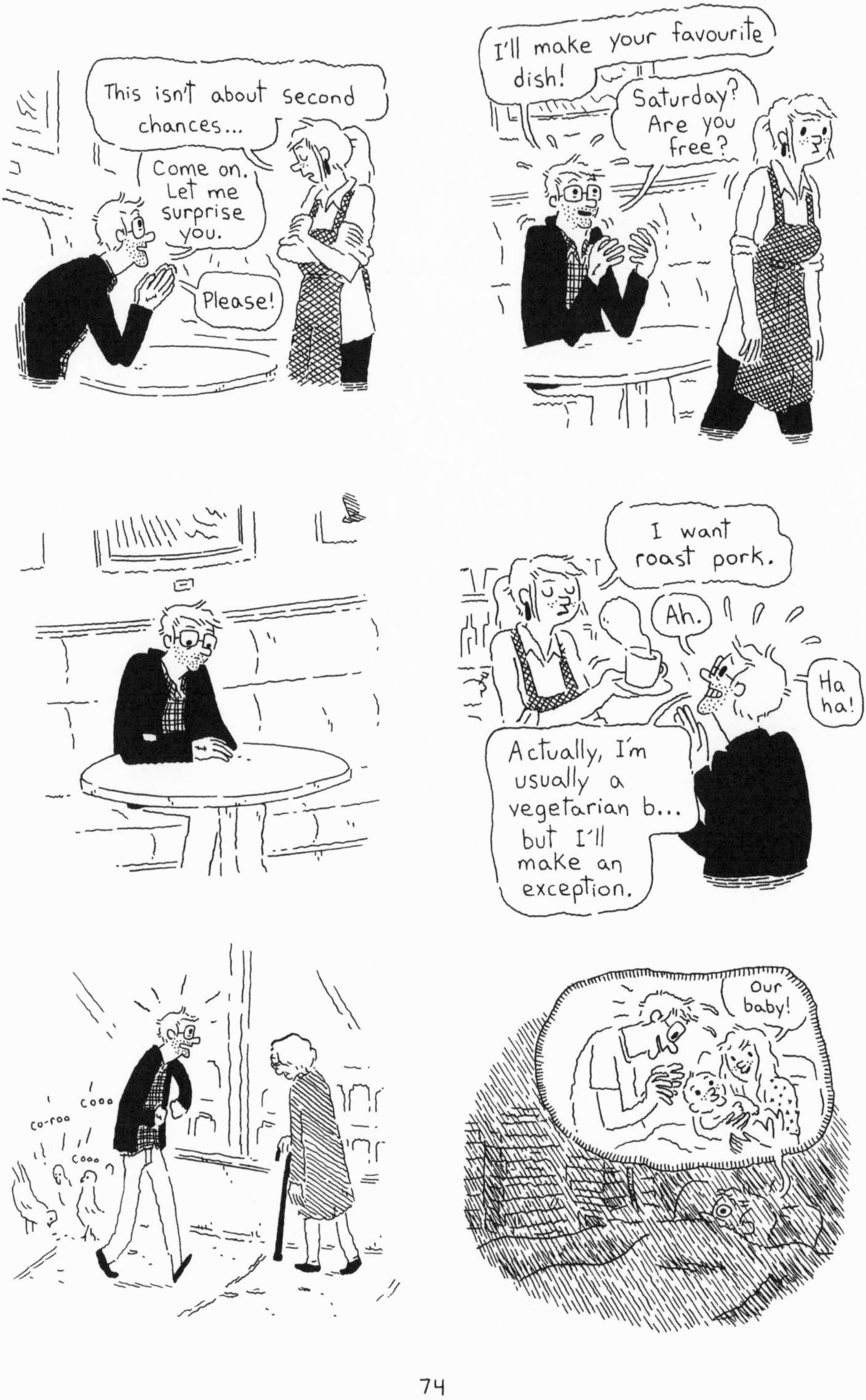
This isn't about second chances...
Come on. Let me surprise you.
Please!
I'll make your favourite dish!
Saturday? Are you free?
I want roast pork.
Ah.
Ha ha!
Actually, I'm usually a vegetarian b... but I'll make an exception.
cooo
co-roo
cooo
Our baby!

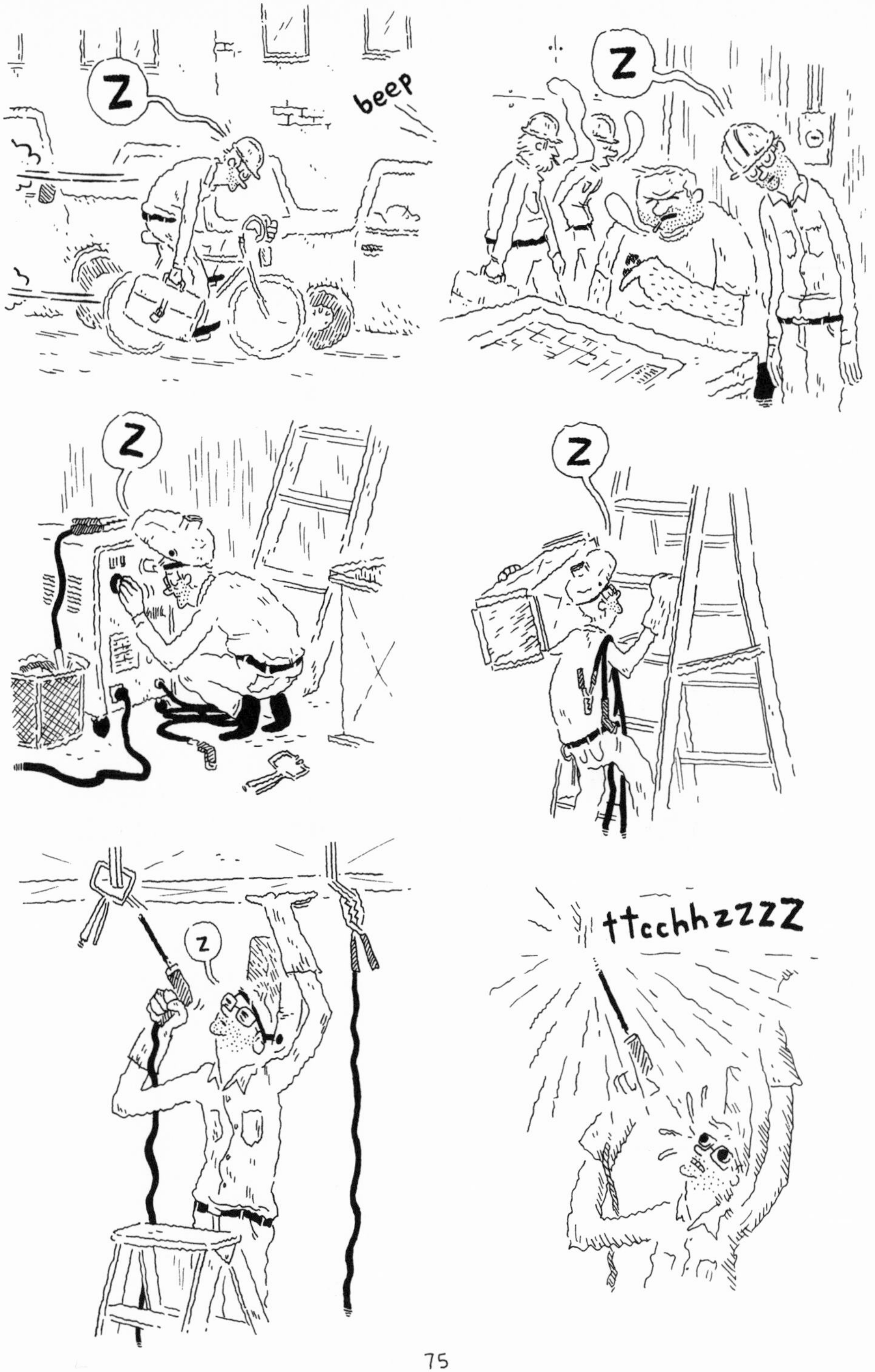
Z
beep
Z
Z
Z
z
ttcchhzzzzZ

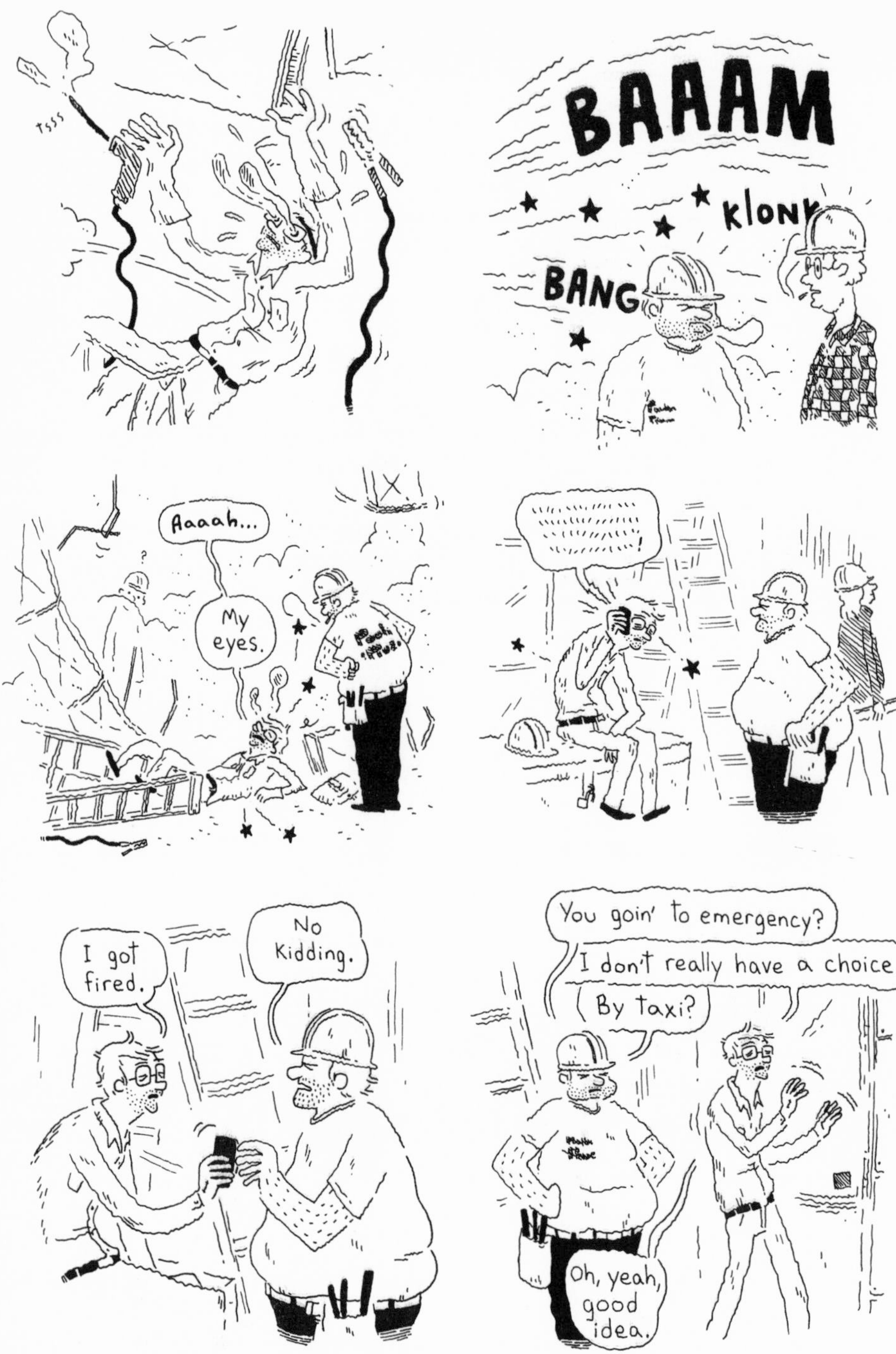
tsss
BAAAM
KLONK
BANG
Aaaah...
My eyes.
I got fired.
No Kidding.
You goin' to emergency?
I don't really have a choice.
By taxi?
Oh, yeah, good idea.

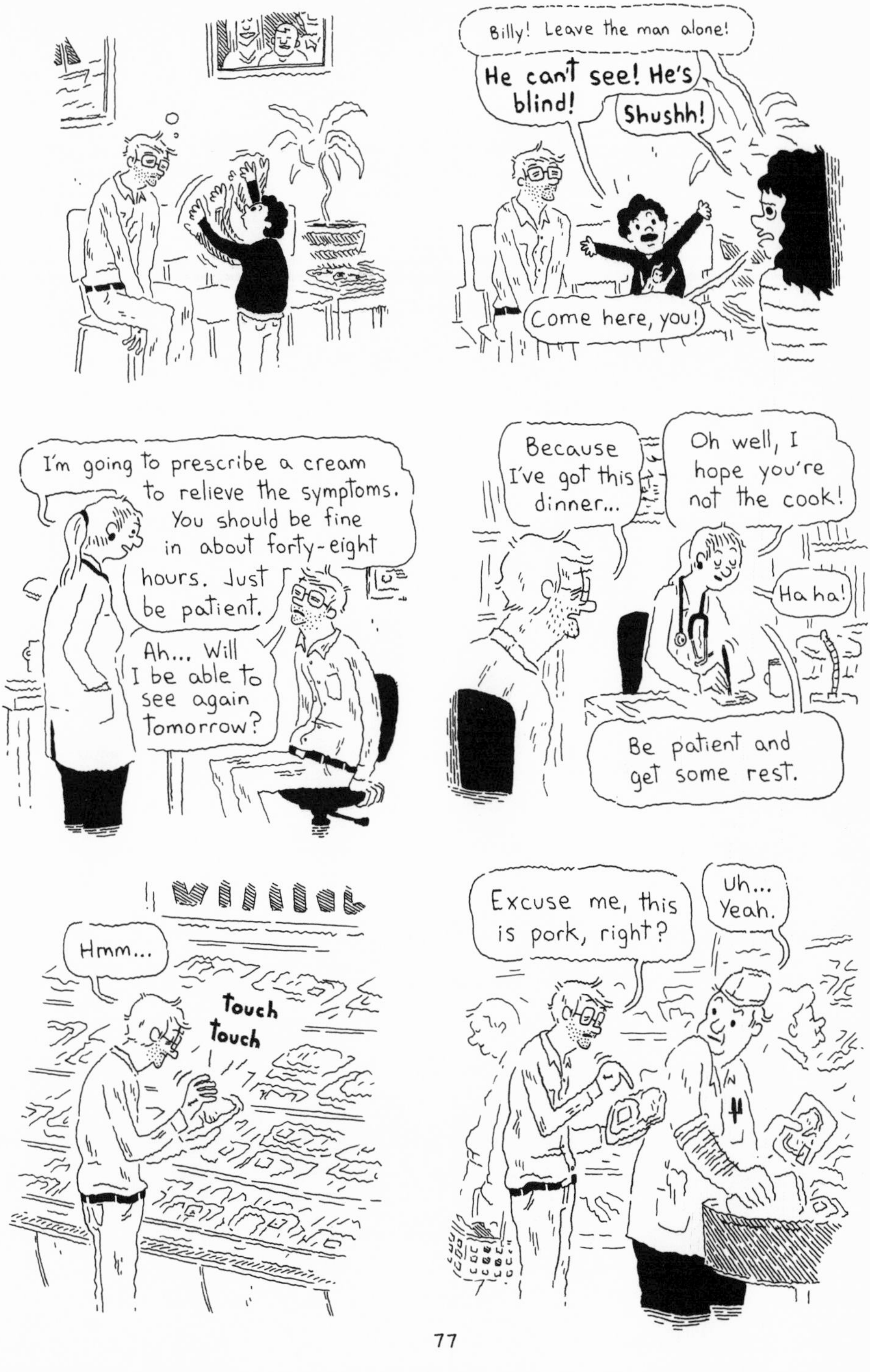
Billy! Leave the man alone!
He can't see! He's blind!
Shushh!
Come here, you!
I'm going to prescribe a cream to relieve the symptoms. You should be fine in about forty-eight hours. Just be patient.
Ah... Will I be able to see again tomorrow?
Because I've got this dinner...
Oh well, I hope you're not the cook!
Ha ha!
Be patient and get some rest.
Hmm...
touch touch
Excuse me, this is pork, right?
Uh... Yeah.

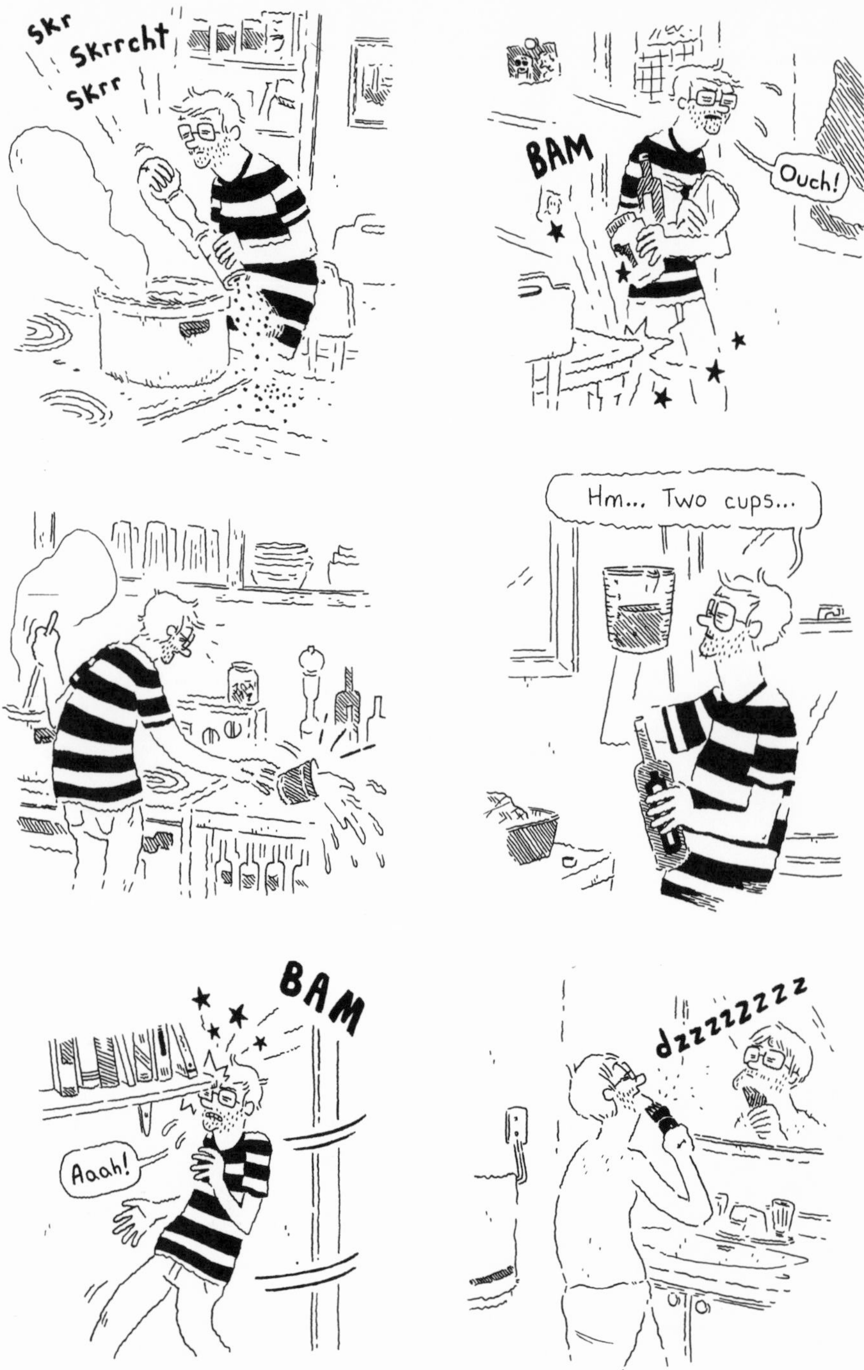
Skr
Skrrcht
Skrr
BAM
Ouch!
Hm... Two cups...
BAM
Aaah!
dzzzzzzzz

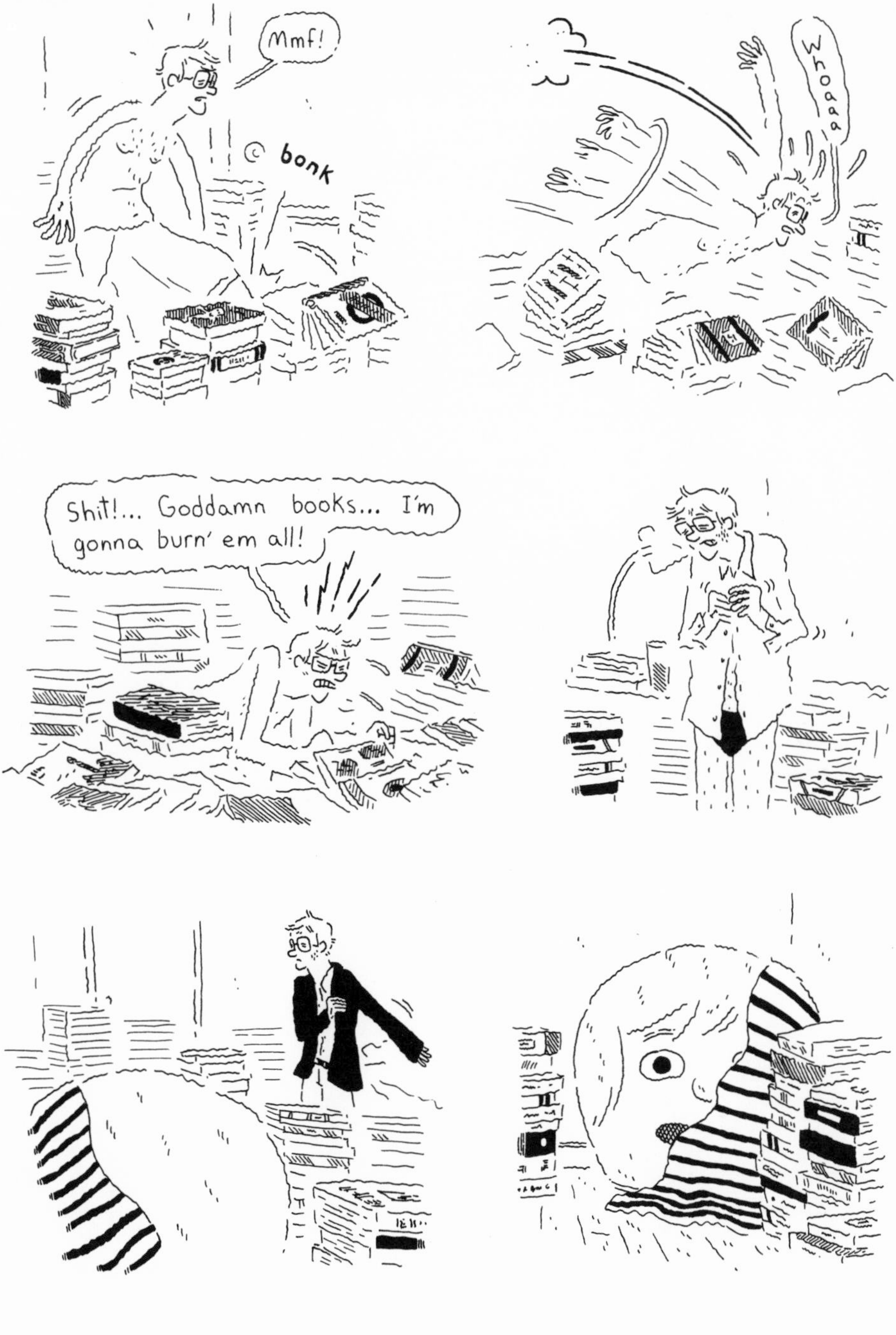
Mmf!
bonk
Whoaaa
Shit!... Goddamn books... I'm gonna burn' em all!

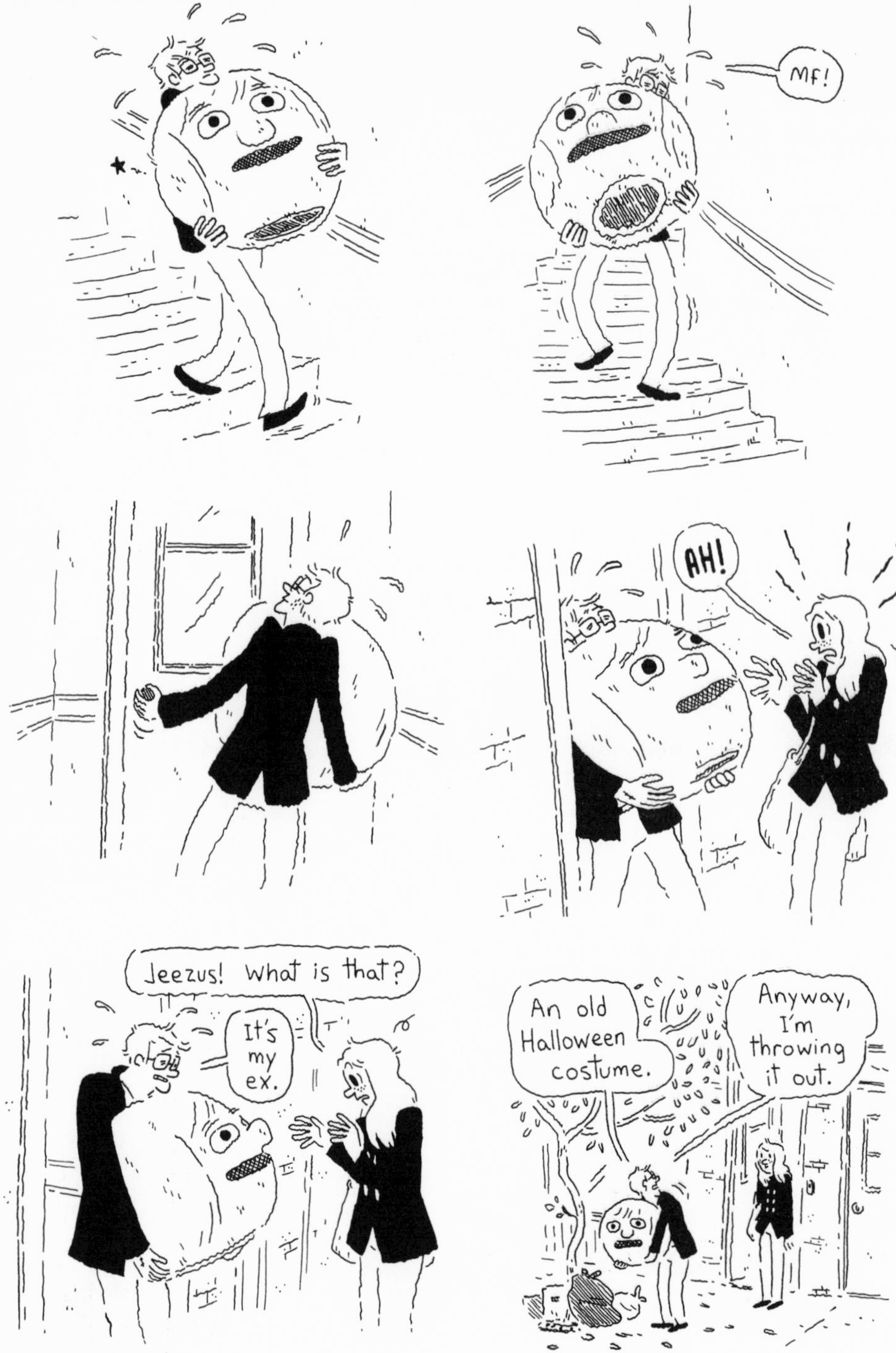
Mf!
AH!
Jeezus! What is that?
It's my ex.
An old Halloween costume.
Anyway, I'm throwing it out.

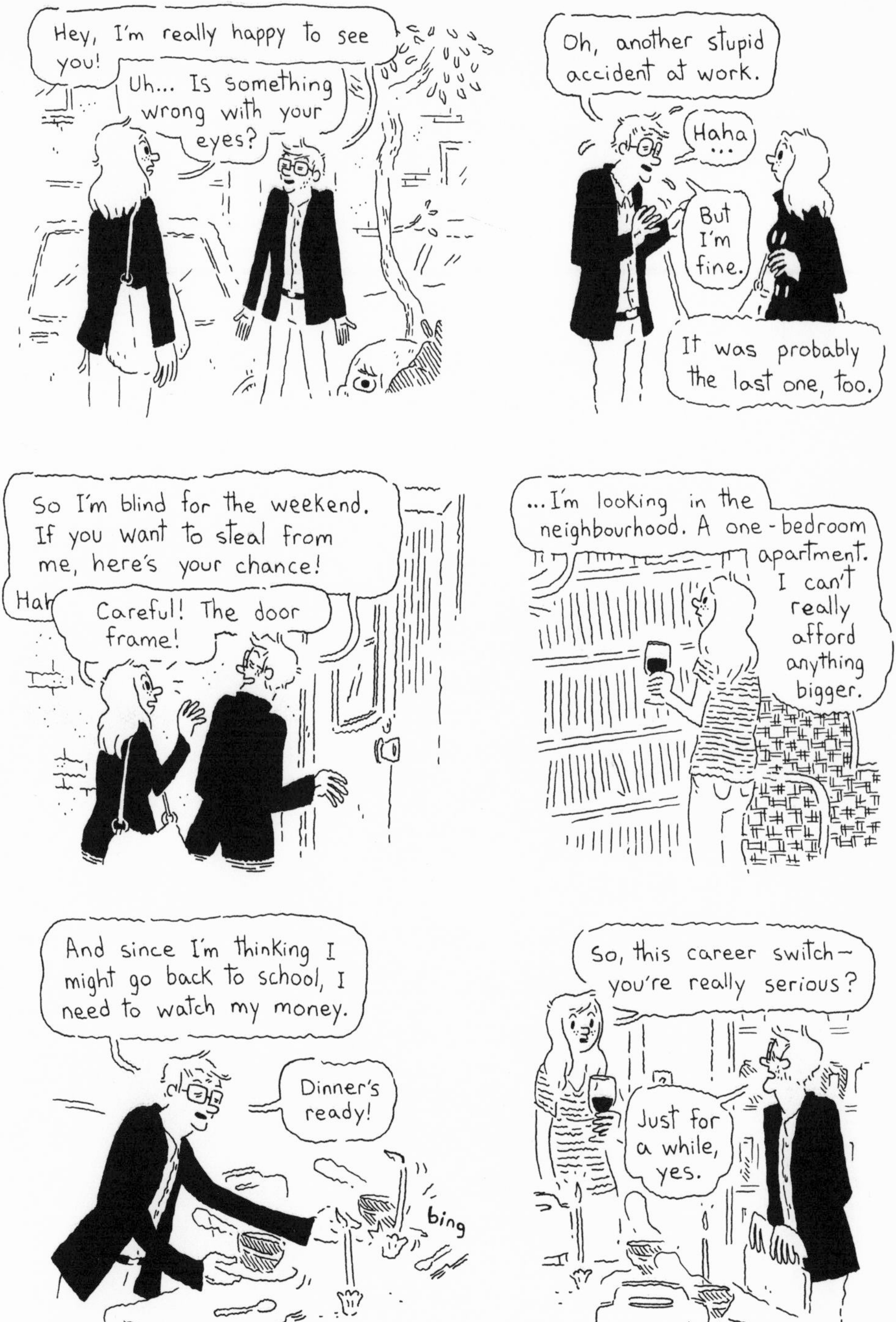
Hey, I'm really happy to see you!
Uh... Is something wrong with your eyes?
Oh, another stupid accident at work.
Haha...
But I'm fine.
It was probably the last one, too.
So I'm blind for the weekend. If you want to steal from me, here's your chance!
Hah
Careful! The door frame!
...I'm looking in the neighbourhood. A one-bedroom apartment. I can't really afford anything bigger.
And since I'm thinking I might go back to school, I need to watch my money.
Dinner's ready!
bing
So, this career switch— you're really serious?
Just for a while, yes.

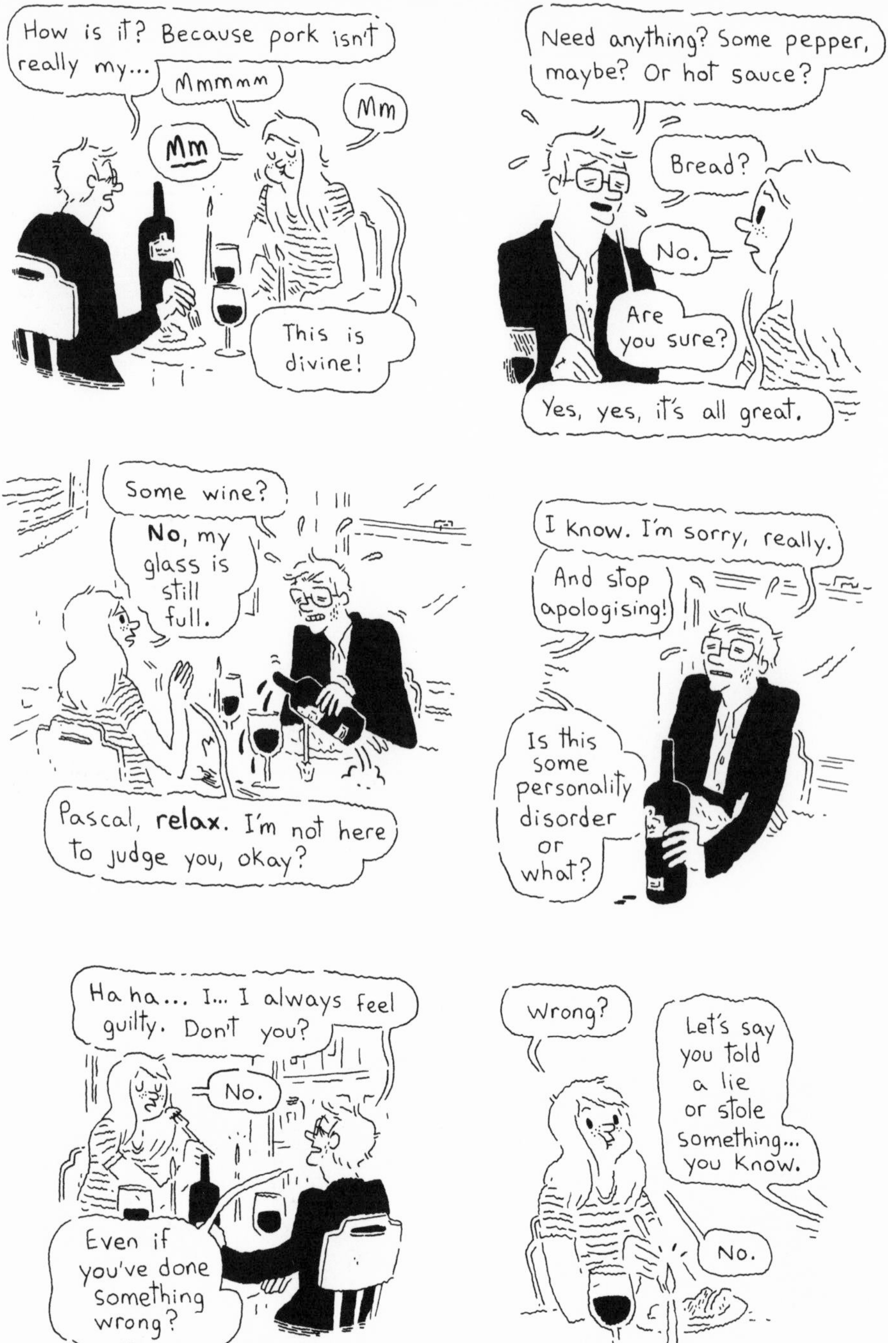

How is it? Because pork isn't really my...
Mmmmm
Mm
Mm
This is divine!
Need anything? Some pepper, maybe? Or hot sauce?
Bread?
No.
Are you sure?
Yes, yes, it's all great.
Some wine?
No, my glass is still full.
Pascal, **relax**. I'm not here to judge you, okay?
I know. I'm sorry, really.
And stop apologising!
Is this some personality disorder or what?
Ha ha... I... I always feel guilty. Don't you?
No.
Even if you've done something wrong?
Wrong?
Let's say you told a lie or stole something... you know.
No.

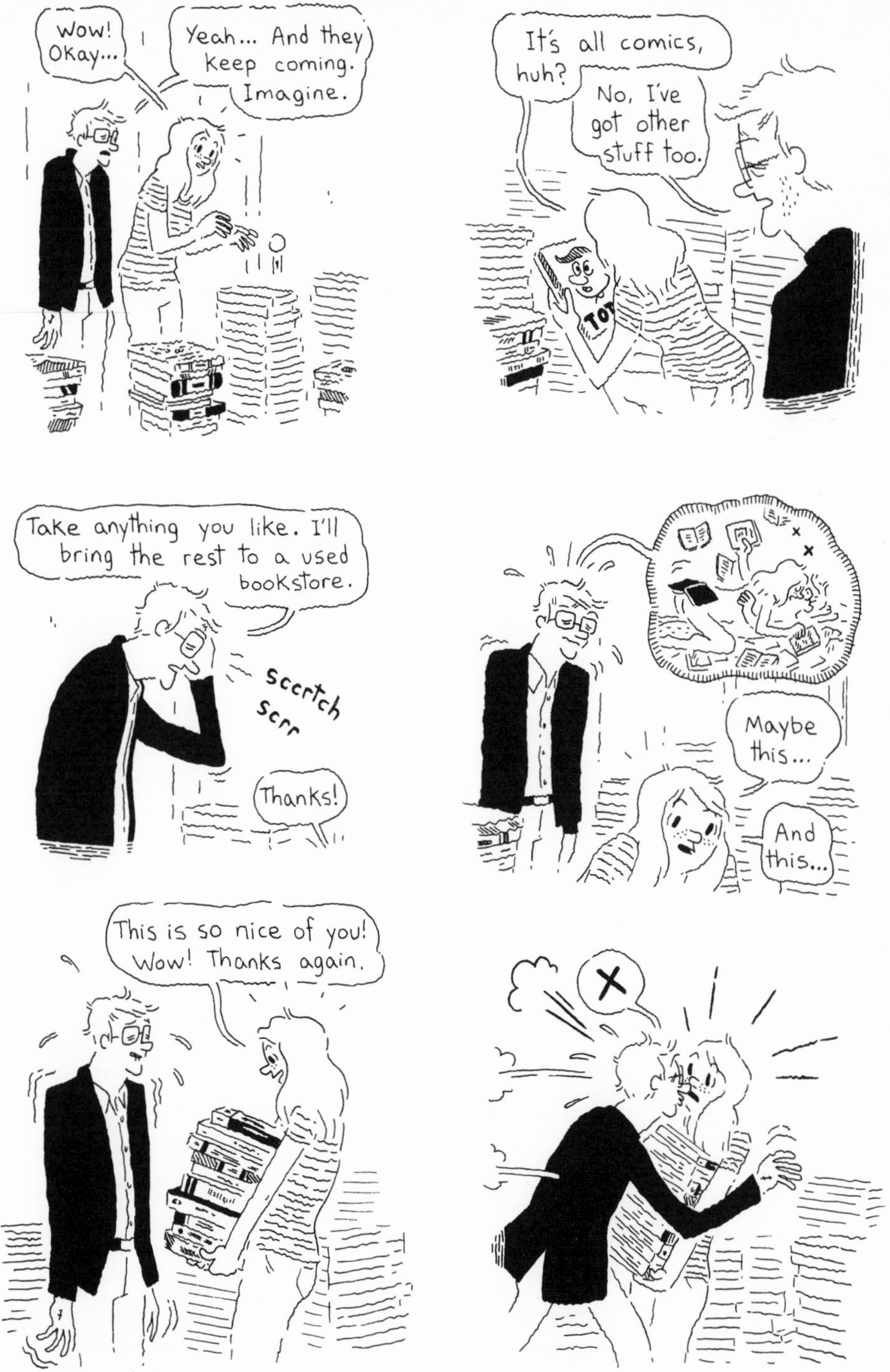
Wow! Okay...
Yeah... And they keep coming. Imagine.
It's all comics, huh?
No, I've got other stuff too.
TOT
Take anything you like. I'll bring the rest to a used bookstore.
Scertch
Scrr
Thanks!
Maybe this...
And this...
This is so nice of you! Wow! Thanks again.

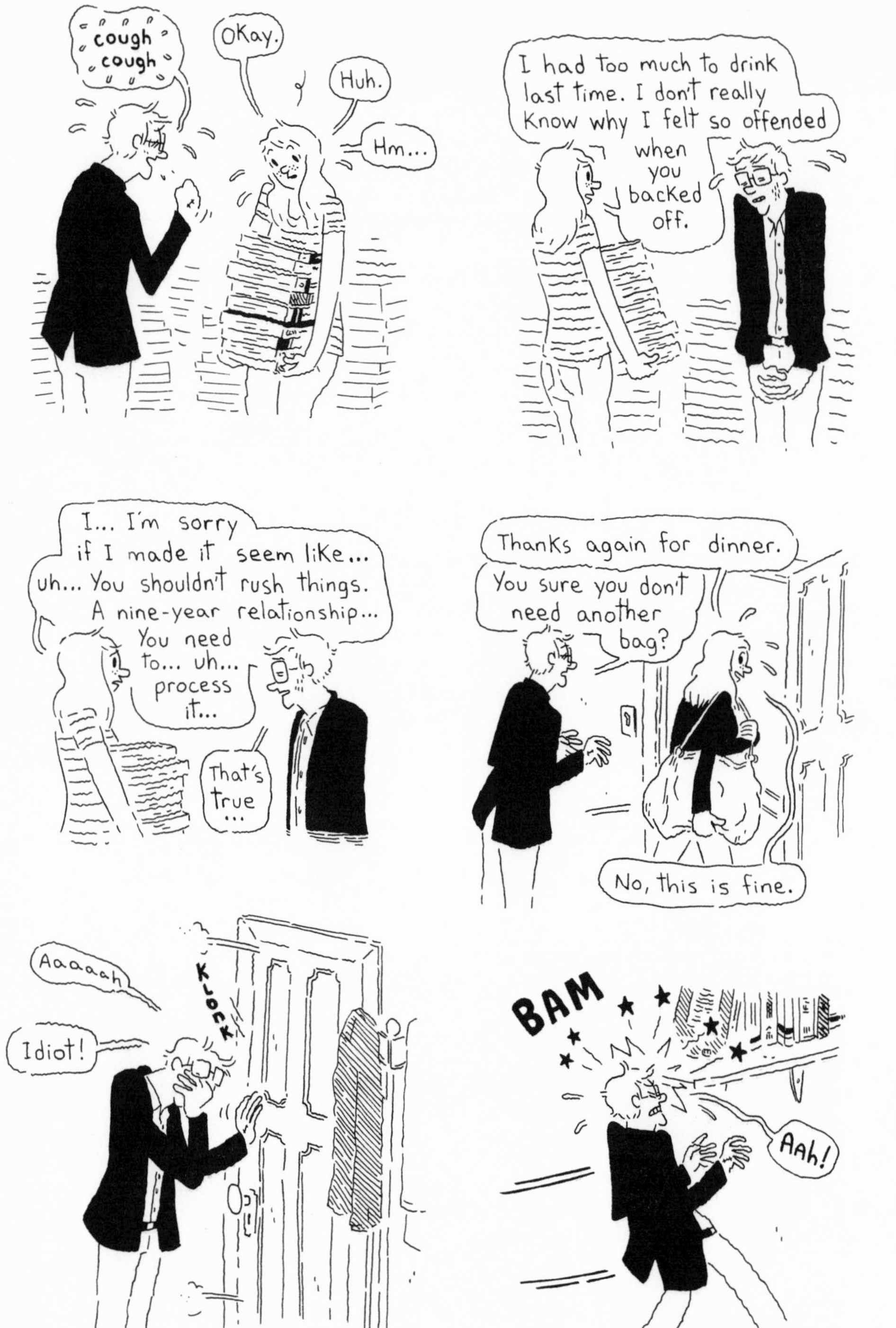

cough cough
OKay.
Huh.
Hm...
I had too much to drink last time. I don't really Know why I felt so offended when you backed off.
I... I'm sorry if I made it seem like... uh... You shouldn't rush things. A nine-year relationship... You need to... uh... process it...
That's true ...
Thanks again for dinner.
You sure you don't need another bag?
No, this is fine.
Aaaaah
KLONK
Idiot!
BAM
Aah!

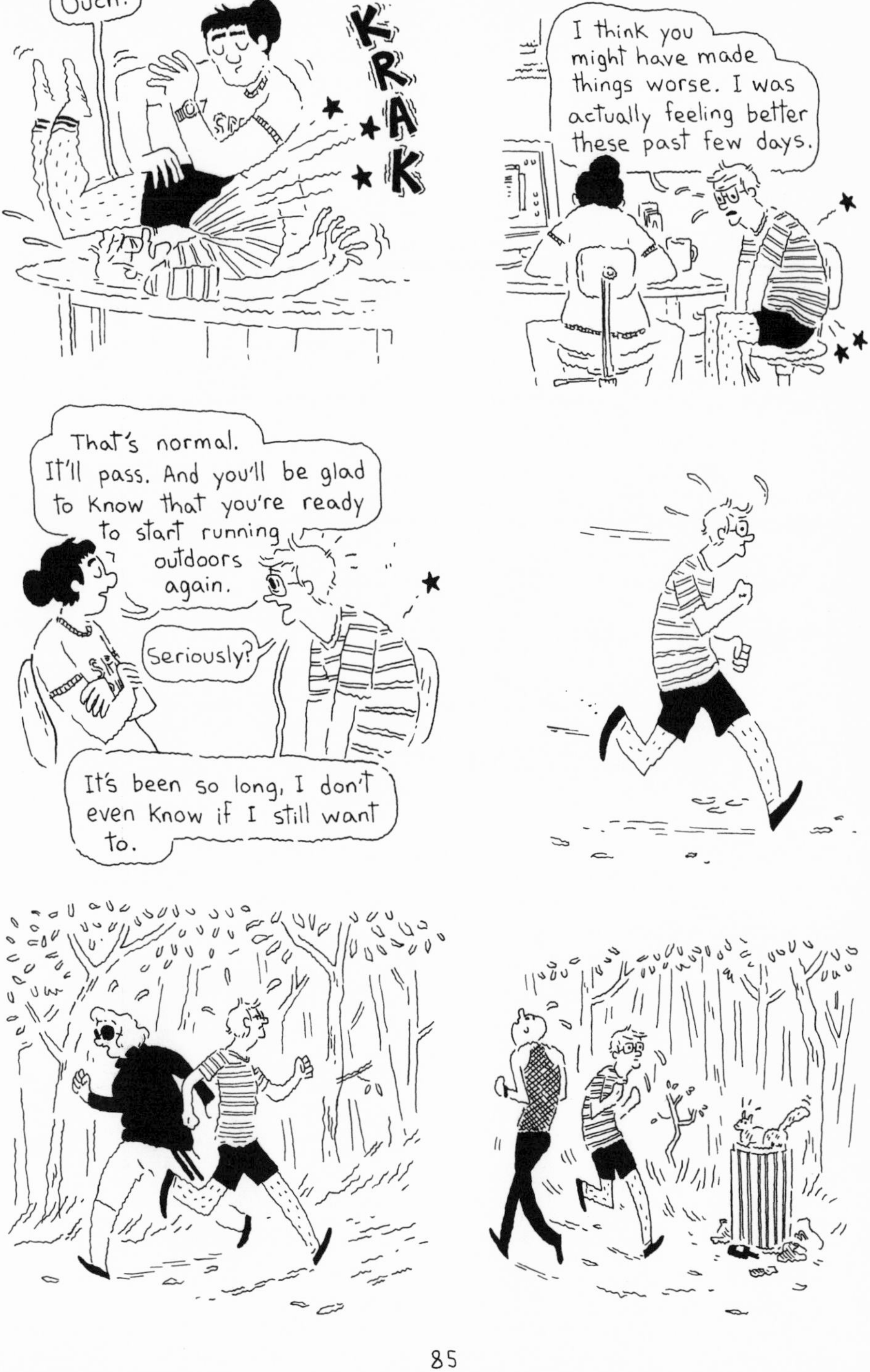
Ouch!
KRAK
I think you might have made things worse. I was actually feeling better these past few days.
That's normal. It'll pass. And you'll be glad to know that you're ready to start running outdoors again.
Seriously?
It's been so long, I don't even know if I still want to.

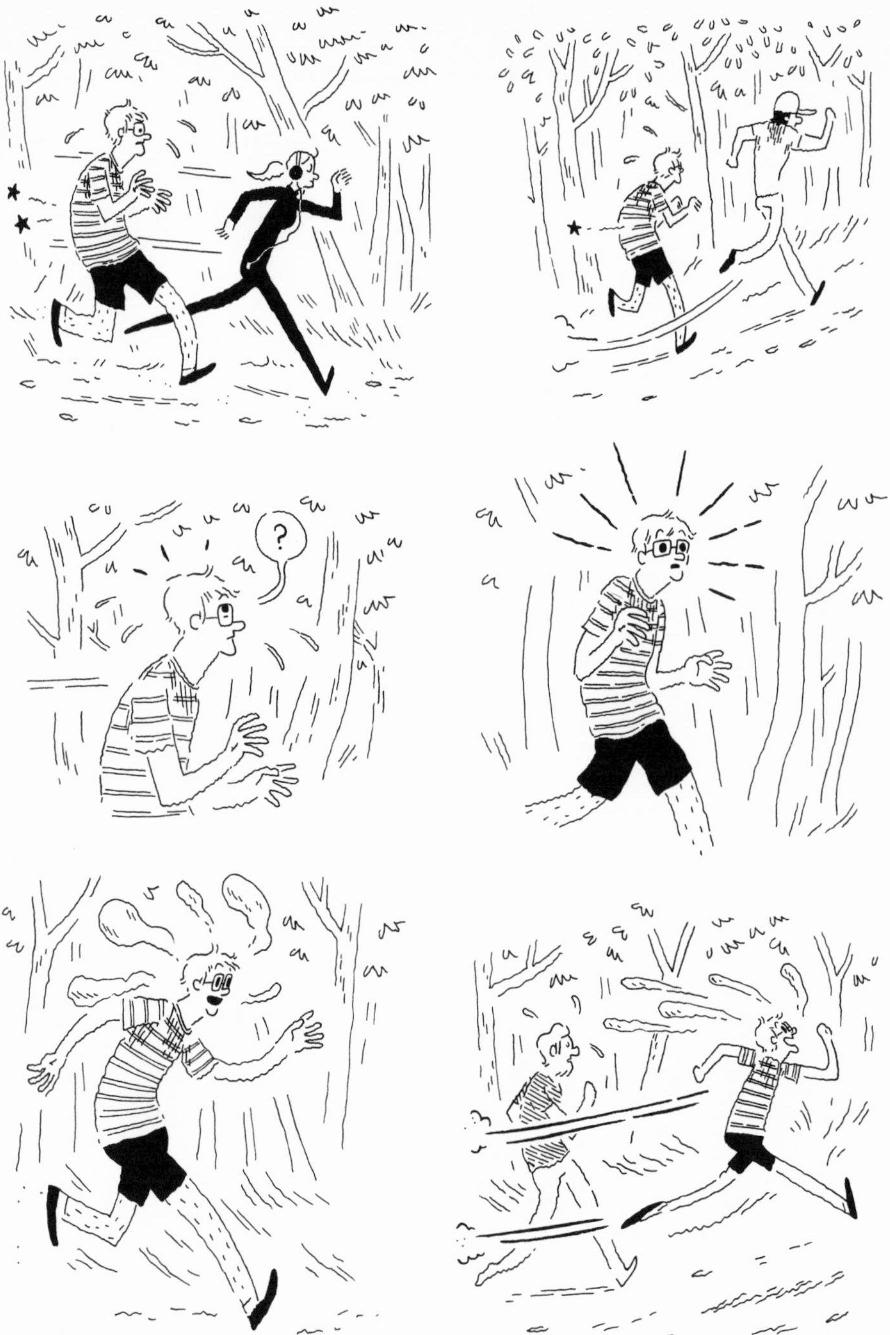
?

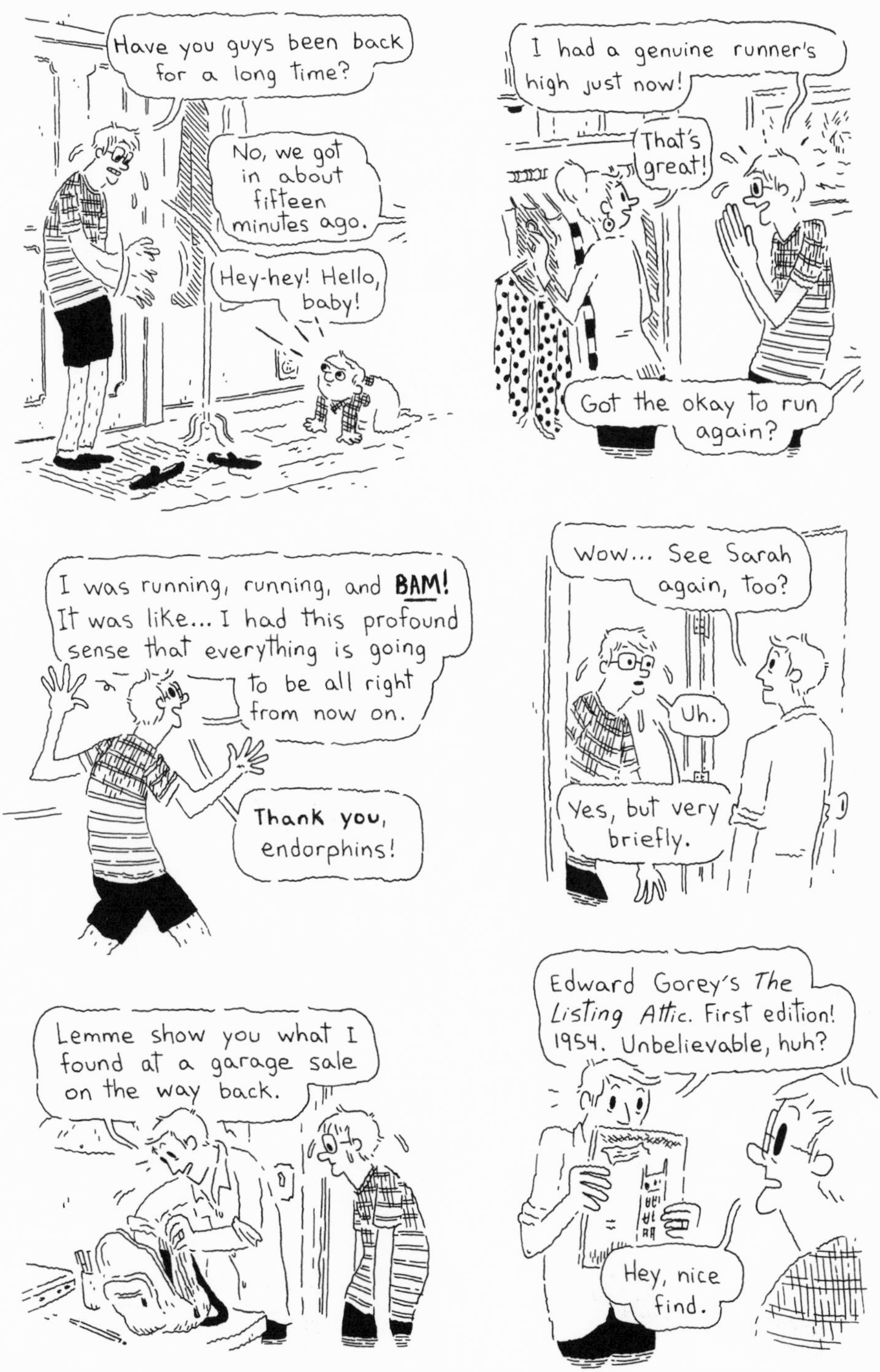
Have you guys been back for a long time?
No, we got in about fifteen minutes ago.
Hey-hey! Hello, baby!
I had a genuine runner's high just now!
That's great!
Got the okay to run again?
I was running, running, and **BAM!** It was like... I had this profound sense that everything is going to be all right from now on.
Thank you, endorphins!
Wow... See Sarah again, too?
Uh.
Yes, but very briefly.
Lemme show you what I found at a garage sale on the way back.
Edward Gorey's *The Listing Attic*. First edition! 1954. Unbelievable, huh?
Hey, nice find.

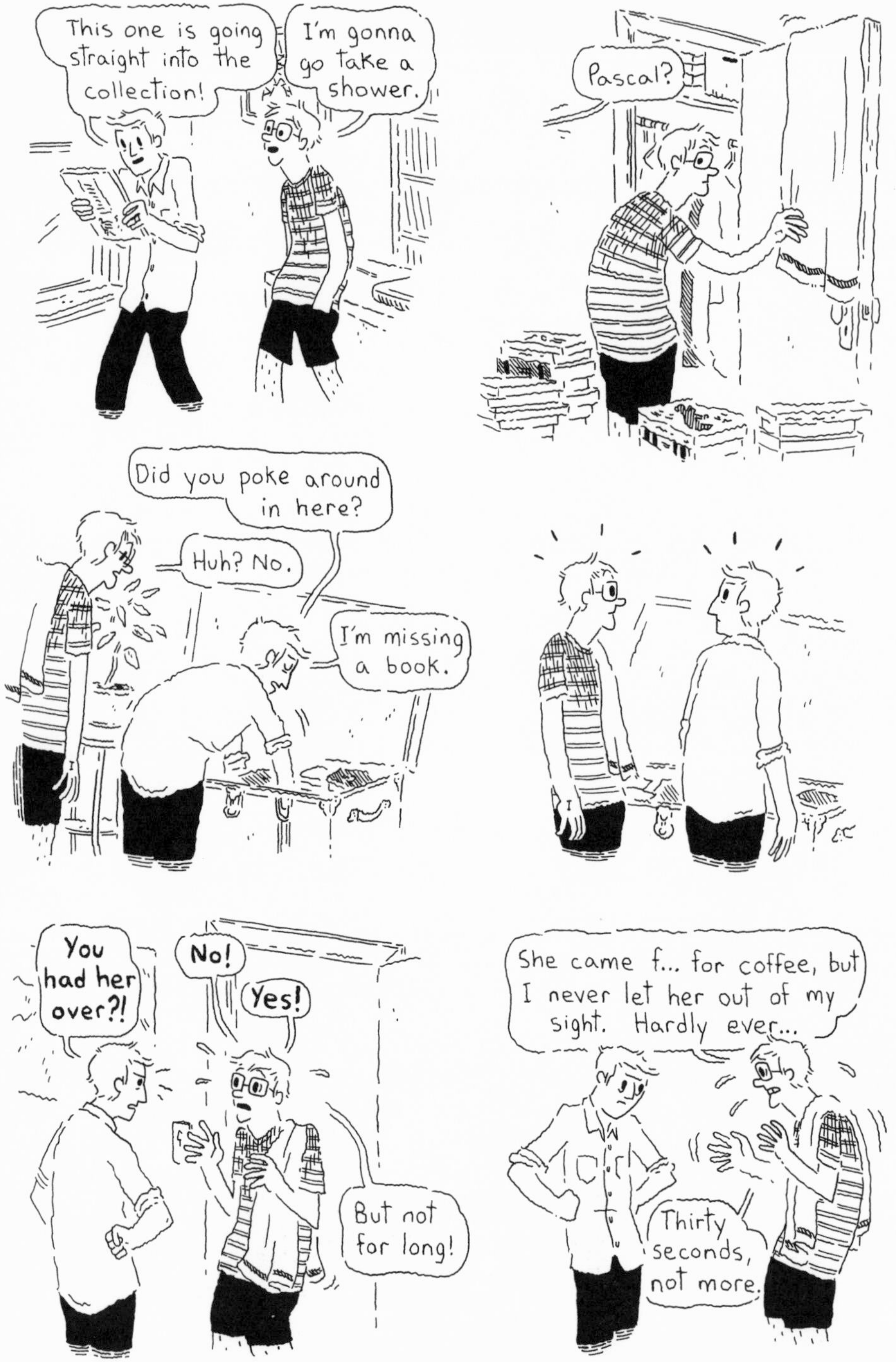
This one is going straight into the collection!
I'm gonna go take a shower.
Pascal?
Did you poke around in here?
Huh? No.
I'm missing a book.
You had her over?!
No!
Yes!
But not for long!
She came f... for coffee, but I never let her out of my sight. Hardly ever...
Thirty seconds, not more.

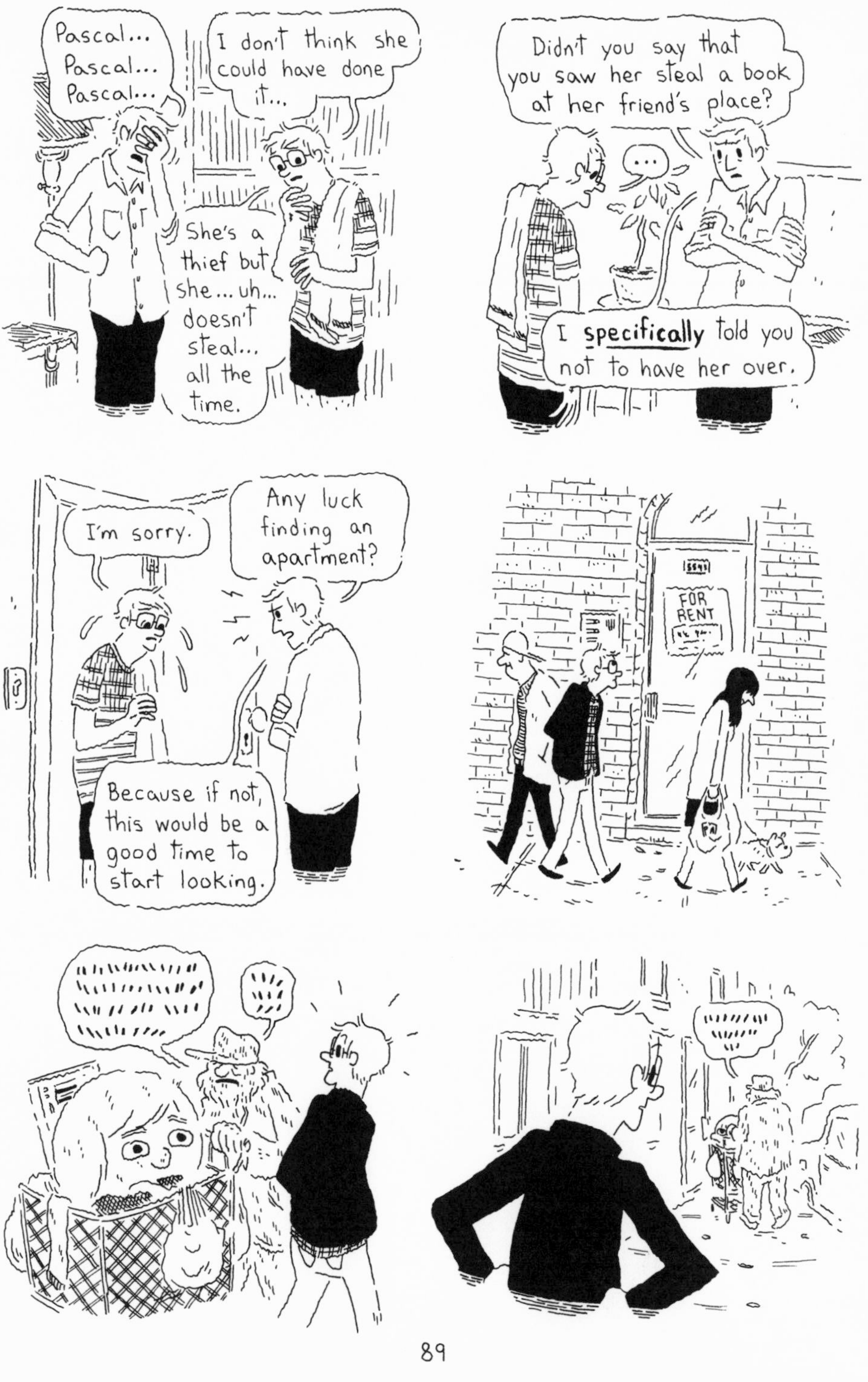
Pascal... Pascal... Pascal...
I don't think she could have done it...
She's a thief but she... uh... doesn't steal... all the time.
Didn't you say that you saw her steal a book at her friend's place?
...
I specifically told you not to have her over.
I'm sorry.
Any luck finding an apartment?
Because if not, this would be a good time to start looking.
FOR RENT

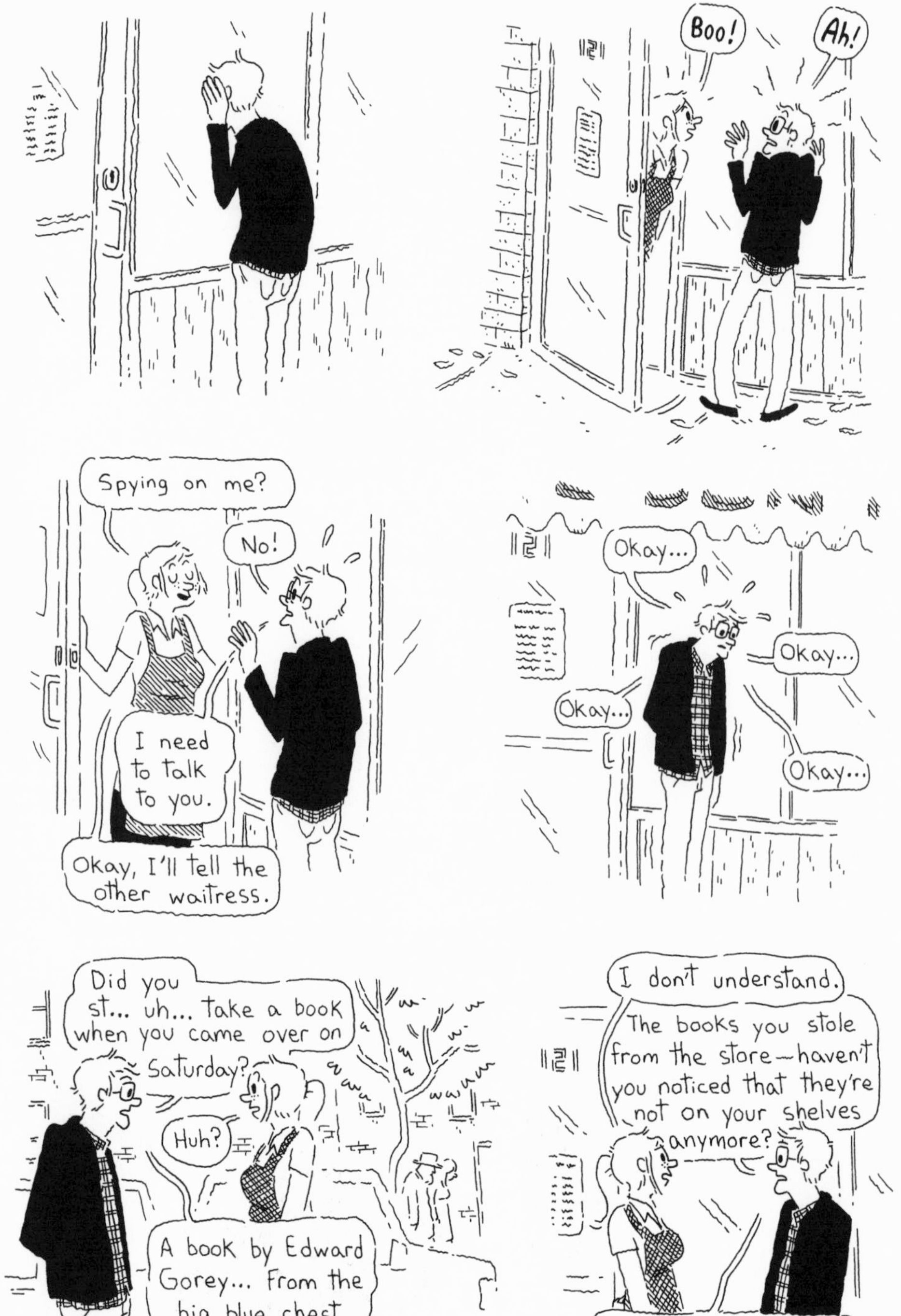
Boo!
Ah!
Spying on me?
No!
I need to talk to you.
Okay, I'll tell the other waitress.
Okay...
Okay...
Okay...
Okay...
Did you st... uh... take a book when you came over on Saturday?
Huh?
A book by Edward Gorey... From the big blue chest.
I don't understand.
The books you stole from the store—haven't you noticed that they're not on your shelves anymore?
Your friend's book, too.

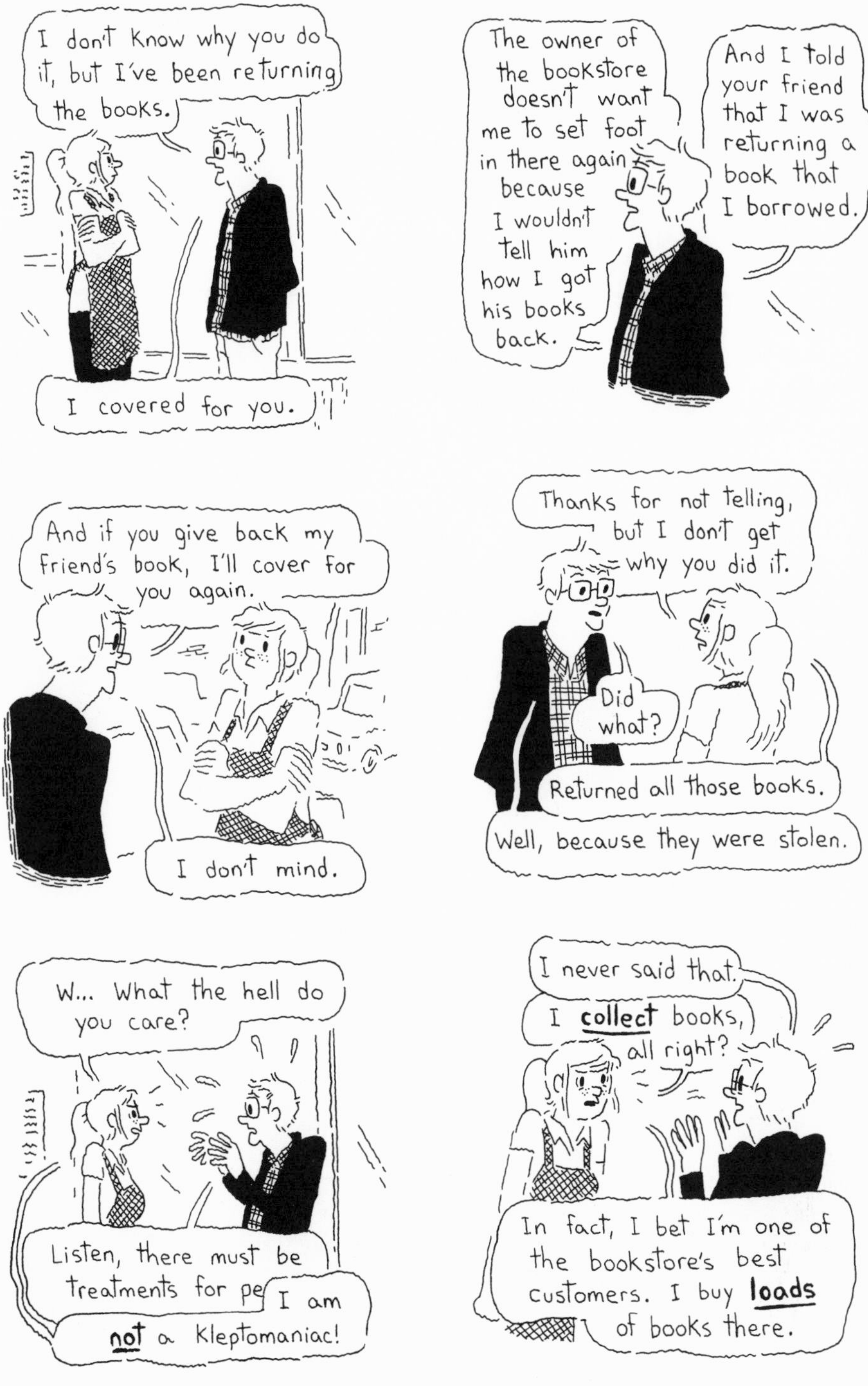

I don't know why you do it, but I've been returning the books.
I covered for you.
The owner of the bookstore doesn't want me to set foot in there again because I wouldn't tell him how I got his books back.
And I told your friend that I was returning a book that I borrowed.
And if you give back my friend's book, I'll cover for you again.
I don't mind.
Thanks for not telling, but I don't get why you did it.
Did what?
Returned all those books.
Well, because they were stolen.
W... What the hell do you care?
Listen, there must be treatments for pe
I am not a Kleptomaniac!
I never said that.
I collect books, all right?
In fact, I bet I'm one of the bookstore's best customers. I buy loads of books there.

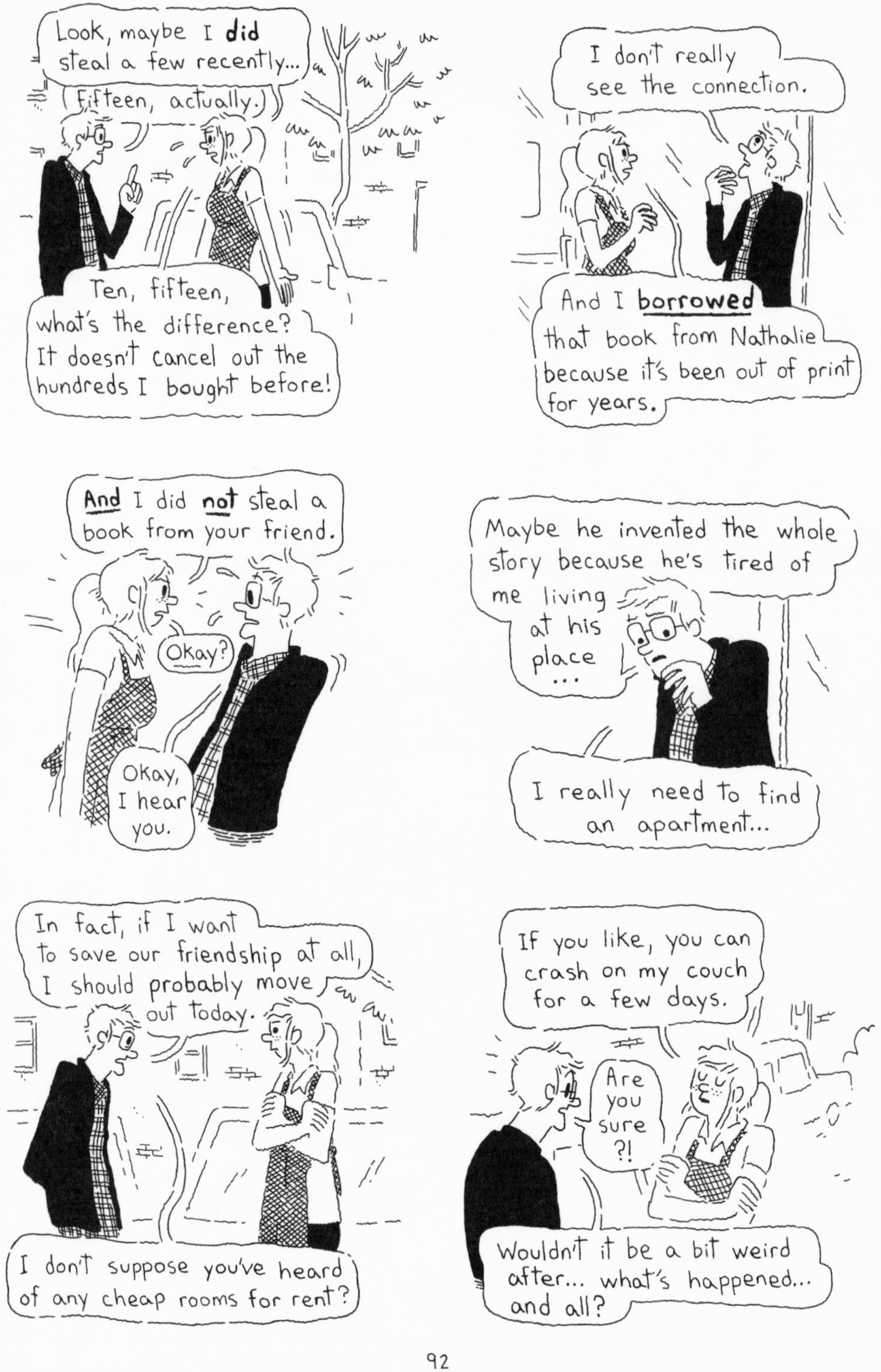
Look, maybe I did steal a few recently...
(Fifteen, actually.)
Ten, fifteen, what's the difference? It doesn't cancel out the hundreds I bought before!
I don't really see the connection.
And I borrowed that book from Nathalie because it's been out of print for years.
And I did not steal a book from your friend.
Okay?
Okay, I hear you.
Maybe he invented the whole story because he's tired of me living at his place...
I really need to find an apartment...
In fact, if I want to save our friendship at all, I should probably move out today.
I don't suppose you've heard of any cheap rooms for rent?
If you like, you can crash on my couch for a few days.
Are you sure?!
Wouldn't it be a bit weird after... what's happened... and all?

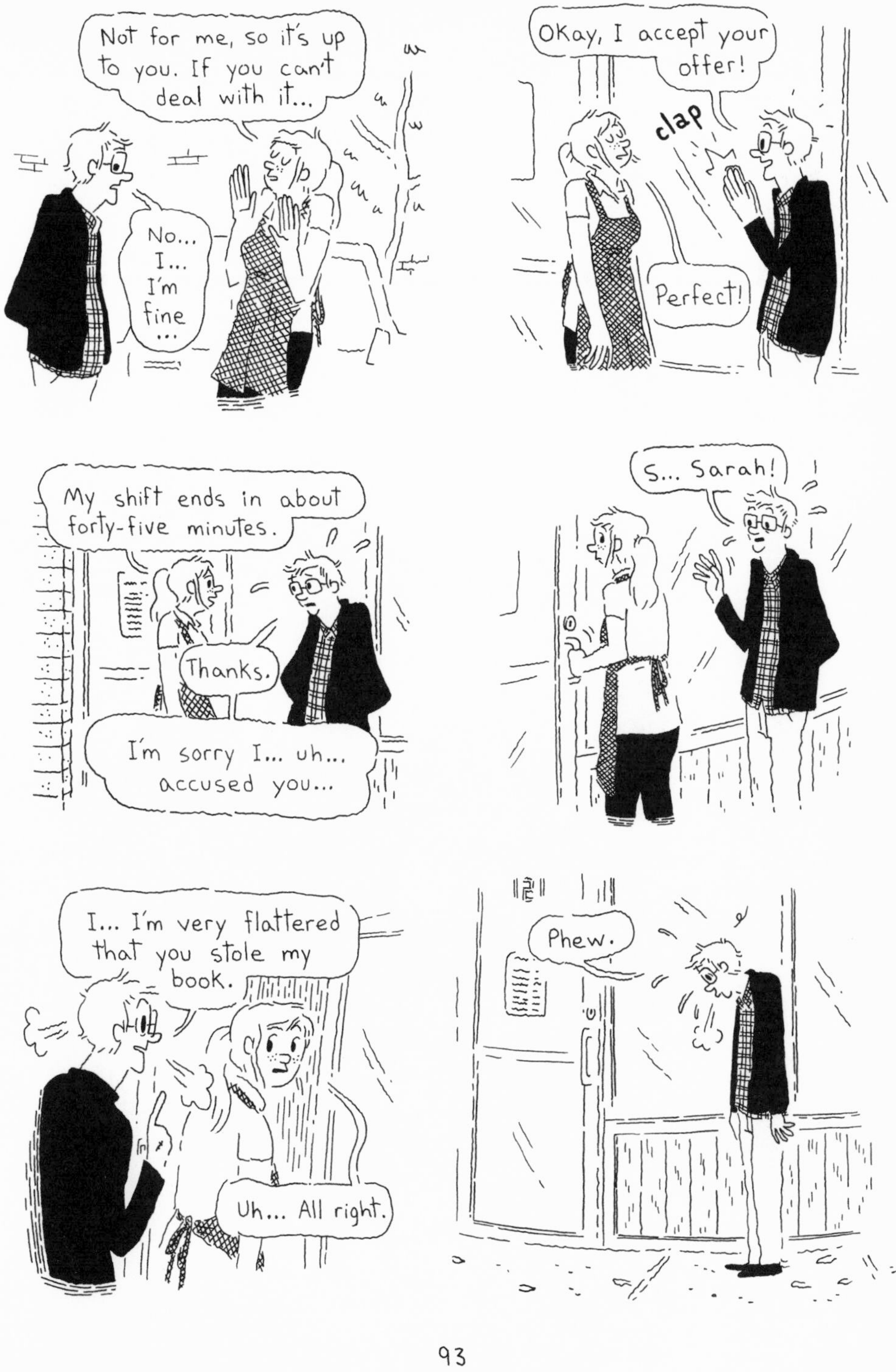
Not for me, so it's up to you. If you can't deal with it...
No... I... I'm fine ...
OKay, I accept your offer!
clap
Perfect!
My shift ends in about forty-five minutes.
Thanks.
I'm sorry I... uh... accused you...
S... Sarah!
I... I'm very flattered that you stole my book.
Uh... All right.
Phew.

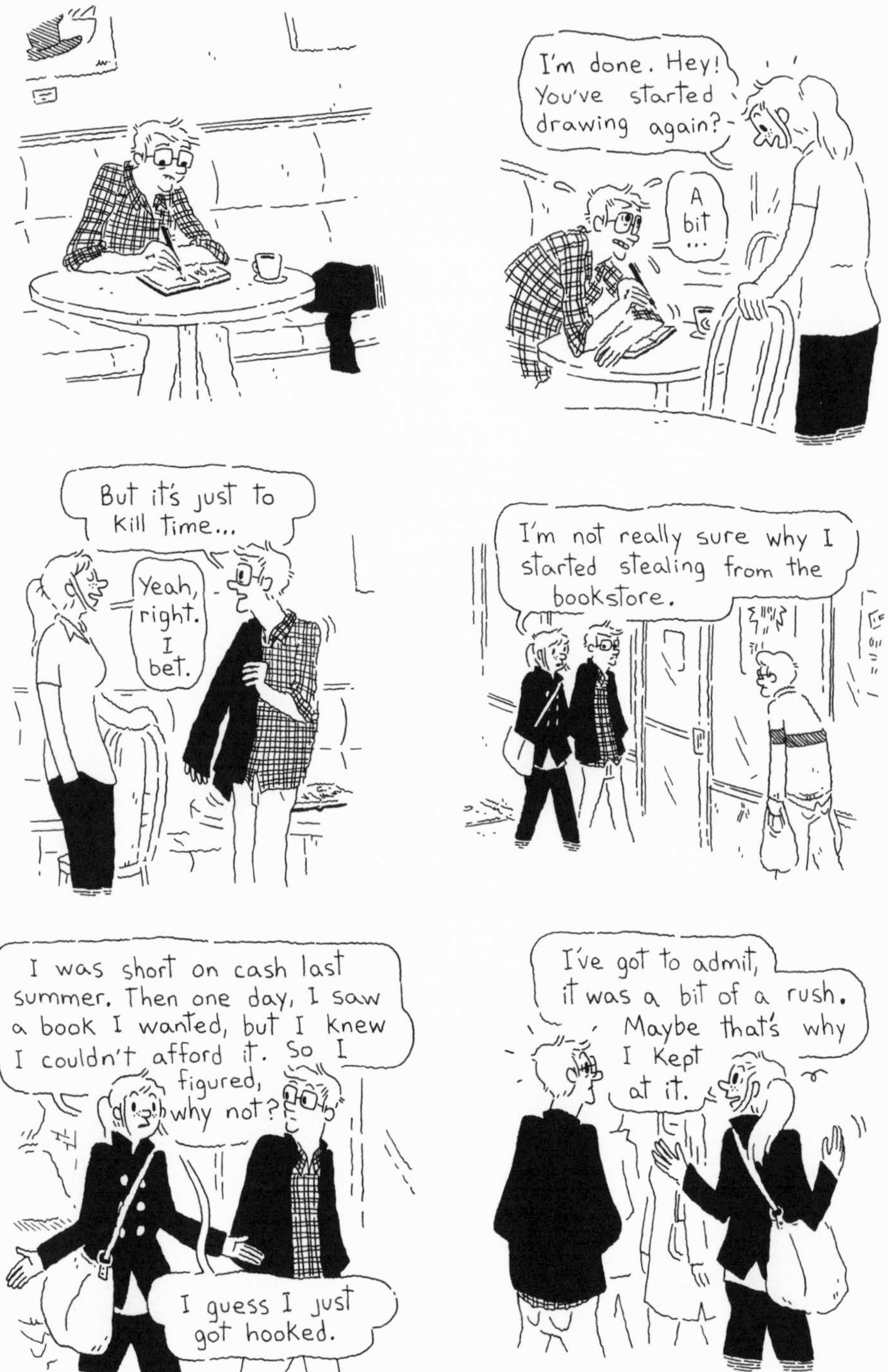
I'm done. Hey! You've started drawing again?
A bit...
But it's just to kill time...
Yeah, right. I bet.
I'm not really sure why I started stealing from the bookstore.
I was short on cash last summer. Then one day, I saw a book I wanted, but I knew I couldn't afford it. So I figured, why not?
I guess I just got hooked.
I've got to admit, it was a bit of a rush. Maybe that's why I kept at it.

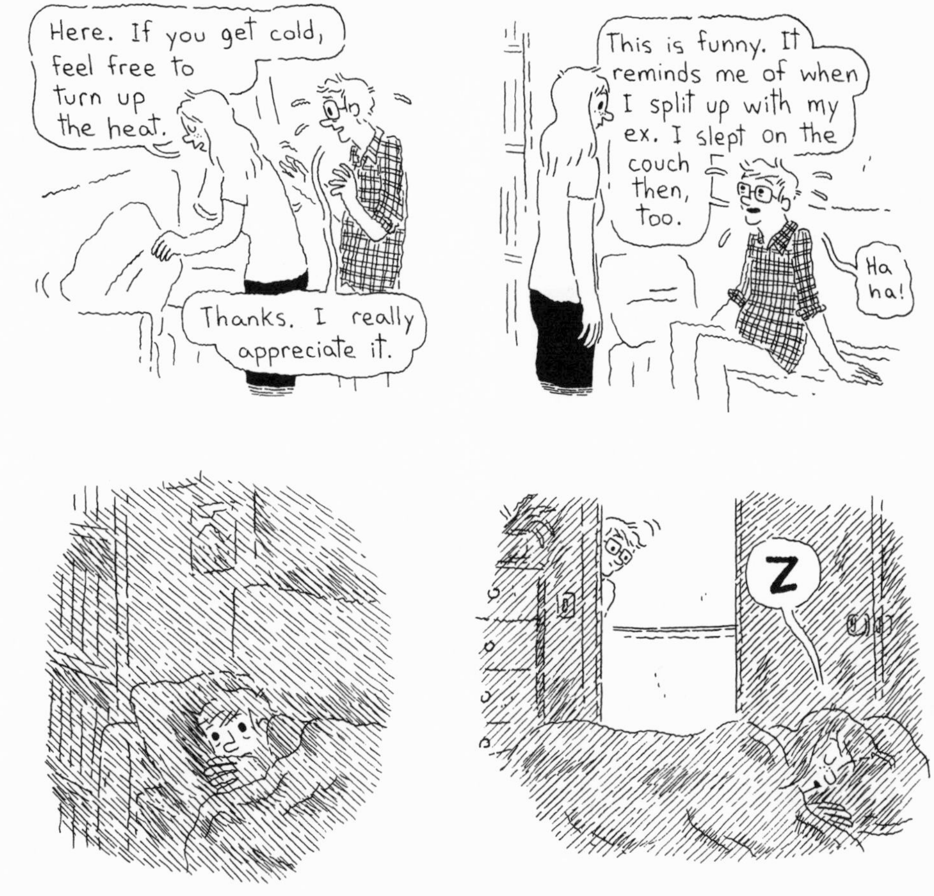
Here. If you get cold, feel free to turn up the heat.
Thanks. I really appreciate it.
This is funny. It reminds me of when I split up with my ex. I slept on the couch then, too.
Ha ha!
Z
Hm.

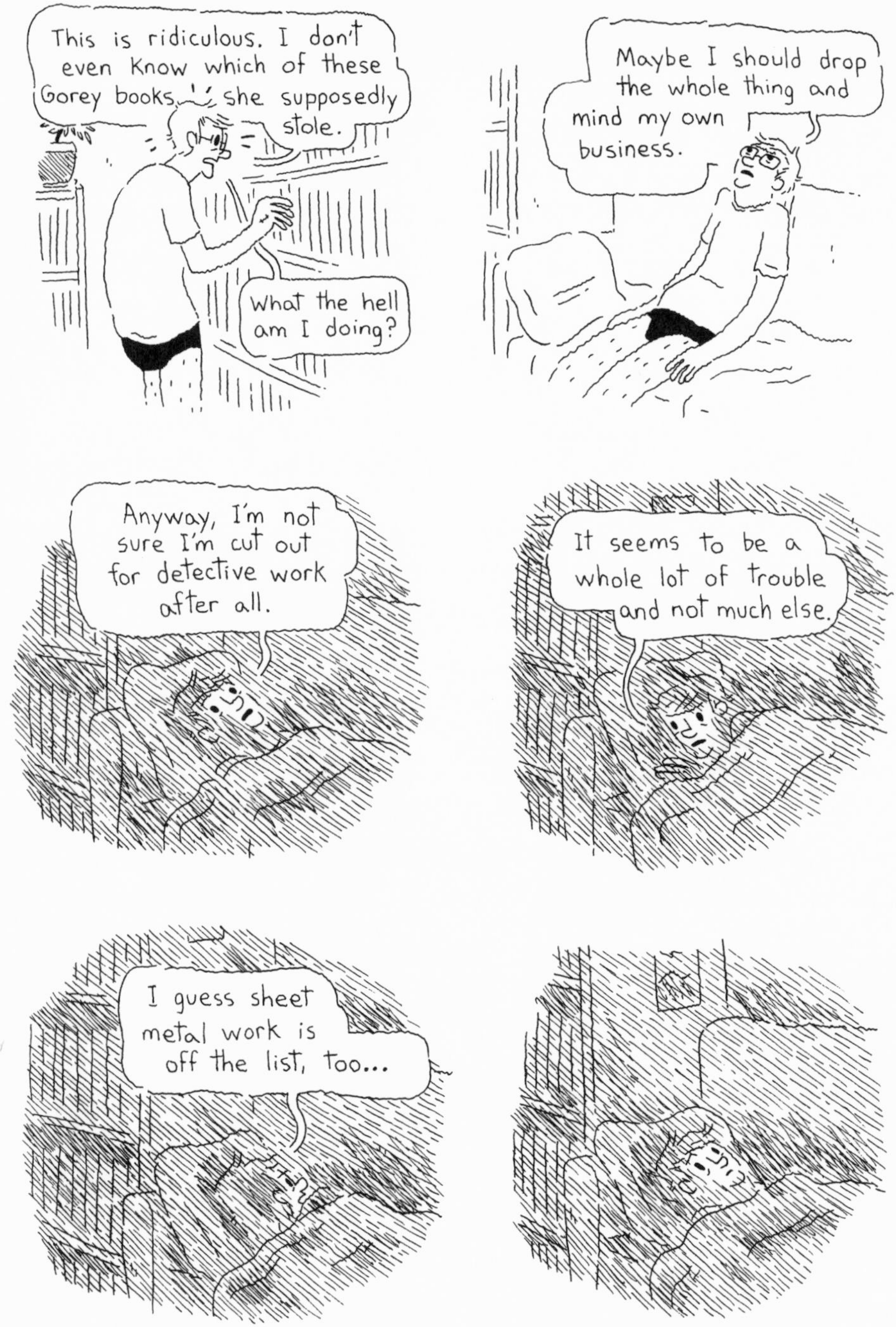
This is ridiculous. I don't even know which of these Gorey books she supposedly stole.
What the hell am I doing?
Maybe I should drop the whole thing and mind my own business.
Anyway, I'm not sure I'm cut out for detective work after all.
It seems to be a whole lot of trouble and not much else.
I guess sheet metal work is off the list, too...

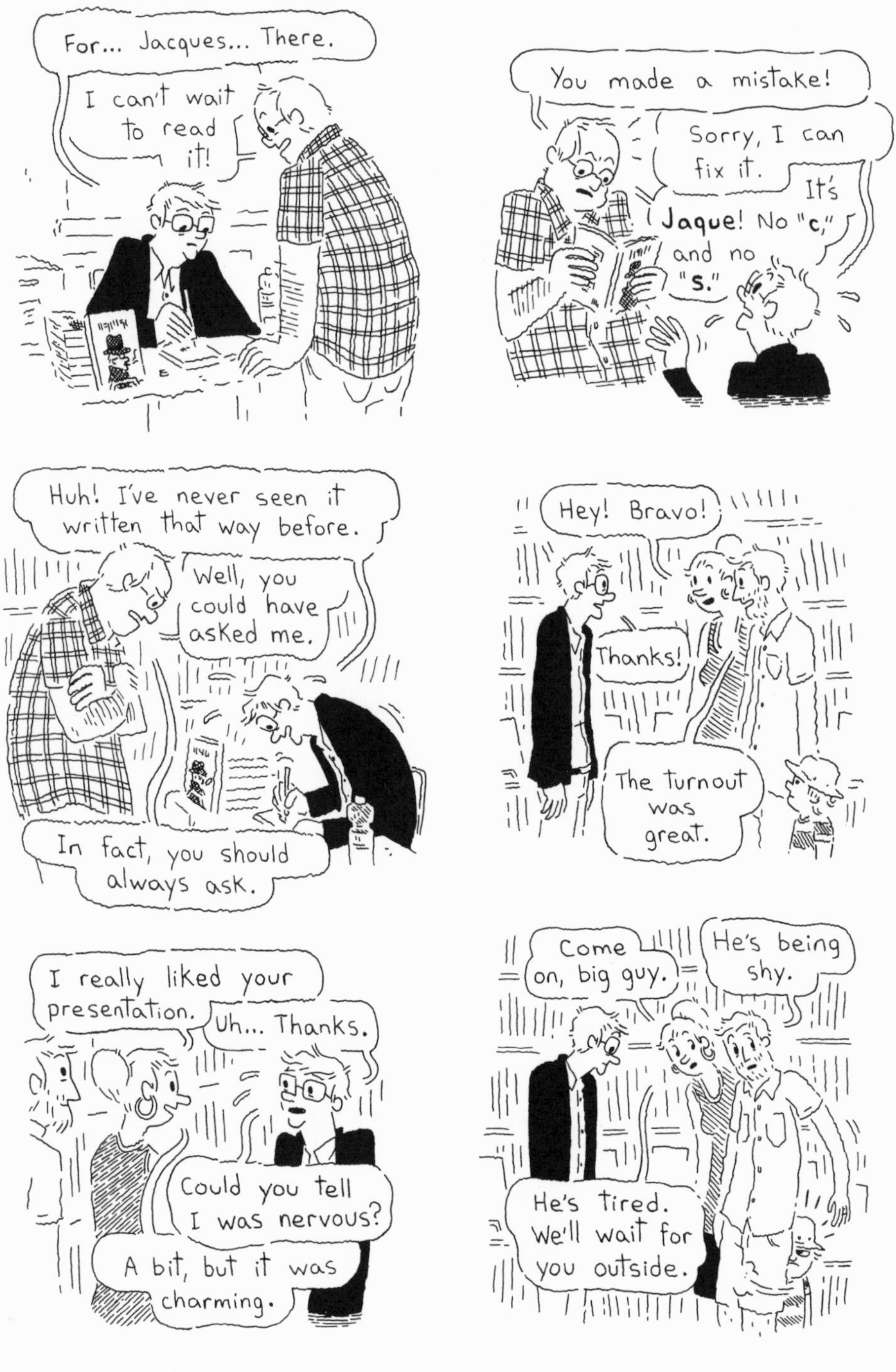
For... Jacques... There.
I can't wait to read it!
You made a mistake!
Sorry, I can fix it.
It's **Jaque**! No "**c**," and no "**s**."
Huh! I've never seen it written that way before.
Well, you could have asked me.
In fact, you should always ask.
Hey! Bravo!
Thanks!
The turnout was great.
I really liked your presentation.
Uh... Thanks.
Could you tell I was nervous?
A bit, but it was charming.
Come on, big guy.
He's being shy.
He's tired. We'll wait for you outside.

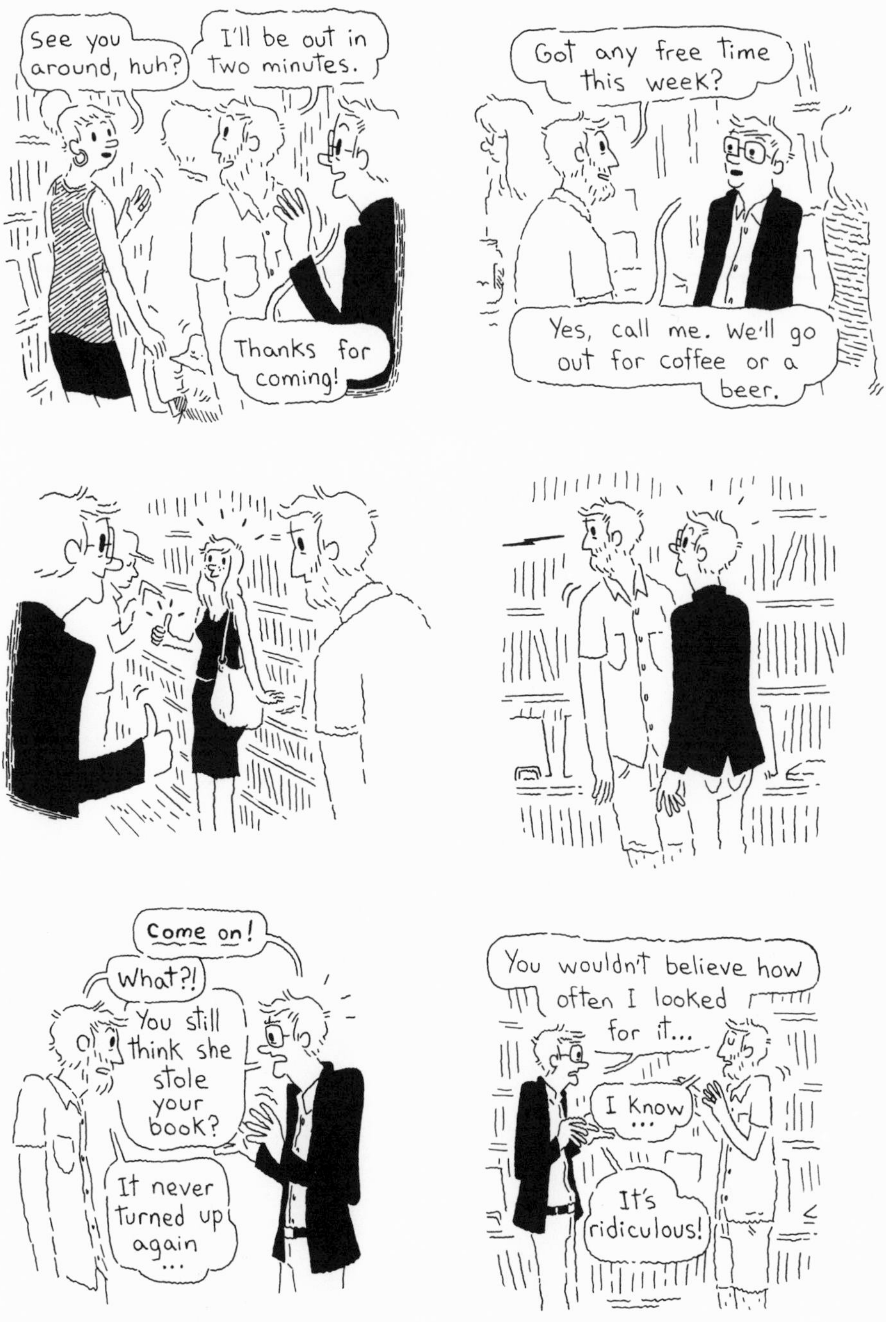
See you around, huh?
I'll be out in two minutes.
Thanks for coming!
Got any free time this week?
Yes, call me. We'll go out for coffee or a beer.
Come on!
What?!
You still think she stole your book?
It never turned up again ...
You wouldn't believe how often I looked for it...
I know ...
It's ridiculous!

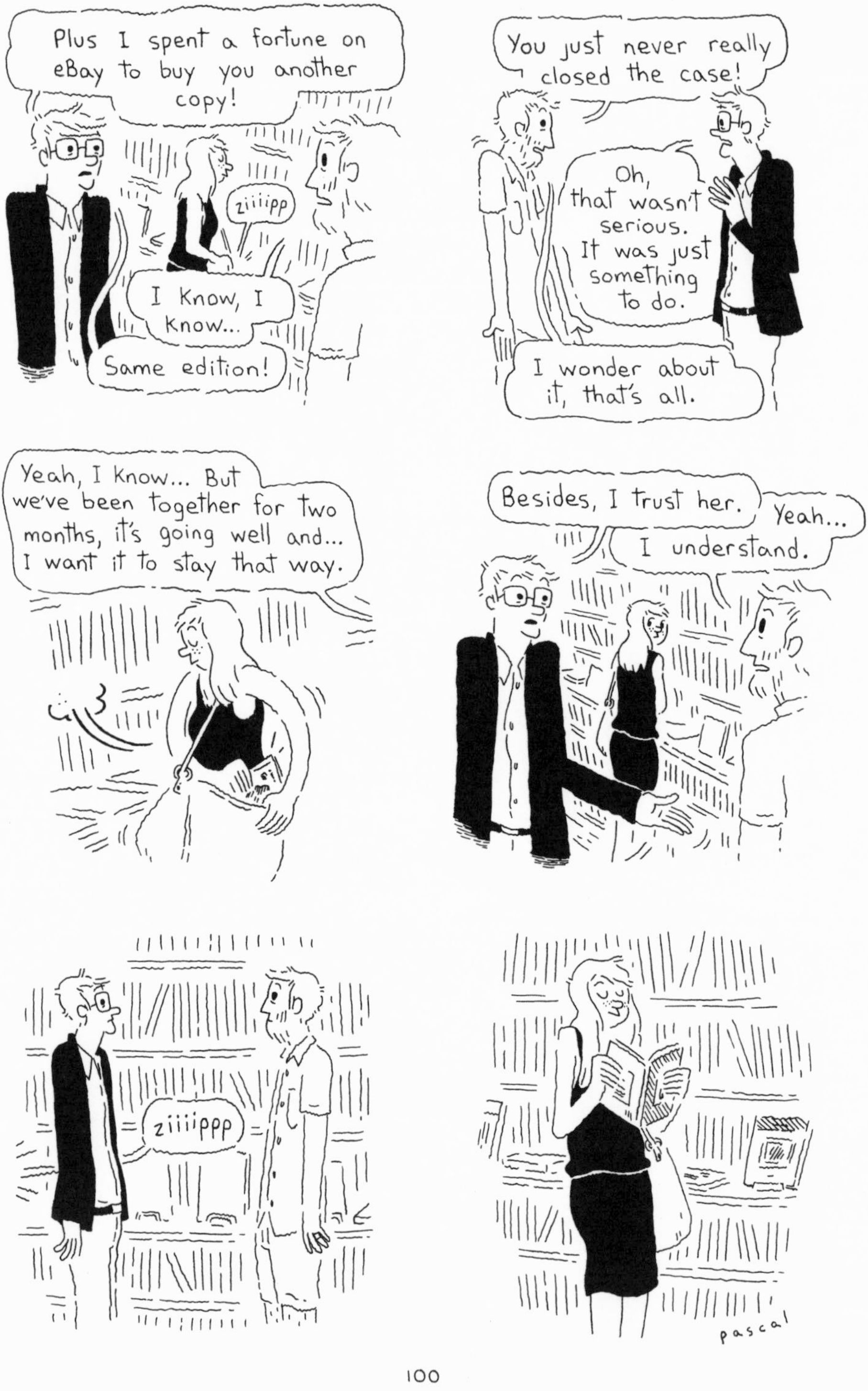

Plus I spent a fortune on eBay to buy you another copy!
ziiiipp
I know, I know...
Same edition!
You just never really closed the case!
Oh, that wasn't serious. It was just something to do.
I wonder about it, that's all.
Yeah, I know... But we've been together for two months, it's going well and... I want it to stay that way.
Besides, I trust her.
Yeah... I understand.
ziiiippp
pascal

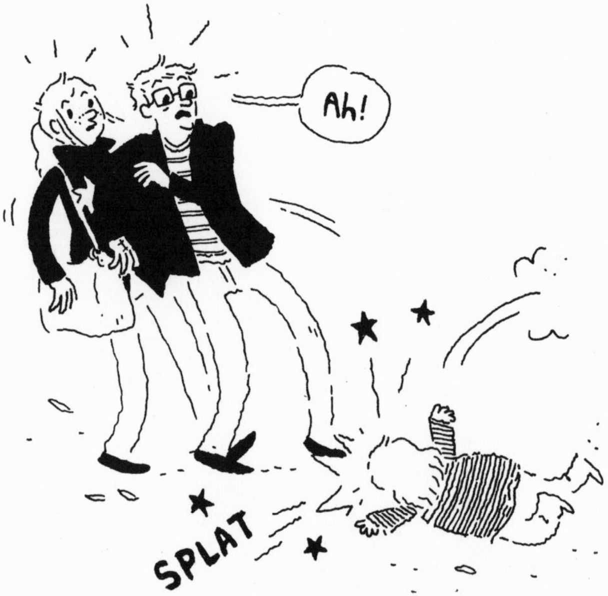
Ah!
SPLAT